Judaism Transcends Catastrophe
God, Torah, and Israel Beyond the Holocaust

Volume IV
Eternal Israel Endures

Jacob Neusner
Editor

Mercer University Press
Macon, Georgia

ISBN 0-86554-495-6

Eternal Israel Endures

Edited and Introduced by
Jacob Neusner

Copyright © 1996
Mercer University Press
Macon, Georgia

All rights reserved.
Printed in the United States of America.

The paper used in this publication meets the minimum requirements of
American National Standard for Information Sciences—
Permanence of Paper for Printed Library Materials,
ANSI Z39.48–1984.

Library of Congress Cataloging-in-Publication Data

Judaism transcends catastrophe: God, Torah, and Israel beyond the Holocaust/
    Jacob Neusner, editor.
    x + 210 pp.   6 x 9" (15 x 23 cm.)
    Includes bibliographical references.
    Contents:
    v. 1. Faith renewed: the Judaic affirmation beyond the Holocaust
    v. 2. God commands.
    v. 3. The torah teaches.
    v. 4. Eternal Israel endures.
    1. Holocaust (Jewish theology). 2. Holocaust, Jewish (1939–1945) — Influence.
    BM645.H6J83   1994–1996   296.3'11   94-38718
        ISBN 0-86554-460-3 (v. 1)
        ISBN 0-86554-461-1 (v. 2)
        ISBN 0-86554-492-1 (v. 3)
        ISBN 0-86554-495-6 (v. 4)
        ISBN 0-86554-519-7 (v. 5)

Contents

Preface vii

Introduction 1

Chapter 1 19
    The Received Faith: Israel in the Dual Torah
       Jacob Neusner

Part One—What Is Israel?

Chapter 2 53
    People of Israel
    Alon Goshen-Gottschein

Chapter 3 65
    The Holy Nation
    Eliezer Berkovits

Chapter 4 73
    The Chosen People
    Bernard J. Bamberger

Chapter 5 81
    The People of the Covenant
    Eugene R. Borowitz

Chapter 6 89
    The Election, The Covenant, and the Mission of Israel
    Samuel E. Karff

Chapter 7 103
    A Religion or a Nation?
    Jonathan Sacks

Part Two—Israel in the Here and Now

Chapter 8 119
   On the Theology of Jewish Survival
   Steven S. Schwarzchild

Chapter 9 133
   The Link between People, Land, and Religion
   in the Structure-of-Faith of Judaism
   Manfred H. Vogel

Chapter 10 157
   Exile and Redemption
   Eliezer Berkovits

Chapter 11 167
   The Personal Messiah
   Steven S. Schwarzchild

Chapter 12 187
   Judaism and the Zionist Problem,
   Zionism and the Jewish Problem
   Jacob Neusner

Preface

The polemic of this anthology, which is meant to be a highly crafted statement and not merely a collection of this and that, a political portrait of ephemerally important folk, is simply stated: "God after Auschwitz" endures as of old, and that is the God of Sinai, known to us through the Torah. Eternal Israel after Auschwitz has not only survived but remained faithful to its election, loyal to its covenant, and true to its vocation of exploring what it means to form a kingdom of priests and a holy people. To be born that eternal Israel, or to find a place in that Israel, for those who are there, abides God's ultimate act of grace: so eternal Israel has always affirmed, and so, whether in or after Auschwitz, eternal Israel today confesses. That confession and affirmation adumbrate not intellectual problems but spiritual mysteries; it is how life is defined and lived for me, and for all of us who embody in our time and place the remnant of that eternal Israel.

In this anthology, I mean to offer the reader the occasion to take up enduring issues of theology as Judaic theologians in our own day have framed those issues. For Christianity, as much as Judaism, formulates its religious experience in the theological categories represented here: (I) the encounter with God in history; (II) finding God in the world, or how we meet God in the here and now (here: God); (III) responding to revelation, or God's self-manifestation (here: Torah); (IV) forming the community of the faithful, in Christian language, the body of Christ (here: eternal Israel), as well as (V) theological thinking about theology. So far as the two religious traditions, Christianity and Judaism, are conceived within a single, shared structure, what Judaic thinkers define as their discipline and task bears relevance to Christian thinking about the same category, and the contrary also is the case. These are the issues of the five volumes:

(1) for the Holocaust in particular, how a religious reading of the massacre of millions of Jewish children, women and men has defined the issues of the last half of the twentieth century, the bases for the affirmation of God beyond the Holocaust (thus: "Judaism transcends catastrophe");

(2) for God, how we know God, where we meet God, the meaning of prayer, other forms of religious encounter and experience;

(3) for the Torah, the definition of the Torah as God's self-manifestation; the issues of how we mediate between the form of that manifestation, which is to say, writing of a particular age, and eternal truths that are made manifest;

(4) for Israel, we want to know how people have thought about the vocation and election of Israel, not only in the aftermath of the Holocaust and the foundation of the state of Israel, but in more enduring categories as well; and how these categories that endure—this is the way of life that God has given us for our service to God, this is the life of faith that we lead in the Torah—have formed a system for the interpretation of what happens in the here and now.

(5) for theology, the account of how theologians have defined their work, the program they have defined for their heirs, the philosophically-minded religious intellectuals of the coming century.

My purpose is to afford access for faithful Christian and Judaic readers to a kind of religious thinking and writing, profoundly Judaic in character, that is possessed of acute relevance but at the same time subjected to wasteful neglect. As I explain in the Introduction, people suppose that "after Auschwitz theology," or "post-Holocaust theology," must deal with only one question, which is, the problem of evil. But that supposition is only partly right, therefore entirely wrong. In fact, Judaic theology from 1945, all of its in one way or another a response to the catastrophe of the German murder of millions of Jews by reason of nothing they ever did but only what they were, which is, born of one Jewish grandparent.

No thinker whom we read in these pages wrote a single line in the oblivion of forgetting or ignoring the revelation of absolute evil that has taken place in our time. But the important thinkers, those whose writing will instruct the coming century, brought to the Holocaust the issues of transcendence, the classical categories and enduring doctrines of the Torah the world calls "Judaism." That is why I think it important to afford access here to moments of theological reflection that form in a variety of idioms and voices a single cogent work sustained, rigorous thought. In post-Holocaust writings I aim to show coherence, cogency, consistency; proportion and balance; authority and commanding mastery; in all, the classical tradition of Judaic theology as it has come to expression in diverse, authentic formulations in our time. I do so in the conviction that first-rate minds provide the rest of us with a model and a standard for our own religious thought, and much first-rate work is encompassed in these pages.

I address Christian as well as Judaic readers because the issues of Christian theology, framed in their own idiom to be sure, run along the same lines as those facing eternal Israel. We want to know what the world can reveal about God, so do they. We explore the responsibilities of the covenant with God that defines our being, so do they. We want to understand what it means to be "Israel," meaning, the people of God assembled before Sinai and children of Abraham, Isaac, and Jacob, and so, by their own word, do they. The dilemmas of faith and temptations of unbelief—how can an all-powerful God have made the world to be what it now is, for instance—confront us both. Judaism and Christianity share a common heritage of revelation, Judaism's written Torah (a term explained in the Introduction), and Christianity's Old Testament. Whatever one of us learns about God in the here and now and in revelation is going to lay claim upon the attention of the other, since by our own word both of us maintain that each party worships and loves the same, one and unique God (along with Islam).

That explains why I choose as my publisher a press conducted by academic colleagues who without apology stand for a clear and explicit religious position, and my publisher has chosen my work because of its comparable recognition that I here make an uncompromisingly religious statement. I take pride in presenting this anthology through the medium of this Southern Baptist university press; valuing the written Torah ("the Old Testament") as the word of God, just as eternal Israel does, that university and its press form an appropriate medium for an account of how God speaks in our place and time. And through theologians' intellect, as much as through saints' deeds and prayers, in responding, we answer the call that comes first and provokes response. Our response may not be the one God wants, but it is an authentic response to a call that, in the end, we maintain, comes to us from God.

Religious faith begins with God, not with us, for the world does not witness to God, but, more often than not, against Him. For me it follows that revelation, in the Scripture we share, the Torah/Bible, forms the beginning of our diverse religious thought. Theology for each of us follows rules of disciplined and rigorous reflection that God in the Torah/Bible has exemplified and that the words of God in the Torah/Bible embody. It is not for us to know why God has made the world the way it is, or to understand the reason why ancient Israel endures through the three great faiths that identify with it, rather than only through us, Israel after the flesh and (we think) the spirit too. But that is how it is, and how it has been for long enough, now, as to defy easy explanation. None of us conceives that theological negotiation is possible; each party believes its torah is the Torah, and that is how God has made us. That Baptists can find in an anthology of Judaic theology a work worthy of their publication forms a tribute to both the Baptists and the intellectual achievement of the theology of Judaism portrayed here. I do not know why God chooses to be heard in one way by Baptists in the Bible, in another way by Holy Israel in the Torah, but I do know that the faith of the Baptists and the steadfastness of holy Israel attest to the glory of one and the same God, and I honor their service as they mine.

This is no history of Judaism either, nor do I promise a thumb-nail account of how nearly two thousand years of thought took place prior to the last half of this century. Right at the outset, I lay out the issues of the Holocaust and then turn to the classical categories. But in each volume, I mean to offer perspective on the issues at hand. That is why I begin with a brief account of how, in the formative age of Judaism and its canon, catastrophe has elicited rational reflection, and, for volumes two through four, how the categories find definition: God, Torah, and Israel in the definitive documents of Judaism. In volume five, the counterpart is my own position on the next task in the theology of Judaism. In these opening statements I offer perspective on what is to follow.

Then I turn to the repertoire of writings on these same topics in our own time, not a survey of popular opinion, which is irrelevant to theology, but a re-presentation of informed thought, which embodies the theological voice. Each speaker is given a brief introduction, in which I explain what I find important in what is to be said.

Readers here take up not individual thinkers' whole systems, but specimens of thought of a number of thinkers on classical problems.

Since I have placed this anthology into the categorical context of Christian theology, I call attention to four other books co-authored by Bruce D. Chilton and myself, on the problem of comparative theology, the first three on the comparison of theological structures, the fourth on the comparison of theological systems, of Judaism and Christianity. These are as follows:

Christianity and Judaism: The Formative Categories. I. Revelation. The Torah and the Bible. Philadelphia: Trinity Press International, 1995.
Christianity and Judaism: The Formative Categories. II. The Body of Faith: Israel and Church. Philadelphia: Trinity Press International, 1996.
Christianity and Judaism: The Formative Categories. III. God in the World. Philadelphia: Trinity Press International, 1997.
Judaeo-Christian Debates. Communion with God, the Kingdom of God, the Mystery of the Messiah. Minneapolis: Fortress Press, 1997.

These works are free-standing but may prove of interest to Judaic and Christian readers interested in the comparison and contrast of the two great traditions of Scripture.

No work of mine can omit reference to the exceptionally favorable circumstances in which I conduct my research. I edited these three volumes as part of my labor of research scholarship, expressed through both publication and teaching at the University of South Florida, which has afforded me an ideal situation in which to conduct a scholarly life. I express my thanks for not only the advantage of a Distinguished Research Professorship, which must be the best job in the world for a scholar, but also of a substantial research expense fund, ample research time, and some stimulating and cordial colleagues. In the prior chapters of my career, I never knew a university that prized professors' scholarship and publication and treated with respect those professors who actively and methodically pursue research.

The University of South Florida, and all ten universities that comprise the Florida State University System as a whole, exemplify the high standards of professionalism that prevail in publicly-sponsored higher education in the U.S.A. and provide the model that privately-sponsored universities would do well to emulate. Here there are rules, achievement counts, and presidents, provosts, and deans honor and respect the University's principal mission: scholarship, scholarship alone—both in the class room and in publication. Here at last I find integrity, governing in the lives of people true to their vocation and their mission.

Jacob Neusner
Distinguished Research Professor of Religious Studies
University of South Florida, Tampa

Introduction

This five-volume anthology systematically presents how the enduring issues of the Judaic faith have transcended catastrophe and shaped the mind of the age beyond. The occasion—a half-century after the liberation of the remnant of suffering Israel, God's holy people, from the German death factories—invites the question, how has the faith, Judaism, recovered its voice? Or has that faith fallen silent, unable to speak beyond the abyss? We know the answer and here celebrate the fact of the renewal of holy Israel, God's people, in the faith of the Torah. That is what this set of theological anthologies proposes to spell out.

Now, had Israel then cast off its covenant with God and thrown its lot in with Satan, the rest of humanity would have deplored but understood its tragic end. But that is not what has happened. With the turning of the century and the daily passing of the generation that accomplished the physical feat of surviving, the time has come to take note of what has taken place among us all. An entire people, overcoming despair and renewing hope, embodied the faith of Job: even though He has slain so great a part of us, yet shall we all trust in Him. It is on that foundation, and only on that foundation, that holy Israel has surpassed death and tasted resurrection. And every faithful Jew who practices Judaism takes part in that resurrection—beyond the shadow of the valley of death, where, in ways we cannot understand, God was with us.

The Torah—the faith's own name for itself—governs holy Israel in God's compelling voice. Nothing has changed. The commanding voice of Sinai has overwhelmed the cacophany of death. For it is now clear that from 1945 to today we have witnessed one of the remarkable moments in the history of theology in the West, Judaic and Christian alike: the power of rigorous thought to think about events that in advance none could even have imagined. The theological minds of eternal Israel in our own day have met a challenge of which few in prior generations can have taken the measure. The Torah (or "Judaism") has triumphed, transcending radical evil, in classical terms, meeting Satan and through holy Israel affirming the living God made manifest in the Torah.

That is not to be taken for granted. Surveying the ruins of the ancient civilization of European Judaism, few imagined that the faith would renew itself, large parts of the Jewish people reaffirming despite and against it all that God rules, God loves. The past half-century has witnessed the unfolding of one of the great religious dramas of all time: how people survived evil beyond imagining and affirmed their heritage of faith. When Israel, the Jewish people, looked outward, around and backward, from 1945, so far as the eye could say lay ruins: villages and towns where the Torah had been proclaimed for a thousand years, now bereft of the presence of holy Israel; great cities, once vital with the vivid affairs of eternal Israel, now in ruins. With everything that flourished in 1939, homes, families, entire societies, now a mass of ashes and an empire of death, who can then have predicted what in fact took place? For it was not the mass-apostasy that the failure of faith would have provoked, but the determination, among religious Jews (Judaists) and secular ones alike, to reaffirm, renew, rebuild. What happened then was not to have been predicted at all: the rebirth of eternal Israel, the reaffirmation of its loyalty to God's word in the Torah, the renewal of faith in the one and only God of all ages. For not only did the remnants of the people, Israel, emerge from death factories where Satan ruled, they renewed their lives by forming a new political entity, the State of Israel, and by rebuilding throughout the world beyond the religious community of Israel that embodies Judaism, that is, the Torah, in the here and now.

Many find in the creation of the State of Israel the response of the people, Israel, to the Holocaust. And they surely find good reason for their view. But the challenge of the Holocaust to faith vastly outweighed the political crisis in which the Jewish people in Europe found itself. And it is here, in particular, that the remarkable renaissance of love for God and obedience to the Torah (variously construed to be sure) formed a response equal in power, but greater in weight and meaning, even to the political one involved in state-building. Israel, the holy people, did more than found the State of Israel. It also found its way to Sinai, once more taking up in these times, in this place, the yoke of the Kingdom of Heaven. Having emerged from the kingdom of Hell, this entire religious community now bears witness to the presence of the living God.

They affirmed the enduring covenant with God. They resumed the holy life of the faith. By word and deed they proclaimed the hope for the salvation of Israel and humanity through the Messiah. So the people Scripture sets forth as God's first love renewed its sustained, and sustaining, life of loving loyalty and obedience to God's Torah. Satan was vanquished by Israel's faith beyond the Holocaust. So, a calamity in many ways unique in history survived, Israel's remarkable rebirth marked the transcendence of catastrophe such as the world has seen only seldom. Why turn to theology to call attention to the renewal of religion? It is because in the profound reflections of the intellectuals of this religion the order, rationality, and coherence of events and faith emerge. Here we find not a narrow theodicy—beyond dogged faith, what theodicy is necessary, and facing the Holcaust, what theodicy is possible?—but a broad and nourishing theology of renewal.

To that religious experience of affirmation and rebirth, theology devotes its best intellectual energies in the pages of these five volumes. Here we see how the first-rate thinkers of the people, Israel, addressed the crisis of the day, on the one side, but also took up the disciplines and tasks of the classical theological heritage of the Torah, on the other. If no generation in the history of Judaism has confronted so critical a catastrophe, none was better served by its thinkers. Even our sages of blessed memory, who carried the Torah beyond the ruins of the Temple and reconstructed the kingdom of priests and the holy people through the Mishnah and the Talmud, accomplished no more towering achievement, nor did they face more intidimating obstacles to faith, than have the theologians of our own half-century.

The anthology shows the ways in which the important Judaic theologians writing in English have thought about the five issues that could not be avoided and had to be met head on: the defining hour of the Holocaust, then the three principal categories of the theological structure of Judaism: God, Torah, and Israel, meaning the eternal people to whom God spoke at Sinai, and then the challenge of the coming century. We here encounter not descriptions of opinion or historical accounts of what various people have thought about the Holcaust, God, Torah, and eternal Israel, and the tasks of theology for generations to come. Rather we read in their own words the theologians' propositions, arguments, passionate advocacy of particular positions. This is theology not recorded but lived in vivid intellects, how thoughtful, rigorous, demanding and restless minds have taken up the critical, anguished issues of a living faith at its time of crisis. The writers assembled here show diverse capacities of learning, acumen, perspicacity, and wit; some write one way, some another. But all of them do precisely what theologians in the traditions of Islam, Christianity, and Judaism are expected to achieve. That is the formulation in well-crafted prose of faith seeking understanding through processes of rationality; sustained and vigorous argument concerning the solution of conceptual problems of a religious character. More than mere philosophers of religion speaking about matters in general, mediating commanding revelation (for Judaism: the Torah) and rigorous, worldly reason, these writers reshape conviction and conscience into intellectually compelling statements of an entirely rational order.

A generation of theologians of Judaism, the one from World War II to the end of the Cold War, which faced the enormous intellectual challenges of the Holocaust, the founding of the State of Israel, now completes its work. The earlier figures, represented by the names of Berkowitz, Herberg and Heschel, have gone to their rest, and the later ones, represented by Borowitz, Fackenheim, and Vogel, now bring their thought to fruition and wisely undertake their valedictory statements. The next generation has yet to coalesce; we simply cannot at this time predict the shape and structure of thought; Judaic theology out of the most recent generation proves still ephemeral and has yet to find either its voice or its agenda. But in the moment of ebb tide, as the waters eddy and seek their new force, a backward perspective illuminates; we can at least take the measure of the high tide that has flowed out. So it is time to inquire into how rigorous religious intellectuals asked themselves the urgent questions precipitated by the greatest catastrophe Israel, the eternal people, has ever faced.

This anthology of five volumes about theological thinking about the Holocaust, God, Torah, and eternal Israel and Judaic theology of the second half of the twentieth century and beyond allows us to take stock of what has happened in the Judaic intellect. The anthology demonstrates that the classic and enduring—chronic in a healthy sense—issues of religious truth, not solely the critical and painful—acute—issue of evil and theodicy, elicited intelligent and profound thought over the past half-century. Not only so, but much that has been written endures as a legacy and a heritage for the thoughtful among the faithful in the century that is now dawning. It is meant to showcase important discussions on the principal categories of the theology of Judaism in the period from World War II to the end of the Cold War.

What makes such an anthology urgent is not only the passing of a generation. It is also that, in general, Jews present themselves as a wholly secular social entity, and the media of religious expression common among their Christian neighbors do not define how Jews make their religious statement. It is the simple fact that while the Jews are a social entity of a single religion, Judaism, or no religion at all (acceptance of any religion other than Judaism marks a person, in functional terms, as no longer part of the Jewish people), the proportion of Jews who also are Judaists, that is, practitioners of Judaism, varies but hardly encompasses the entire community. Not only so, but even among Judaists, serious encounter with the intellectual heritage of Israel takes place only in modest proportion. Faith without learning (an oxymoron in Judaic piety) is very common; faith surpassing understanding, which two generations from 1945 to the present in fact embodied, is not fully grasped.

God

It follows that, because of the prevailing secularity of the Jews' public discourse (and not merely its mediocrity), the modest place accorded to Judaists in the scheme of the Jews' ethnic existence, and the uncomprehending disdain for the reality of God's presence in and through eternal Israel, many, Jewish and gentile, have missed the astonishing intellectual events of our time. If attentive to the better publicized theological discourse, the more discerning will have judged the theological response to the Holocaust shallow and predictable. If God is all-powerful, then what does the Holocaust tell us about God? And if God is not all-powerful, then the Holocaust "proves" there is no God. So the issue of theodicy has exacted, and not only from theologians by any means, many sleepless nights. Many people now suppose that the only theological issue important in Judaism is theodicy, which is to say, theologies that focus upon "God after Auschwitz."

All Judaic theology from 1945 and onward, I think, for centuries to come, will have to qualify as "after-Auschwitz"-theology, not only for chronological reasons, but for substantive ones. We have learned facts about this world that, before the rule of Satan, we could never have conceived. A central religious task of rigorous thinking will always require confrontation with these facts, as much as, for the prophets, the demise of Northern Israel and the destruction of Jerusalem in 586 precipitated deep thought on how God acts in history. But what the catastrophe teaches, how eternal Israel has responded, the commanding voice of Sinai, the renewed encounter with the living God in prayer and acts of service—these all together form that theology in the shadow of the Holocaust. The reason is that, beyond the shadows, there has been much illumination: eternal Israel, responding to the living God, renewed its covenant in the Torah. That is the story of the rebirth of Judaism throughout the world, on the one side, and the message, too, of the theologians whom we meet in these five books. In an exact sense, for all who mourn for Israel's millions, murdered by the Germans from 1933 through 1945, every breath is an act of affirmation: we, Israel, choose to live, despite it all, because of the call of the One to whom we respond.

That is why all Judaic theology is a "Holocaust-theology." But few presently understand that every piece of religious expression, encompassing the entirety of Judaic theological writing, forms a response to the issue of the Holocaust; there is no other fact of transcendent religious character that compares in our time, or, many would maintain, in all time. Here I show a different picture. It encompasses not only the reaffirmation of God beyond the gates of Hell. It extends also to how thinkers have worked on a wide front, all of them under the shadow of the catastrophe of the Holocaust, but all of them engaged by classic issues and the revealed Torah. True, that statement contradicts how people presently assess the condition of eternal Israel and of Judaism. Any observer, following public life, would have supposed there has been paralysis in the encounter with the classic challenges to systematic thought.

I here make manifest that that is not the case. I show how thought has taken place in the main lines of theology of Judaism not despite the Holocaust nor solely in response to the Holocaust but in the renewal of the religious life of reflection in the aftermath of the Holocaust: how people mediated between new experience and received truth. The enduring categories of thought—God, Torah, Israel—continue to form the definitive outline of truth. For that forms the challenge to thought, which is to say, the religious mind transcends events and transforms them into enduring truth, making occasion into eternity. For the secular Jews, these questions come to formulation in secular speech: fiction, poetry, film, music; and they are given a secular articulation in politics and social thought. For the religious Jews there is yet another response. It takes two forms, the inchoate, profound expression of live as it is lived under the covenant with the Almighty: the life of faith and trust, hope, patience, and service, which the Torah teaches. And, it takes the second form of reflection on the meaning and truth of that life, reflection in the form of not only prayer or poetry or artful gesture, but sustained and rigorous thought, lucidly set forth in crafted prose. Secular Jews dominate the public square. But religious ones—Judaists, not only Jews—have also found voices, and in this anthology, these voices gain their hearing.

Israel

In this same context—the distinction between the secular and the religious in the life of the Jews—a further complication must be introduced. When in the theology of Judaism we speak of "Israel," we do not mean the State of Israel in particular but the eternal, holy people. That people, of whom Scripture speaks, to whom God gives the

Torah, of course encompasses the Jewish part of the population of the State of Israel, but it is not limited to that one sector of the Jewish people, not at all. In fact, the name, "Israel," bears a variety of meanings. In the Torah, "Israel" always speaks not of a place nor yet of a state but only, invariably, of the people Israel, the extended family of Abraham and Sarah, Isaac and Rebecca, Jacob and Leah and Rachel; the kingdom of priests and the holy people. In all Judaic theology, and in all Jewish ethnic writing, before 1948, when people spoke of "Israel" they meant the Jewish people. All other usages in which "Israel" appeared referred to the same sense, e.g., in Hebrew, "land of Israel," did not mean, "the land, Israel," but "the Land that belongs in particular to Israel, the people." In the liturgy of Judaic prayer, "Israel" refers to the elect people of Israel, to whom God gave the Torah, wherever they live; it does not refer to a particular place or to a particular group of Jews as distinct from all others.

The confusion between the received, theological meaning carried by the word "Israel" began in 1948, when the Jewish State, founded by the Zionist movement, to which, as a matter of fact, most of the Jews in the world and in the Land of Israel subscribed, called itself "the State of Israel." Now that formulation, "the State of Israel" by contrast quite properly speaks of the Jewish state, located in the Land of Israel (as the Jewish people have always known that place). When the Psalmist speaks of "The guardian of Israel does not slumber nor sleep," he means, of course, "the guardian of the holy people," and not "the guardian of the Land of Israel," or obviously of "the political entity, the State of Israel." "Israel" as the holy people to whom God revealed the Torah, identified in the here and now as Israel the Jewish people, obviously should not to be confused with the contemporary State of Israel, a this-worldly fact, to be sure bearing profound religious meaning to Judaism. Since people refer to the State of Israel simply as "Israel," I distinguish the State of Israel from the holy people of Israel of whom the Torah speaks by referring to the latter as "eternal Israel." That will sidestep the difficulties in sense and meaning brought about by calling a secular state by a name that bears its own, distinct theological referent.[1]

So it is time to distinguish the ethnic from the religious, the secular from the theological, out of the voices of a half-century of pained and anguished reflection upon, not merely response to, the catastrophe of the ages that took place between 1933 and 1945. For those who see Israel not as an ethnic group alone but as God's people, those who interpret the world not in its own terms alone, but as testimony to the Almighty, those who distinguish this world's facts from eternal truths, those who view humanity "in our image, after our likeness," the issues surpass ethnic testimony about sound social policy or political action. Judaists, without apology, without shame, see the world under the aspect of God's rule, find in the Torah surpassing truth, appreciate the Israel of this world in its transcendent setting.

Torah

The profoundly secular character of the Jews' public life and therefore shared discourse in the USA and Europe obscures the equally deep, rooted religious faith of Judaists' inner life. This book and its companions give testimony to the living faith, Judaism—which calls itself "the Torah," which sees itself as the "Israel" of which the Torah speaks and which identifies itself as the statement of the eternal God, creator of heaven and earth, ruler of all worlds, and ultimate redeemer of humanity. Specifically, they show how Judaic thinkers, rooted in the absolute and unshakeable givenness of God's presence in history and rule over Israel, responded in rigorous, rational, theological ways to the defining moments of our day.

Theology in this context refers to systematic and rigorous reflection on religious questions; faith seeking understanding through processes of rationality; sustained and vigorous argument concerning the solution of conceptual problems of a religious character. In Judaism, theology has taken a variety of forms, important ideas expressing themselves through patterns of behavior as much as through propositions of belief. But in times past, and in our own day, rigorous and systematic religious thought has yielded a harvest of sustained, proportioned, coherent theological writing. This anthology means to portray how Judaic theology in the past half-century has conducted its work of making sense of the world measured by the dimensions of

(1) the Holocaust events themselves
(2) the revealed Torah
(3) the one, unique, and only God who is made manifest in the Torah at Sinai
(4) the eternal, holy nation, Israel, God's first love
(5) the presence, in eternal Israel, of rigorous, philosophically-insistent intellects and their theological program for time to come.

Knowing what we have learned in this awful century, how do we read the Torah, think about the power and mercy of God, make sense of the mystery of Israel? And what tasks face us in the coming generation?

The Holocaust: What makes the theological adventure of Judaic religious thought compelling and of broad interest to a wide audience of religious faithful, Christian and Judaic alike, over the past fifty years? The gates of the death factories, built by the Germans in World War II, closed finally in 1945. No event in the history of humanity bears more profound implications for our understanding of Torah, Israel, and God, not the fall of Man and Woman, not the Golden Calf, not the exile of the lost tribes, not the destruction of the Temple in 586 B.C.E., nor again in 70, not the massacre of Rhineland Jewries in the First Crusade, nor the expulsion of the Jews from Spain, nor the advent of Communism, nor the empowerment of Fascism and Nazism. Seen by themselves or all together, these turnings in time made sense on the received cartography of the known ways, God's and humanity's. But the received solutions to the problem of evil—Job's or Jeremiah's for instance—for many proved insufficient, incommensurate to what now has happened. Consequently, Judaic thinkers writing in the American language faced a challenge of reflection, critical thought, and sustained, rigorous intellection. Some directed their attention to the problem of evil and the issue of theodicy.

God, Torah, Israel

But others took up the ancient discipline of rationality in quest of religious truth and broadened the discussion. The Holocaust for them presented the occasion, even the provocation. But it did not define the issues. These, for eternal Israel, had been determined at Sinai, when, God having made the world and brought Israel into being and assembled the holy people before the mountain, completed the trilogy by giving the Torah. Creation, revelation, redemption defining the workings of the unfolding system that Sinai set forth, God, Torah, and Israel constituted the structure by which all reality, here and above, natural and supernatural, would be ordered. So for those who surpassed the occasion, the Holocaust stood for a new beginning in the unending encounter, in intellect, with the living God of Sinai's Torah.

Now, a half-century later, it is time to take stock of the work of a generation that has run its course. Clearly, two distinct kinds of theology require attention, "Holocaust-theology," and "theology that takes account of the Holocaust." The former, as is clear, rightly insist that all thought within the Torah find its defining program in the catastrophe of 1933–1945 (whether or not completed by the miracle of 1948 to the present day represented by the creation of the State of Israel, the Jewish state, in the Land of Israel). The latter carry forward the classical program of Judaic theological thought—how to live the holy life that God has commanded to covenanted Israel, how to reflect intelligently on the defining categories of that sanctified community's existence, God, Torah, Israel. Among these latter thinkers, the Holocaust found full recognition; but those events were not permitted to silence thought or impose upon the full and transcendent program of intellectual reflection constraints of what are, ultimately, an adventitious character. For they did not permit episodes to define eternal issues, but only to contribute new facts to the contemplation of those issues. So far as the Holocaust contained defining moments on the character of humanity and the holiness of Israel, it was to make, and it did make, its full, ample, and necessary contribution. But the Holocaust for this second set of writers, the more classical ones in education and sensibility, was to be faced within the received and eternal framework of the Torah.

The Theological Adventure in Contemporary Judaism

Ample evidence, part of which is laid out in these five anthologies, demonstrates that, transcending catastrophe, great intellects of Judaism accomplished two remarkable tasks of an intellectual character, and they did so forthrightly and courageously.

First, they faced head-on what came to be called "the Holocaust." A formidable corpus of writing by systematic thinkers of Judaism took up the problems of religious belief presented by the events of 1933–1945, when millions of Jews, men and women and upwards of a million children, were murdered by reason of not their faith but the mere fate of having been born into a Jewish family. In fiction, poetry, film, music, as well as in the media of sustained and rigorous thought in the form of ideas carefully crafted and persuasively set forth, the issue of the catastrophe was framed. Certainly, no generation has ever confronted a more insistent or formidable challenge than finding ways to think theologically about the unthinkable.

The faithful of Christianity and Judaism alike have found in the results not only important religious ideas, commensurate to the enormous dimensions of the challenge, but also the occasion for the renewal of faith. That is why the religious response to the Holocaust has rightly won for itself so rich a response of public appreciation. These anthologies do not have to provide a reprise of that protracted chapter in post-Holocaust theology of Judaism. But within the demanding discipline of reasoned thought about religious questions that theology comprises, a specific, theological formulation of matters was set forth. And that has to be appreciated to make sense of everything else. The achievement of the theologians—as distinct from philosophers, poets, film makers, composers, novelists, moralists, and publicists—was to insist that the Holocaust ask not a thin question of theodicy, but a thick question of encounter: God was there, the Torah was there, with eternal Israel in Auschwitz.

Second, some of these same thinkers and others as well in the same period, under the shadow of the same tremendous events, furthermore took up the received agenda of Judaic theology, that is, the program of mediating between revelation, the Torah, and the present hour that defines the work of theology in that religious tradition. From the formation of the classical and authoritative writings of Judaism, called all together "the Torah," to our own day, each generation has taken up the labor of making its own what the ages had handed on, the fundament of faith for which the Torah stands. The past half-century has witnessed a remarkable display of how enduring and historically-rooted intellectual traditions have taken over and made their own the newest of humanity's, and eternal Israel's, discoveries. When thinking about God, Torah, and Israel, the three generative categories of thought, the Judaic theologians took up an age-old discipline of continuous reflection, always aware of the catastrophe in Europe, but never struck dumb by it. This corpus of religious thinking of a rigorous character in Judaism shows us how Judaism not only faced the Holocaust but also, through appeal to enduring theological disciplines, transcended it as well. And it is to that labor of intellectual transcendence that these three anthologies are devoted.

What justifies the work in the proportions that characterize these anthologies—the Holocaust forming only part of the portrayal of the encounter with God in our time—is simple. While ready access to the first of the two massive enterprises of Judaic theology, both in its conventional form and in the unconventional formulations of the second half of the twentieth century, is easily gained in numerous and widely-appreciated works, to the second labor, the more classical, few have afforded an opening. That is to say, we may readily find anthologies of Judaic theological and Jewish ethnic responses to the Holocaust, and many of these have rightly enjoyed a massive hearing. But the paramount status rightly accorded to the theological challenge of the Holocaust has tended to obscure this other kind of theology that the generation beyond the Holocaust has formulated.

That is the theology that has continued the ages-old discussion of the enduring issues of Judaic faith to which the greater part of these volumes is devoted. Theologians of mighty power met the challenge, only to find their work neglected in favor of other kinds of expression, because of the paramount secularity characteristic of the Jewish world. For the secular taste, the Holocaust validated atheism; God could not stop those events, so is not God; or God could stop them but did not, so is evil. For the religious perception, God is always, everywhere, eternally God, without qualification, condition, or apology. In the context of the iron, incorruptible faith of eternal Israel since its origins, silence before the unknowable hardly defined a task beyond accomplishment. So the secular reading of the Holocaust prevailed in public life.

But of course for those of us who find our being in God's Israel and the purpose of our being in God's Torah, the Holocaust is reduced in its dimensions when treated as an event only in this world's terms. So reading the Holocaust in the narrowly political, secular, and ethnic reading of the catastrophe—or in terms essentially secular people assume pertain to theology impoverishes. More happened at Auschwitz and the other capitals of evil embodied than this world contains. And we have known the reality of pure evil from of old; for our paradigm, if there is no ultimate evil, there also is no meaning to the ultimate redemption. And God is diminished. But in the structure of a this-worldly reading of existence that predominates in Israel, the Jewish people, as distinct from eternal Israel in the here and now, how the received, enduring dimensions of the Torah are to be measured has scarcely attracted attention.

Theodicy

The issues of religious encounter with the living God that religious Jews—practitioners of Judaism, called Judaists—find urgent but secular, ethnic Jews scarcely acknowledge are not addressed in theodicy alone, or in declarations that there was a God but he died in Auschwitz and similar formulations. Consequently, when people take up the examination of the theology of Judaism in the generation now completing its work, they take for granted one issue defines discourse. That issue is the one of theodicy, framed as "God after Auschwitz." People have taken for granted that, when we turn to theology, all we shall discuss is what we can know about God in light of the revelations of systematic murder of the people, Israel, in Europe. That is a legitimate issue; it is not the only one.

It is a broadly held impression that, in the aftermath of the murder of nearly six million Jews in Europe in world war II and also the creation of the State of Israel, the theology of Judaism has given itself over to the enormous problem of theodicy presented by the former, and the political concerns defined in response to the creation and maintenance of the latter. So God is no longer God in creation, revelation, and redemption, as Judaism has always encountered God. God is now subject to human judgment, requiring explanation and defense. But we in holy and eternal Israel have known more about God than the works of this day's history. We have defined our existence in more dimensions than the political and the empowered. Not only so, but theologians, who undertake in each generation to mediate the Torah to the acutely-present moment, have set forth rigorously argued systems, or components of systems, that provide rational and philosophically-defensible re-presentations of the received and revealed Torah of Sinai.

It is time to right the balance. That is not by an opposite and equal distortion, namely, re-presenting the theology of Judaism in the last half-century under the aspect of Sinai but not of Auschwitz. No theologian of Judaism has imagined such a vision; it were folly. All theologians of Judaism from 1945 onward have written in full consciousness of the events of 1933 to 1945, and every one of them in every line acknowledged those events. No religious thinking in Judaism has aimed at obscuring or diminishing the dreadful power of the ultimate revelation of evil—the counterpart and opposite of Sinai. But all of those represented in these pages have conducted the theology of Judaism in a different way.

The Holocaust-theologians start where they finish: at Auschwitz, The theologians who transcend catastrophe and move, as time moves, beyond the Holocaust, conduct their thought in a different realm. They surpass calamity and transcend the Holocaust by continuing the ancient and lasting conversation with the Torah, speaking of this morning's headlines in the language of eternity. Specifically, theologians who carry on beyond the Holocaust do so by placing that theology of Judaism in its own, enduring context, under the aspect of Sinai that of course illuminates all life, all time, all being, even unto death. What some have called "the commanding voice of Auschwitz" then is taken in to the commanding voice of Sinai. In this setting, one immense event casts its shadow over all that has come before and over all that will follow; but it is not the whole of time, nor does it set forth the entirety of truth.

Theology

I have throughout used a term not defined at all, "theology." An entire volume in this anthology, the final one, is devoted to the Judaic definition of theology. But to begin with, we turn to the definition of the particular kind of thinking that is represented in these anthologies: theological thinking, not philosophy, not "Jewish thought" (which rarely is defined but generally means, Jews thinking about Jewish things), and not history, literature, or anything else but itself.

To state matters simply: theology philosophically sets forth religion. That statement paraphrases the definition of Ingolf U. Dalferth,

> Theology is not philosophy, and philosophy is not a substitute for religious convictions. But whereas religion can exist without philosophy, and philosophy without religion, theology cannot exist without recourse to each of the other two. It rationally reflects on questions arising in pre-theological religious experience and the discourse of faith; and it is the rationality of its reflective labor in the process of faith seeking understanding which inseparably links it with philosophy. For philosophy is essentially concerned with argument and the attempt to solve conceptual problems, and conceptual problems face theology in all areas of its reflective labors.[2]

Accordingly, by the definition of theology that is before us, what we here examine is contemporary Judaic theologians' systematic and rigorous reflection on religious questions; faith seeking understanding through processes of rationality; sustained and vigorous argument concerning the solution of conceptual problems of a religious character.

To understand the claim of this anthology, a clear definition of theology is required at the very outset. For that purpose I reverse the elements of the definition provided by Dalferth. The predicate becomes the subject in this way:

(1) *where* we have rational reflection on questions arising in religious experience and the discourse of faith,
(2) *there* we have theology.

When we find reflective labor on the rationality—the cogency, harmony, proposition, coherence, balance, order, and proper composition—of statements of religious truth, e.g., truth revealed by God, then we have identified a theological writing. In these pages I present numerous, sustained examples of reflective labor on the rationality of statements of religious truth and consequence:

> God commands.
> The Torah teaches.
> Eternal Israel endures.

Those three theologoumena encompass the entire theology that Judaism has maintained and today sustains as God's truth. They form Judaism in its theological manifestation.

Concern with argument, the attempt to solve conceptual problems—these characterize that writing. By themselves, of course, they do not mark a writing as theological. Argument concerning conceptual problems yields theology when the argument deals with religion, the conceptual problems derive from revelation. Only the source of the givens of the writing—revelation, not merely reasoned analysis of this world's givens—distinguishes theology from philosophy, including, as a matter of fact, philosophy of religion. But that suffices.

To make this point clear, let me refer to the canonical documents and how they make their points. Take for example that splendid formulation of religion as philosophy, the Mishnah. The Mishnah states its principles through method of natural history, sifting the traits of this-worldly things, demonstrating philosophical truth—the unity of one and unique God at the apex of the natural world—by showing on the basis of the evidence of this world, universally accessible, the hierarchical classification of being. That is a philosophical demonstration of religious truth. The Talmud of Babylonia states its principles through right reasoning about revealed truth, the Torah. The Torah (written, or oral) properly read teaches the theological truth that God is one, at the apex of the hierarchy of all being. That is a theological re-presentation of (the same) religious truth. But that re-presentation in the two Talmuds (and in the Midrash-compilations, not treated here) also exhibits the traits of philosophical thinking: rigor, concern for harmonies, unities, consistencies, points of cogency, sustained argument and counter-argument, appeal to persuasion through reason, not coercion through revelation. In our time, as through the past centuries, in Judaism, the methods of philosophy applied to the data of religious belief and behavior produced theology. The method of philosophy shapes the message of religion into a re-statement characterized by rationality and entire integrity.

Since I have made reference to the received and classical documents of Judaism, a very brief account of the sources out of which all authentic Judaism thought proceeds is here required. That is important for the understanding of the opening chapter of each of these volumes, which provides the starting point of all Judaic theological thought, which is, the canonical definition of the several categories that form Judaism. A brief account of that authoritative canon must start with the end-product, which is, the Torah as defined at the end of the formation of Judaism.[3] For many people, both Christian and Jewish, take for granted that "Judaism" is pretty much the same thing as "the Old Testament," and if they know the word "Torah" at all, they mean by it "the Pentateuch," the Five Books of Moses, Genesis, Exodus, Leviticus, Numbers, and Deuteronomy.

But Judaism is no more the religion of the Old Testament alone than Christianity is the religion of the New Testament alone. "Torah" for Judaism is the counterpart to "Bible" for Christianity. Just as Christianity reads the Old Testament in the light of the New, so Judaism reads what it knows as "the written Torah" in the complementary and fulfilling setting of "the oral Torah." So to understand the enduring conversations about religious truth that theologian of Judaism conducts, we have to acquire a very exact knowledge of the sources of religious truth that the Torah comprises. What then is this "Torah" that forms "the Bible" for Judaism?

It is the Torah in two media, written and oral. That Torah, called in due course "the one whole Torah of Moses, our rabbi," was formulated and transmitted by God to Moses in two media, each defining one of the components, written and oral. The written is Scripture as we know it, encompassing the Pentateuch, Prophets, and Writings. The oral part of the Torah came to be written down in a variety of works, beginning with the Mishnah, ca. 200 C.E. The canon of the Judaism the theology of which is described here is made up of extensions and amplifications of these two parts of the Torah. The written part is carried forward through collections of readings of verses of Scripture called Midrash-compilations. The oral part is extended through two sustained, selective commentaries and expansions, called talmuds, the Talmud of the Land of Israel, a.k.a. the Yerushalmi (ca. 400 C.E.), and the Talmud of Babylonia, a.k.a., the Bavli (ca. 600 C.E.).

In literary terms, then, the formation of Judaism reached its fruition in extensions of the oral Torah and the written Torah. For the oral Torah, the formative age came to its conclusion when the Talmud of Babylonia set forth the theological statement of Judaism by expressing the religious convictions of the Talmud of the Land of Israel in accord with a profound reconsideration of the philosophical norms of the Mishnah, ca. 200. C.E. Joining the method of the Mishnah to the messages of the prior Talmud, the framers of the second Talmud thereby defined the theological, including the legal, norms of Judaism. For the written Torah, the Midrash-compilations of the successive ages, corresponding to the two Talmuds and associated with them, carry forward the same modes of discourse and express in their ways the same hermeneutics.

The Talmuds' distinctive hermeneutics, which contains within itself the theology of the Judaism of the dual Torah, is exposed not in so many words but in page-by-page repetition; it is not articulated but constantly (even tediously) instantiated; we are then supposed to draw our own conclusions. The unique voice of the second of the two Talmuds, the Talmud of Babylonia, which bears that hermeneutic, speaks with full confidence of being heard and understood; and that voice is right; we never can miss the point. For the hermeneutic itself—insistence on the presence of philosophy behind jurisprudence, law behind laws, total harmony among premises of discrete and diverse cases pointing to the unique and harmonious character of all existence, social and natural—properly understood, bears the theological message: the unity of intellect, the integrity of truth.

As the Mishnah had demonstrated the hierarchical classification of all natural being, pointing at the apex to the One above, so the second Talmud demonstrated the unity of the principles of being set forth in the Torah. The upshot is that Judaism would set forth the religion that defined how humanity was formed "in our image, after our likeness," not to begin with but day by day: in the rules of intellect, the character of mind. We can be like God because we can think the way God thinks, and the natural powers of reason carry us upward to the supernatural origin of the integrity of truth—that sentence sums up what I conceive to be the theological consequence of the Talmud's hermeneutics.

The Talmud of Babylonia therefore forms the pinnacle and the summa—what we mean when we speak of "Judaism"—because from the time of its closure to the present day it defined not only Judaic dogma and its theological formulation but also Judaic discourse that carried that dogma through to formulation in compelling form. Not only so, but the entire documentary heritage of the first six centuries of the Common Era was recast in that Talmud. And that body of writing was itself a recapitulation of important elements of the Hebrew Scriptures and in its basic views indistinguishable in theological and legal character from elements of the Pentateuch's and Prophets' convictions and requirements. Scripture itself ("the written Torah") would reach coming generations not only as read in the synagogue on the Sabbath and festivals, but also, and especially, as recast and expounded in the Talmud in the school houses and courts of the community of Judaism.

Other received documents that had reached closure during that long period of time—the Mishnah, the Tosefta, the Talmud of the Land of Israel itself, the score of Midrash-compilations—furthermore flowed into the Talmud of Babylonia. So each prior writing found its proper position, in due proportion, within the composite of the Bavli. And the Bavli made of the entire heritage of the revealed Torah, oral and written, not a composite but a composition, whole, proportioned, coherent. That is what I mean by, "the Talmudic re-presentation," that is, the second Talmud's re-presentation of the Torah given by God to our rabbi, Moses, at Mount Sinai.

That re-presentation was accomplished through one medium: a governing, definitive hermeneutics, the result of applied logic and practical reason when framed in terms of the rules of reading a received and holy book. I need not hide my conviction that the persuasive power of the Talmud's hermeneutics explains the Talmud's success in taking the primary position in the canon of Judaism. That conviction admittedly is subjective, resting as it does on the unprovable premise that ideas and attitudes account of conduct and social policy. But it is the indubitable fact that the second Talmud effected the re-presentation of all that had gone before. Given the Talmud's priority of place among all Judaic writings, before and since for all time, I set forth an objective fact when I maintain that the Talmud also stated in its distinctive way, through its particular hermeneutics, the authoritative theology of the Judaism for which it formed the summa. Religious belief and right behavior to express that belief

—both would find definition in its pages, exposition and exegesis in accord with its modes of analytical thought. With the Bavli, the theological text had been inscribed; all the rest was commentary.[4] The commentary would flourish from then to now; the exegesis of that exegesis would define the future history of Judaism.

For the later history of Judaism, from late antiquity to the present day, theology would take a distinctive, and I think, unique form. It provoked rigorous argument, rather than merely laying out well-defined propositions. In this way it guided the conduct of theological thought, rather than merely defining its propositions and syllogistic goals. When the sages of Judaism chose to make their statements of norms, they began in the Talmud, worked within its categories, framed their ideas in accord with its intellectual discipline, and spoke in its language about its problems. They did so in the (descriptively-valid) conviction that the Talmud had made the full and authoritative statement of the Torah of Sinai, oral, covering the Mishnah and Midrash-compilations, and written, covering Scripture, as well. That is why everything to come would validate itself as a commentary to the text set forth by the Talmud out of all the prior texts that all together comprised the Torah.

It remains to explain that a well-known Judaism is not treated here. Specifically, In this setting, I do not address "the Judaism of Holocaust and Redemption," which from 1967 to the very recent past enjoyed enormous power in the life of American Jews. It was the Judaic religious system formed around the events of the Holocaust in Europe and the creation of the State of Israel, and held that the principal task of the Jews (not "eternal Israel") is to remain Jewish (without a supernatural definition of what that meant, that is, without a Judaism) and to support through political and philanthropic activity the State of Israel. It was enormously influential among American Jews, accounting to them why they should remain different from gentiles, but defining the difference in this-worldly terms, with no bearing on the conduct of everyday life and affairs. Profoundly secular in every way, that Judaism elicited the kind of devotion that, under other circumstances, religions ordinarily do.

But as a matter of fact, by any definition of religion and theology, that Judaism was no religion and had no theology. It was, and in its surviving pockets still is a chapter of the politics and sociology of Jewish Americans, itself an element in the politics and sociology of Americans in general. "Holocaust and Redemption" writing has no place in the theology of Judaism, except as rigorous theologians have transformed the issues, as they have, into the occasion for profound theological reflection. "The Judaism of Holocaust and Redemption" formed a Judaic system—an account of the way of life, world view, and definition of the social entity of a particular version of "Israel," but even though powerful in Reform and Conservative Judaisms, it was not a Judaic religious system, lacking as it did a serious confrontation with God and with issues of transcendence and holiness.[5]

Clearly, my focus is on issues of faith seeking understanding, the rational, philosophical construction of religious belief. It is not on the facts of who said what; I do not describe what pretty much everybody has thought, and I entirely ignore the institutional embodiments of the faith in the partisan seminaries and organizations of synagogues, e.g., Reconstructionist, Orthodox, Reform, Conservative, humanistic, and the like. In these pages the sects of contemporary Judaism play no role at all, because the issues that divide them are trivial and personal. Not only so, but locally-important theologians are not surveyed, since the criteria of selection emphasize the excellence of thought, not the ephemeral influence of the thinker. None of the worldly facts of episodic popularity bears theological consequence; all form mere accidents of local politics and sociology.

Episodically-famous personalities, joined to such institutions and occasions of ritual celebration by them, mean nothing. Mediocrity lays no claim upon the future. We are not here to celebrate platitudes and banalities. Conventional thinking fails the challenges of classical faith, and routine and full minds do not require a hearing that is not compelled by politics. Writers in the English language, and those whose works translated into English, that are not treated here are not neglected; they are rejected. Nor do I choose to pay attention to what by the standards of the Torah are simply heresies, on the one side, or rationalizations for apostasy, on the other. That is why I ignore some local icons, whose writing I find merely homiletical, on the one side, and theologians whose theology consists of the announcement that there is no God, on the other. For different reasons, neither class of theologians of Judaism deserves a hearing when the faithful come together rigorously to analyze the faith.

At stake here are issues alone. And I should maintain the catholic character of the writing, coming as it does from theologians identified with Orthodox, Reform, Conservative, and other Judaisms, resident in the English-speaking world or overseas, justifies that decision. Here are no party platforms nor partisan voices, celebrated here but unknown there, but rather, sober efforts at purveying truth—God's truth, so far as, in this world, we gain access to it. That is why this anthology presents not a historical-biographical repertoire covering everybody who was around at that time, but a sampler of vivid thinking and provocative, engaged writing. I bear sole responsibility for the judgments represented by inclusion and exclusion; nothing is tacit.

I have chosen writing that means to persuade, not merely inform; writing from heart to heart; writing that sets forth in the medium of words a deeply-felt religious sentiment, attitude, emotion, or conviction. In these pages readers meet embodiments of faith, hope, love for God, in the words of exemplary figures. That is why readers may expect to be not merely informed as to information but invited to participate in the thought and argument of interesting minds on important questions. When people go to a museum formed as a storehouse, they acquire information; they are left inert and unchanged. But when they go to a museum designed to teach, instruct, and engage, they enter into the experience of what is placed on display. They are affected and changed. Here they describe in vigorous advocacy of propositions, fully analyzed, amply documented, the encounter with God that has brought regeneration and renewal after the unparalleled catstrophe of our century.

Endnotes

[1] I have spelled out the many meanings imputed to "Israel" in various Judaic religious systems in my *Judaism and its Social Metaphors. Israel in the History of Jewish Thought* (New York: Cambridge University Press, 1988).

[2] Ingolf U. Dalferth, *Theology and Philosophy* (Oxford: Basil Blackwell Ltd., 1988) vii.

[3] By "Judaism" throughout these pages I mean one Judaic system in particular, the Judaism of the dual Torah, oral and written. The canon of that Judaism in particular is what is described in this and following paragraphs. Other Judaic systems have flourished and do today. Here the focus is upon the system that predominated and now continues, in a variety of modulations, to define Judaism for most practitioners of (a) Judaism, and to provide a principal source for all the others. That operative definition is descriptive, of course. All of the Judaic theologians represented in this anthology appeal to that one canonical literature and acknowledge its authority and authenticity as represented of God's revelation to eternal Israel.

[4] We of course should not ignore the fact that the labor of extension, amplification, application, and commentary in the richest sense went forward, and now goes forward, in a variety of directions. But no contemporary Judaic system begins elsewhere than in the Talmud and the oral part of the Torah represented by it. In the seminaries of all Judaic systems, and in the synagogues of all contemporary Judaisms, the Torah is presented in both the written and the oral components, though, I hasten to add, different Judaisms take up, each its own position on what fits into that entire Torah and how the Torah ia to be received and re-presented.

[5] Reading that Judaism in its correct, secular framework, I have dealt with that matter at some length in *Stranger at Home. Zionism, "The Holocaust," and American Judaism* (Chicago: University of Chicago Press, 1980).

Chapter 1

The Received Faith: "Israel" in the Dual Torah

Jacob Neusner

In many ways, for Christians (and others) the most difficult category of the theology of Judaism to grasp is "Israel." That is because today "Israel" is used to refer only to the state of Israel. But that usage is very recent; in fact, in Judaism, "Israel" refers to a social entity that is holy, that is called into being in the service of God and stands in a covenanted relationship with God through the Torah. Christians then will grasp what, in the context of theology, we mean by "Israel" when they remember that for them, "the Church," "the body of Christ," forms the structural and functional counterpart to the position of "Israel" in the received literature and liturgy of Judaism, from the Hebrew scriptures onward.

This brings us to the confusing fact that "Israel" in Judaism refers to the holy people of God, children of Abraham, Isaac, and Jacob, who stood at Sinai and received the Torah and entered the covenant with God, while "Israel" in the world today refers to the State of Israel. People today think of "Israel" as the Jewish State in the Land of Israel (a.k.a., "Palestine"), a political entity, equivalent to the U.S.A. But in Judaism, "Israel" has a different meaning altogether, a transcendent, supernatural significance: "people of God," "holy people," "children of Abraham, Isaac, and Jacob," and equivalent theological formulations.

We have therefore to realize that, when we study Judaism, we are not dealing with the Jews as a diverse set of ethnic groups, but with "Israel" as a theological formation, corresponding in the here and now to those Jews who identify themselves as practitioners of Judaism. It is somewhat complicated to realize that a religious community, "Israel," and an ethnic group or set of ethnic groups, "the Jews," coincide. That is because while all Judaists, or practitioners of Judaism, also are by definition Jews, members of the ethnic group, not all Jews are Judaists. If we define a Jew as the child of a Jewish mother (that is the definition of the law of Judaism) who either practices Judaism or does not practice any religion, then matters become clearer. All such Jews of ethnic definition may without an act of conversion adopt Judaism as their religion; all other human beings may adopt Judaism as their religion only through an act of conversion.

This brings us to the task at hand: the description of the category, Israel, in the received Judaism of the dual torah. "Israel" forms a principal part of the theology of

---

*From *The Jewish Return into History*. Copyright © 1978 by Emil L. Fackenheim. Reprinted by permission of Georges Borchardt, Inc. for the author.

Judaism in particular, because when people call themselves "Israel," and mean by that that same group of which the Hebrew Scriptures or "Old Testament" speaks, they claim for themselves a standing and a status that the simple facts of daily life do not, and cannot, validate. This is an act of theological faith, not sociological description. They compare themselves to some other social group and allege that they are like that other group or continue it or embody it in the here and now. In so doing, they evoke in explaining who they are what we may call a social metaphor. For the statement,"we are Israel," means to allege, "we are like that Israel of old" of which the Scriptures speak. The same is so when Christian residents of a given locale call themselves "the Church," or "the body of Christ." Then they speak of what is not seen, though very real. In both of these cases, the claim that "we" are "Israel," or "we" are "the body of Christ," form instances of metaphors invoked to explain the character and standing of a social entity. When we speak of social metaphors, we refer, therefore, to the things to which a group of people compare themselves in accounting for their society together.

"Israel"—that is, a theory of who "we" are in relationship to the Israel of the Torah—is the basic and required element of all theology of Judaism. There can be no Judaism without a clear statement of who and what is "Israel." The identification of "Israel" has preoccupied thinkers of all Judaisms from the beginning to the present. (It is, furthermore, a critical element in the thought of the many secular thinkers who produces what they call "philosophies of Judaism" or "of Jewish existence," or of Zionism, or of other secular readings of the Jews viewed solely in this worldly terms.) The making of Judaic systems commenced with the formation of the Pentateuch in the aftermath of the destruction of the first Temple of Jerusalem in 586 B.C. From that time to the present day the definition of "Israel," who belongs, who does not, and to what sort of social entity do "Israelites" adhere in forming (an) "Israel," has formed a remarkably pervasive theme in all of Judaisms. When we take up the systemic treatment by a Judaism of the category, "Israel," we address one critical and indicative issue of the Judaic system under study. The centrality of thought on "Israel" for all Judaisms from then to now may be assessed not only in the encounter with the record of the past.

For the theology of Judaism, the definition of an "Israel"—what it is and who belongs to it—takes the form of spelling out the rules of relationship. For to define one social entity, an "Israel," the sages of the Judaism of the dual Torah not only explain how that entity relates to some other. They also—and especially—compare and contrast that entity to some other. Accordingly, when the sages wish to think about "Israel" or "an Israel," their ordinary mode of thought is to ask to what "Israel" or "an Israel" is to be compared, hence in what ways it is like, and in what ways it is unlike, that to which it is compared. These then form the contrastive and analogical processes of reflection—metaphorical thinking.

How come "Israel," the social group imagined as a principal component of the formation of all of creation, took such a prominent place in the theology of Judaism? The reason is that the doctrine of what is "Israel" and who is Israel, as worked out over seven hundred years, held the whole system together. The story begins after 586 B.C.E. From that time forward all Judaisms that came into being framed a theory of "Israel," meaning, the group that a given Judaism identified as its social base. From the reconstitution of the Jews in the Land of Israel some three generations after the destruction of the first temple in 586 B.C.E., reflection on the character and composition of that social entity began with the self-conscious question: who is Israel and what are the conditions for being Israel? Every Judaism required answers to that question, which formed a definitive trait of the social ecology in which all Judaisms took shape. The urgency of the issue, "Israel," may be explained by reference to the reconstruction of the story of the group accomplished, out of materials referring to the period before 586, by authorships after that turning point.

Specifically, that point of entry into reflection on the issues of group life—the identification of an appropriate definition, a social metaphor for the group—was dictated by the interpretation placed upon the events of the sixth century by the emergent scripture, the Pentateuch or Five Books of Moses. That document, composed in part from revised materials deriving from the period before the destruction in 586, treated as critical the issues of the on-going life of the community, seen as not a given but a gift, and its relationship to the land that it possessed, interpreted as subject to diverse stipulations. The upshot was the doctrine of the experience of exile and return, and that doctrine imparted to the social entity formed by the Jews of the Land a heightened reality, treating as problematic and uncertain what, in the view of others, was simply another fact of the social life of humanity in that region. Accordingly, any Judaism required for a complete statement of its system a doctrine of who and what is Israel, the social group.

From the formation of the Pentateuch in ca. 450 B.C.E., every Judaism addressed the issue of who is Israel. Each appealed to its social metaphor in stating an answer to that question. The reason that the definition of what, and who, (an) Israel is played so critical role in all Judaism is not difficult to imagine. It was, specifically, the unsettling and disorienting experience selected and composed into an account of Israelite society by the authorship of Scripture in its final version. That authorship selected as normative two experiences, the one, the exile from Jerusalem and destruction of the Temple, the other, the return to Zion and rebuilding of the Temple. The paradigm of exile and return made it difficult to think of the life of the group as a given, a fixed star in the firmament of reality. Rather, that unsettling account of the life of the group portrayed the group's collective existence as a gift and not a given, as something subjected to stipulations and conditions, e.g., a covenant with God. The terms of the covenant, involving life on the land endowed with moral traits, uncertainty of the on-going existence of the group unless certain conditions were met, the notion that the group came from somewhere and was en route to some further destination—these terms highlighted the issue of who is Israel, and what an Israel is.

That framing of events into the pattern at hand represents an act of powerful imagination and interpretation, a symbolic transaction. It is an experience that is invented, because no one person or group both went into "exile" and also "returned home." Diverse experiences have been sorted out, various persons have been chosen, and the whole has been worked into a system by those who selected history out of happenings, and models out of masses of persons. We say "selected," because no Jews after 586 B.C.E. actually had experienced what in the aggregate Scripture says happened. None both went into exile and then came back to Jerusalem. So, to begin with, Scripture does not record a particular person's experience.

More to the point, if it is not autobiographical, writing for society at large the personal insight of a singular figure, it also is not an account of a whole nation's story. The reason is that the original exile encompassed mainly the political classes of Jerusalem and some useful populations alongside. Many Jews in the Judea of 586 never left. And, as is well known, a great many of those who ended up in Babylonia stayed there. Only a minority went back to Jerusalem. Consequently, the story of exile and return to Zion encompasses what happened to only a few families, who identified themselves as the family of Abraham, Isaac, and Jacob, and their genealogy as the history of Israel. Those families that stayed and those that never came back had they written the Torah would have told as normative and paradigmatic a different tale altogether.

That experience of the few that formed the paradigm for Israel beyond the restoration taught as normative lessons of alienation. Let me state with emphasis the lessons people claimed to learn out of the events they had chosen for their history: the life of the group is uncertain, subject to conditions and stipulations. *Nothing is set and given, all things a gift: land and life itself. But what actually did happen in that uncertain world—exile but then restoration—marked the group as special, different, select.*

There were other ways of seeing things, and the Pentateuchal picture was no more compelling than any other. Those Jews who did not go into exile, and those who did not "come home" had no reason to take the view of matters that characterized the authorship of Scripture. The life of the group need not have appeared more uncertain, more subject to contingency and stipulation, than the life of any other group. The land did not require the vision that imparted to it the enchantment, the personality, that, in Scripture, it received: "The land will vomit you out as it did those who were here before you." And the adventitious circumstance of Iranian imperial policy—a political happenstance—did not have to be recast into return. So nothing in the system of Scripture—exile for reason, return as redemption—followed necessarily and logically. Everything was invented: interpreted—much as with the force and power of metaphor.

That experience of the uncertainty of the life of the group in the century or so from the destruction of the First Temple of Jerusalem by the Babylonians in 586 to the building of the Second Temple of Jerusalem by the Jews, with Persian permission and sponsorship returned from exile, formed the paradigm. With the promulgation of the "Torah of Moses" under the sponsorship of Ezra, the Persians' viceroy, at ca. 450 B.C.E., all future Israels would then refer to that formative experience as it had been set down and preserved as the norm for Israel in the mythic terms of that "original" Israel, the Israel not of Genesis and Sinai and the end at the moment of entry into the promised land, but the "Israel" of the families that recorded as the rule and the norm the story of both the exile and the return. In that minority genealogy, that story of exile and return, alienation and remission, imposed on the received stories of pre-exilic Israel and adumbrated time and again in the Five Books of Moses and addressed by the framers of that document in their work over all, we find that paradigmatic statement in which every Judaism, from then to now, found its structure and deep syntax of social existence, the grammar of its intelligible message.

To be (an) "Israel"—the social component of a Judaism—from then to now has meant to ask what it means to be Israel (the secular formulation of the same issue is in terms of "who is a Jew?") The original pattern meant that an Israel would be a social group the existence of which had been called into question and affirmed—and therefore always would be called into question, and remained perpetually to be affirmed. Every Judaism then would find as its task the recapitulation of the original Judaism. That is to say, each made its own distinctive statement of the generative and critical resentment contained within that questioning of the given, that deep understanding of the uncertain character of the existence of the group in its normal location and under circumstances of permanence that (so far as the Judaic group understood things) characterized the life of every other group but Israel. What for everyone else (so it seemed to the Judaisms addressed to the Israels through time) was a given for Israel was a gift.

What all the nations knew as how things *must* be Israel understood as how things *might not be*: exile and loss, alienation and resentment, but, instead of annihilation, renewal, restoration, reconciliation, and (in theological language) redemption. So that paradigmatic experience, the one beginning in 586 and ending in ca. 450, written down in that written Torah of Moses, made its mark. That pattern, permanently inscribed in the Torah of God to Moses at Sinai, would define for all Israels over all time that matter of resentment demanding recapitulation: leaving home, coming home. An "Israel"—any "Israel"—would then constitute a social entity engaged by exile and return. But that covered a wide range of possibilities. In the theology of Judaism were fully realized the most important possibilities: Israel as holy people, Israel as extended family, Israel as sui generis, Israel as different from the rest of all humanity, non-Israel.

Now we understand the ambiguity of "Israel" in the theology of Judaism and in the secular ideologies of the Jewish ethnic group, "the Jewish people." While in today's world we take for granted that the word "Israel" refers to "the Jewish people," we also define our most vexed issues in terms of "who is Israel," meaning, "who is a Jew?" and "what is Israel?" meaning, "where should Jews live? what kind of a social entity do they, and should they, constitute?" Not only so, but when the founders of the Jewish state called it, "the State of Israel," they made a powerful statement indeed. What they said was, "to be 'Israel' means to form a political entity, a state, the Jewish state, the Jewish state located here in the Land of Israel. Then those who do not live in that place fall outside of "Israel," meaning, "the State of Israel." Clearly, therefore, when in contemporary Jewish discourse people talk about "Israel," they mean a variety of things and deliver a considerable judgment indeed.

In today's world the word "Israel" commonly is made to refer to the State of Israel, and the word "Israeli" to a citizen of that nation. "Israel" also may refer to a particular place, namely, the State of Israel or the Land of Israel. But that narrow and particularly political, enlandised and empowered meaning is new, beginning, as it does, in 1948. Long prior to that time, and even today, there has been a second and distinct meaning, "Israel" as "all Jews everywhere," the people of Israel. This "Israel" defined as "the Jewish people," sometimes spelled with a capital P as "the Jewish People," identifies "Israel" with a trans-national "community." It is a very important meaning of the word, for Scripture's many references to "Israel," as in "the Guardian of Israel does not slumber or sleep" then are taken to refer to that people or People. Throughout the liturgy of the synagogue, "Israel" always refers to the people, wherever they live, and not to the State of Israel today.

The fact that these two meanings, the one particular to a state, the other general to a scattered group, contradict one another alerts us to a problem. It is that a single word may stand for two things. And, as we shall see in the pages of this book, it may stand for many more. Indeed, thinking about "Israel" leads us deep into the generative processes of the theology of Judaism. In their reflection on that to which "Israel" is to be compared and contrasted, in their selection, from a repertoire of metaphors available from Scripture, of a particular set of comparisons, in their mode of thought on the matter, whether philosophical and abstract, whether political and concrete, our sages of blessed memory tell us the fundamental affirmation of the theology of Judaism: land, state, people—Israel all.

Now let us survey the unfolding of the conception of Israel in the oral Torah: The Mishnah's framers' thinking about "Israel" treated that social entity as intransitive, bearing no relationships to any other distinct social entity. The opposite of "Israel" in the Mishnah is "the nations," on the one side, or "Levite, priest," on the other: always taxonomical, never defined out of relationship to others within the same theoretical structure. As we shall see, the opposite of "Israel" in the Yerushalmi became "Rome," and Israel found itself defined as a family, with good and bad seed.

Now the nations were differentiated, and a different world-order conceived; Israel entered into relationships of comparison and contrast, not merely hierarchy, because Christianity, sharing the same Scriptures, now called into question the very status of the Jews to constitute "Israel."

The Mishnah defines "Israel" bears two identical meanings: the "Israel" of (all) the Jews now and here, but also the "Israel" of which Scripture— the Torah—spoke. And that encompassed both the individual and the group, without linguistic differentiation of any kind. Thus in the Mishnah "Israel" may refer to an individual Jew (always male) or to "all Jews," that is, the collectivity of Jews. The individual woman is nearly always called *bat yisrael,* daughter of (an) Israel(ite). Sages in the Mishnah did not merely assemble facts and define the social entity as a matter of mere description of the given. Rather, they portrayed it as they wished to. They imputed to the social group, Jews, the status of a systemic entity, "Israel." To others within Jewry it was not at all self-evident that "all Jews" constituted one "Israel," and that that one "Israel" formed the direct and immediate continuation, in the here and now, with the "Israel" of holy writ and revelation.

The Mishnaic identification of Jewry in the here and now with the "Israel" of Scripture therefore constituted an act of metaphor, comparison, contrast, identification and analogy. It is that Judaism's most daring social metaphor. Implicitly, moreover, the metaphor excluded a broad ranger of candidates from the status of (an) "Israel," the Samaritans for one example, the scheduled castes of Mishnah-tractate Qiddushin Chapter Four, for another. Calling (some) Jews "Israel" established the comprehensive and generative metaphor that gives the Mishnaic system its energy. From that metaphor all else derived momentum.

The Mishnah defines "Israel" in antonymic relationships of two sorts, first, "Israel" as against "not-Israel," gentile, and second, "Israel" as against "priest," or "Levite." "Israel serves as a taxonomic indicator, specifically part of a more encompassing system of hierarchization; "Israel" defined the frontiers, on the outer side of society, and the social boundaries within, on the other. To understand the meaning of "Israel" as the Mishnah and its associated documents of the second and third centuries sort matters out, we consider the sense of "gentile." The authorship of the Mishnah does not differentiate among gentiles, who represent an undifferentiated mass. To the system of the Mishnah, whether or not a gentile is a Roman or an Aramaean or a Syrian or a Briton does not matter. That is to say, differentiation among gentiles rarely, if ever, makes a difference in systemic decision-making.

And, it is also the fact, to the system of the Mishnah, that in the relationship at hand, "Israel" is not differentiated either. The upshot is that just as "gentile" is an abstract category, so is "Israel." "Kohen" is a category, and so is "Israel." For the purposes for which Israel/priest are defined, no further differentiation is undertaken. That is where for the Mishnaic system matters end. But to the Judaic system represented by the Yerushalmi and its associated writings, "gentile" may be Roman or other-than-Roman, for instance, Babylonia, Media, or Greece. That act of further differentiation—we may call it "speciation"—makes a considerable difference in the appreciation of gentile. In the Mishnah's authorship's "Israel," therefore we confront an abstraction in a system of philosophy.

The centrality of "Israel" in the analogy of a people holy as the temple was holy marked the Mishnaic system. "Israel" was a species of the genus, people or nation. But, in the system of the Mishnah's authorship, "Israel," the genus, possessed only the sole species, Israel. The issue of who and what is "Israel" profoundly troubled the Mishnah's authorship. For the question that provoked sustained thought finds definition in the points of emphasis of the Mishnah's theology as a whole. The holiness of the life of "Israel," the people, a holiness that had formerly centered on the temple, now endured and transcended the physical destruction of the building and the cessation of sacrifices. The Mishnah's theology stated in countless details that "Israel" the people was holy, the medium and the instrument of God's sanctification.

What required sanctification, in particular, were the modalities of life lived in community, procreation, nourishment, family, land, time, village, temple. The system then instructed "Israel" to act as if "Israel," the Jewish people, like the temple of old, formed a utensil of the sacred. Two points of ordinary life formed the focus for concrete, social differentiation in the foundations of the Mishnah's theology of sanctification: food and sex, the latter governing valid marriage. What people ate, how they conducted their sexual lives, and whom they married or to whom they gave their children in marriage would define the social parameters of their group. These facts indicate who was kept within the bounds, and who was excluded and systematically maintained at a distance. That is why and how sanctification functions to define the social thinking and therefore to lend shape to metaphors of the social entity of a system.

How does this work in detail? The word and category "Israel" reach definition in relationship to other species of its genus, if [1] nation, then Israel/not gentile, if [2] caste, then Israel/not priest. These definitions viewed in this worldly terms self-evidently tell us much about what "Israel" is when compared with (other) nations or (other) castes, but nothing about what "Israel" *is*. That is what we mean by "Israel" as transitive and not intransitive. In the theology of the Mishnah "Israel" draws upon metaphors of a hierarchical character—nation, caste, while "Israel" in the pages of the Talmud of the Land of Israel and related Midrash-compilations appeals to metaphors of a concrete and societal character or of family, or it is represented as utterly other and *sui generis*.

When in the Mishnah "Israel" stands alone, not as a qualifier or partitive, it ordinarily functions as a contrastive, that is, Israel *and not*, ... specifically, either, *not an outsider*, or *not a higher caste*. The best way to find out what meanings attach to the word "Israel" thus is to investigate the antonyms, and two are of fundamental importance. If the authorship of the Mishnah heard "Israel," one might think of the opposite as gentile (or Samaritan, heretic); or he might hear "Priest, Levite." All senses of the word "Israel" in the Mishnah fall within one or the other classification, e.g., "Israel as nation," whether a political or a supernatural entity, Israel, not Samaritan, Israel as individual Israelite—all of these senses draw to begin with upon "Israel" as "not gentile." "Israel" as a caste within Israel the people is by far the most common.

While in Scripture, and later on in the Yerushalmi and related writings, Israel also is treated as an extended family, the Mishnah's authorship rarely makes use of that category. Like Israel *sui generis*, the meaning of "Israel" as family when it does occur always bears supernatural, not narrowly familial or genealogical, meaning or occurs in a liturgical context, which is the same thing. When "fathers" or "ancestors" is joined to the noun, "Israel," a supernatural sense intrudes, e.g., "God of the fathers of Israel" (*m. Bik.* 1:4), "All Israelites are sons of princes" (which is ordinarily understood to allude to their being children of Abraham) (*m. Šabb.* 14:4)—this for purposes of ritual classification. Not every genealogical reference demands the sense of "family" at all, e.g., "the children of Israel" (*m. Neg.* 2:1) is simply synonymous with "Israel" the social entity, pure and simple. These usages are not commonplace and play no role in the formulation of the law, to which the bulk of the Mishnah is devoted.

We now reach the second of the two very common usages, namely, *Israel-not-priest*, that is, Israel in contradiction to *kohen*, that is, priest, or, less commonly, to Levite. Israelite society was deemed divided into castes: priests, Levites, Israel, and on downward. "Israel" in the sense of the caste yields Israel as "common folk," always defined in contradiction to Levites and *Kohanim* or priests, occurs throughout, e.g., Yoma 7:1: "For Israel unto itself, . . . for the priests unto themselves." The temple had its courtyard into which Israelites were permitted to enter, with inner spaces open to priests but closed to Israelites (e.g., *m. Sukk.* 5:4). Related distinctions separate Israel from Nazirites, those who have taken the oath specified at Numbers 6, *mamzerim*, offspring of a couple that can never legally marry (*m. Ma'aś. S.* 5:4), or other special cultic categories.

So who really is "Israel"? When we ask the authorship of the Mishnah to tell us in explicit terms how they define (an) "Israel," they direct our attention to the one passage in which they systematically answer that question. It is framed, as a question of social definition must be, in terms of who is in and who is out. (An) "Israel" then is defined within the categories of inclusion and exclusion, which implicitly yields the definition that all who are out are out and all who are in are in, and, all together, the ones that are in (implicitly) constitute the social entity or social group at hand. When the Mishnah's authorship wishes to define "Israel" by itself and on its own terms, rather than as a classification among other classifications in an enormous system of taxonomy, "Israel" may be set forth as an entity not only in its own terms but also *sui generis*. But, as we now expect, the context will be defined by supernatural considerations.

All "Israelites"—persons who hold the correct opinion—constitute "Israel." There is no passage of the Mishnah and related literature more concrete and explicit than the one at hand on who is in and who is out. *But the "in" is not within this world at all.* It is who enters or has a share of the world to come. Then all those "Israelites" who constitute in themselves the social entity, the group, "Israel," form a supernatural, not merely a social entity—and no wonder all metaphors fail. The premise is that we speak only of Israel, and the result is the definition of Israel in terms we should not have anticipated at all: not Israel as against non-Israel, gentile, nor Israel as against non-Israel, the priest, but Israel as against those who deny convictions now deemed—explicitly—indicatively and normatively to form the characteristics of "Israel"[ite]. Here is an "Israel" that, at first glance, is defined not in relationships but intransitively and intrinsically. To state the result simply: in what follows, Israel is implicitly *sui generis*.

A. All Israelites have a share in the world to come,
B. as it is said, "your people also shall be all righteous, they shall inherit the land forever; the branch of my planting, the work of my hands, that I may be glorified" (Isa 60:21).
C. And these are the ones who have no portion in the world to come:
D. He who says, the resurrection of the dead is a teaching which does not derive from the Torah, and the Torah does not come from Heaven; and an Epicurean.
E. R. Aqiba says, "Also: He who reads in heretical books,
F. "and he who whispers over a wound and says, 'I will put none of the diseases upon you which I have put on the Egyptians, for I am the Lord who heals you' (Exod 15:26)."
G. Abba Saul says, "Also: He who pronounces the divine Name as it is spelled out."

m. Sanhedrin 11:1

Israel is defined inclusively: to be "Israel" is to have a share in the world to come. "Israel" then is a social entity that is made up of those who share a common conviction, and that "Israel" therefore bears an other-worldly destiny. Other social entities are not so defined within the Mishnah—and that by definition!—and it must follow that (an) "Israel" in the conception of the authorship of the Mishnah is *sui generis*, in that other social entities do not find their definition within the range of supernatural facts pertinent to "Israel;" an "Israel" is a social group that endows its individual members with life in the world to come; an "Israel"[ite] is one who enjoys the world to come. Excluded from this "Israel" are "Israel"[ite]s who within the established criteria of social identification exclude themselves. The power to define by relationships does not run out, however, since in this supernatural context of an

Israel that is *sui generis*, we still know who is "Israel" because we are told who is "not-Israel," now, specific non-believers or sinners. These are, as we should expect, persons who reject the stated belief.

    A.   Three kings and four ordinary folk have no portion in the world to come.
    B.   Three kings: Jeroboam, Ahab, and Manasseh.
    C.   R. Judah says, "Manasseh has a portion in the world to come,
    D.   "since it is said, 'And he prayed to him and he was entreated of him and heard his supplication and brought him again to Jerusalem into his kingdom' (2 Chron 33:13)."
    E.   They said to him, "To his kingdom he brought him back, but to the life of the world to come he did not bring him back."
    F.   Four ordinary folk: Balaam, Doeg, Ahitophel, and Gehazi.

m. Sanhedrin 11:2

Not only persons, but also classes of Israelites are specified, in all cases contributing to the definition of (an) Israel. The excluded classes of Israelites bear in common a supernatural fault, which is that they have sinned against God. So much for the first document of the Oral Torah. We turn now to the formulations in the Talmud of the Land of Israel, which came to closure in the century after the conversion of the Roman Empire to Christianity, where we find ourselves in a quite different world.

The profound shift in characterization of "Israel" that took place in the late fourth and fifth century documents responded to the crisis presented by the political triumph of Christianity. Now "Israel" found definition on its own terms, and not principally in relationship to "non-Israel," whatever that, in context, may have meant. "Israel" now bore an absolute, not a relative meaning, with concrete, not abstract valence. The documents that carried forward and continued the Mishnah exhibit striking changes, in particular within those writings brought to closure at the end of the fourth century and in the hundred years thereafter, and the representation of "Israel" followed suit. These writings, over all, present us with a Judaic system interested in sanctification in the here and now and also in salvation at the end of time, a system in which the teleology bore in its wake an eschatological doctrine of a salvific character.

When sages wished to know what (an) "Israel" was, in the writings produced at the end of the fourth century they reread the story of Scripture's "Israel's" origins for the answer. To begin with, as Scripture told them the story, "Israel" was a man, Jacob, and his children are "the children of Jacob." That man's name was also "Israel," and, it followed, "the children of Israel" comprised the extended family of that man. By extension, "Israel" formed the family of Abraham and Sarah, Isaac and Rebecca, Jacob and Leah and Rachel. "Israel" therefore invoked the theory of genealogy to explain the bonds that linked persons unseen into a single social entity; the shared traits were imputed, not empirical. That social theory of "Israel"—a simple one, really, and easily grasped—bore consequences in two ways. First, children in general are admonished to follow the good example of their parents. The deeds of the patriarchs and matriarchs therefore taught lessons on how the children were to act. Of greater interest in an account of "Israel" as a social theory, "Israel" lived twice, once in the patriarchs and matriarchs, a second time in the life of the heirs as the descendants relived those earlier lives. The stories of the family were carefully reread to provide a picture of the meaning of the latter-day events of the descendants of that same family. Accordingly, the lives of the patriarchs signaled the history of Israel.

The polemical purpose of the claim that that abstraction, "Israel," was to be compared to the family of the mythic ancestor lies right at the surface. With another "Israel," the Christian Church, now claiming to constitute the true one, Jews found it possible to confront that claim and to turn it against the other side. "You claim to form 'Israel after the spirit.' Fine, and *we* are Israel after the flesh—and genealogy forms the link, that alone." (Converts did not present an anomaly, of course, since they were held to be children of Abraham and Sarah, who had "made souls," that is, converts, in Haran, a point repeated in the documents of the period.) That fleshly continuity formed of all of "us" a single family, rendering spurious the notion that "Israel" could be other than genealogically defined. But that polemic seems to me adventitious and not primary. At the same time the theory provided a quite separate component to sages' larger system.

The theology of Israel as family supplied an encompassing theory of society, accounting for that sense of constituting a corporate social entity that clearly infused the documents of the Judaism of the dual Torah from the very outset. Such a theory explained not only who "Israel" as a whole was. It also set forth the responsibilities of Israel's social entity, its society; it defined the character of that entity; it explained who owes what to whom at why, and it accounted for the inner structure and interplay of relationship within the community, here and now, constituted by Jews in their villages and neighborhoods of towns. Accordingly, "Israel" as family bridged the gap between an account of the entirety of the social group, "Israel," and a picture of the components of that social group as they lived out their lives in their households and villages. An encompassing theory of society, covering all components from least to greatest, holding the whole together in correct order and proportion, derived from "Israel" viewed as extended family.

That theory of "Israel" as a society made up of persons who because they constituted a family stood in a clear relationship of obligation and responsibility to one another corresponded to what people much later would call the social contract, a kind of compact that in palpable ways told families and households how in the aggregate they formed something larger and tangible. The web of interaction spun out of concrete interchange now was spun out of not the gossamer thread of abstraction and theory but the tough hemp of family ties. "Israel" formed a society because "Israel" was compared to an extended family. That, sum and substance, supplied to the Jews in their households (themselves a made-up category which, in the end, transformed the relationship of the nuclear family into an abstraction capable of holding together quite unrelated persons) an account of the tie from household to household, from village to village, encompassing ultimately "all Israel."

If "we" form a family, then we know full well what links us, the common ancestry, the obligations imposed by common ancestry upon the cousins who make up the family today. The link between the commonplace interactions and relationships that make "us" into a community, on the one side, and that encompassing entity, "Israel," "all Israel," now is drawn. The large comprehends the little, the abstraction of "us" overall ("the circumcised," for instance) gains concrete reality in the "us" of the here and now of home and village, all together, all forming a "family." In that fundamental way, the theology of "Israel" as family therefore provided the field-theory of "Israel" linking the most abstraction component, the entirety of the social group, to the most mundane, the specificity of the household. One theory, framed in that theology of such surpassing simplicity, now held the whole together. The theology of family provided an encompassing theory of society, an account of the social contract encompassing all social entities, Jews' and gentiles' as well.

We survey how "Israel" as family comes to expression in the document that makes the most sustained and systematic statement of the matter, *Genesis Rabbah*. In this theory we should not miss the extraordinary polemic utility, of which, in passing, we have already taken note. "Israel" as family also understood itself to form a nation or people. That nation-people held a land, a rather peculiar, enchanted or holy, Land at that, one that, in its imputed traits, was as *sui generis*—as (presently we shall see) in the metaphorical thought of the system at hand, Israel also was. Competing for the same territory, Israel's claim to what it called the Land of Israel—thus, *of Israel* in particular—now rested on right of inheritance such as a family enjoyed, and this was made explicit. The passage shows how high the stakes were in the claim to constitute the genealogical descendant of the ancestors.

1. A. "But to the sons of his concubines, Abraham gave gifts, and while he was still living, he sent them away from his son Isaac, eastward to the east country" (Gen 25:6):

B. In the time of Alexander of Macedonia the sons of Ishmael came to dispute with Israel about the birthright, and with them came two wicked families, the Canaanites and the Egyptians.

C. They said, "Who will go and engage in a disputation with them."

D. Gebiah b. Qosem [the enchanter] said, "I shall go and engage in a disputation with them."

E. They said to him, "Be careful not to let the Land of Israel fall into their possession."

F. He said to them, "I shall go and engage in a disputation with them. If I win over them, well and good. And if not, you may say, 'Who is this hunchback to represent us?' "

G. He went and engaged in a disputation with them. Said to them Alexander of Macedonia, "Who lays claim against whom?"

H. The Ishmaelites said, "We lay claim, and we bring our evidence from their own Torah: 'But he shall acknowledge the firstborn, the son of the hated' (Deut 21;17). Now Ishmael was the firstborn. [We therefore claim the land as heirs of the first-born of Abraham.]"

I. Said to him Gebiah b. Qosem, "My royal lord, does a man not do whatever he likes with his sons?"

J. He said to him, "Indeed so."

K. "And lo, it is written, 'Abraham gave all that he had to Isaac' (Gen 25:2)."

L. [Alexander asked,] "Then where is the deed of gift to the other sons?"

M. He said to him, " 'But to the sons of his concubines, Abraham gave gifts, [and while he was still living, he sent them away from his son Isaac, eastward to the east country]' (Gen 25:6)."

N. [The Ishmaelites had no claim on the land.] They abandoned the field in shame.

Genesis Rabbah LXI:VII

The metaphor now shifts, with the notion of Israel today as the family of Abraham, as against the Ishmaelites, also of the same family, gives way. But the theme of family records persists. Canaan has no claim, for Canaan was also a family, comparable to Israel—but descended from a slave. The power of the theology of family is that it can explain not only the social entity formed by Jews, but the social entities confronted by them. All fell into the same genus, making up diverse species. The theory of society before us—that is, the theory of "Israel"—thus accounts for the existence, also, of all societies, and, as we shall see when we deal with Rome, the theory of "Israel" does so with extraordinary force.

O. The Canaanites said, "We lay claim, and we bring our evidence from their own Torah. Throughout their Torah it is written, 'the land of Canaan.' So let them give us back our land."

P. Said to him Gebiah b. Qosem, "My royal lord, does a man not do whatever he likes with his slave?"

Q. He said to him, "Indeed so."

R. He said to him, "And lo, it is written, 'A slave of slaves shall Canaan be to his brothers' (Gen 9:25). So they are really our slaves."

S. [The Canaanites had no claim to the land and in fact should be serving Israel.] They abandoned the field in shame.

The same theology serves both "Israel" and "Canaan." Each formed the latter-day heir of the earliest family, and both lived out the original paradigm. The mode of thought at hand imputes the same genus to both social entities, and then makes its possible to distinguish among the two species at hand. We shall see the same mode of thought—the family, but which wing of the family—when we consider the confrontation with Christianity and with Rome, in each case conceived in the same personal way. The theology applies to both and yields its own meanings for each. The final claim in the passage before us moves away from the theology of family. But the notion of a continuous, physical descent is implicit here as well.

Families inherited the estate of the founders, and "Israel" was a family with a sizable heritage and inheritance. Thinking not in terms of abstractions but in personal and concrete ways, sages personalized, but, through the invented personalities, were able to make perfectly clear statements for themselves. Along these same lines, when the Church theologians-historians faced the task of explaining the connection between diverse nations or peoples and the Church, they worked out relationships between the king of a country and Jesus, as in the case of the correspondence between Jesus and Abgar, which accounted for the place of the Church of Edessa within the family of Christianity. Since the Church understood that not only Jesus' blood relatives, but also his disciples, standing in a supernatural relationship with him, entered into the original communion, the invented discipleship of kings made a place, within a larger social theory of the Church, for the new and diverse groups. When, in the fourth century, a principal world-ruler did convert, the Church had an understanding of the role of persons and personalities in the history of salvation. The mode of thought before us, therefore, finds ample place in a larger scheme of thinking about society and the relationships of its components.

Families have histories, and "Israel" as family found in the record of its family -history those points of coherence that transformed events into meaningful patterns, that is, the history of the social unit, the nation-family, as a whole. This matter is simply expressed by the common wisdom, like parent, like child, the apple does not fall far from the tree, and the like. Whether true or false, that folk wisdom surely accounts for the commonsense quality of sages' search, in the deeds of the patriarchs and matriarchs, for messages concerning the future history of the children. But sages assuredly were not common folk. They were philosophers, and their inquiry constituted a chapter in the history of what used to be called natural philosophy, and what today we know as social science. Specifically, sages looked in the facts of history for the laws of history. They proposed to generalize, and, out of generalization, to explain their own particular circumstance. That is why we may compare them to social scientists or social philosophers, trying to turn anecdotes into insight and to demonstrate how we may know the difference between impressions and truths. Genesis provided facts concerning the family. Careful sifting of those facts will yield the laws that dictated why to that family things happened one way, rather than some other.

Among these social laws of the family history, one took priority, the laws that explained the movement of empires upward and downward and pointed toward the ultimate end of it all. Scripture provided the model for the ages of empires, yielding a picture of four monarchies, to be followed by Israel as the fifth. Sages repeated this familiar viewpoint (one we shall rehearse when we consider "Israel" as *sui generis*, now for quite other reasons). In reading Genesis, in particular, they found that time and again events in the lives of the patriarchs prefigured the four monarchies, among which, of course, the fourth, last, and most intolerable was Rome. Israel's history falls under God's dominion. Whatever will happen carries out God's plan, and that plan for the future has been laid out in the account of the origins supplied by Genesis. The fourth kingdom, Rome, is part of that plan, which we can discover by carefully studying Abraham's life and God's word to him.

1. A. "Then the Lord said to Abram, 'Know of a surety [that your descendants will be sojourners in a land that is not theirs, and they will be slaves there, and they will be oppressed for four hundred years; but I will bring judgment on the nation which they serve, and afterward they shall come out with great possessions']" (Gen 15:13-14):
    B. "Know" that I shall scatter them.
    C. "Of a certainty" that I shall bring them back together again.
    D. "Know" that I shall put them out as a pledge [in expiation of their sins].
    E. "Of a certainty" that I shall redeem them.
    F. "Know" that I shall make them slaves.
    G. "Of a certainty" that I shall free them.
         Genesis Rabbah XLIV:XVIII

No. 1 parses the cited verse and joins within its simple formula the entire history of Israel, punishment and forgiveness alike. Not only the patriarchs, but also the matriarchs, so acted as to shape the future life of the family, Israel. One extended statement of the matter suffices. Here is how sages take up the detail of Abraham's provision of a bit of water, showing what that act had to do with the history of Israel later on. The intricate working out of the whole then encompasses the merit of the patriarchs, the way in which the deeds of the patriarchs provide a sign for proper conduct for their children, the history and salvation of Israel .

2. A. "Let a little water be brought" (Gen 18:4):
    B. Said to him the Holy One, blessed be he, "You have said, 'Let a little water be brought' (Gen 18:4). By your life, I shall pay your descendants back for this: 'Then sang Israel this song, "spring up O well, sing you to it" ' (Num 21:7)."
    C. That recompense took place in the wilderness. Where do we find that it took place in the Land of Israel as well?
    D. "A land of brooks of water" (Deut 8:7).
    E. And where do we find that it will take place in the age to come?
    F. "And it shall come to pass in that day that living waters shall go out of Jerusalem" (Zech 14:8).

G. ["And wash your feet" (Gen 18:4)]: [Said to him the Holy One, blessed be he,] "You have said, 'And wash your feet.' By your life, I shall pay your descendants back for this: 'Then I washed you in water' (Ezek 16:9)."

H. That recompense took place in the wilderness. Where do we find that it took place in the Land of Israel as well?

I. "Wash you, make you clean" (Isa 1:16).

J. And where do we find that it will take place in the age to come?

K. "When the Lord will have washed away the filth of the daughters of Zion" (Isa 4:4).

L. [Said to him the Holy One, blessed be he,] "You have said, 'And rest yourselves under the tree' (Gen 18:4). By your life, I shall pay your descendants back for this: 'He spread a cloud for a screen' (Ps 105:39)."

M. That recompense took place in the wilderness. Where do we find that it took place in the Land of Israel as well?

N. "You shall dwell in booths for seven days" (Lev 23:42).

O. And where do we find that it will take place in the age to come?

P. "And there shall be a pavilion for a shadow in the day-time from the heat" (Isa 4:6).

Q. [Said to him the Holy One, blessed be he,] "You have said, 'While I fetch a morsel of bread that you may refresh yourself' (Gen 18:5). By your life, I shall pay your descendants back for this: 'Behold I will cause to rain bread from heaven for you' (Exod 16:45)"

R. That recompense took place in the wilderness. Where do we find that it took place in the Land of Israel as well?

S. "A land of wheat and barley" (Deut 8:8).

T. And where do we find that it will take place in the age to come?

U. "He will be as a rich grain field in the land" (Ps 82:16).

V. [Said to him the Holy One, blessed be he,] "You ran after the herd ['And Abraham ran to the herd' (Gen 18:7)]. By your life, I shall pay your descendants back for this: 'And there went forth a wind from the Lord and brought across quails from the sea' (Num 11:27)."

W. That recompense took place in the wilderness. Where do we find that it took place in the Land of Israel as well?

X. "Now the children of Reuben and the children of Gad had a very great multitude of cattle" (Num 32:1).

Y. And where do we find that it will take place in the age to come?

Z. "And it will come to pass in that day that a man shall rear a young cow and two sheep" (Isa 7:21).

AA. [Said to him the Holy One, blessed be he,] "You stood by them: 'And he stood by them under the tree while they ate' (Gen 18:8). By your life, I shall pay your descendants back for this: 'And the Lord went before them' (Exod 13:21)."

BB. That recompense took place in the wilderness. Where do we find that it took place in the Land of Israel as well?

CC. "God stands in the congregation of God" (Ps 82:1).
DD. And where do we find that it will take place in the age to come?
EE. "The breaker is gone up before them . . . and the Lord at the head of them" (Mic 2:13).

Genesis Rabbah XLVIII:X

Everything that Abraham did brought a reward to his descendants. The enormous emphasis on the way in which Abraham's deeds prefigured the history of Israel, both in the wilderness, and in the Land, and, finally, in the age to come, provokes us to wonder who held that there were other children of Abraham, beside this "Israel." The answer—the triumphant Christians in particular, who right from the beginning, with Paul and the evangelists, imputed it to the earliest generations and said it in so many words—then is clear. We note that there are five statements of the same proposition, each drawing upon a clause in the base verse. The extended statement moreover serves as a sustained introduction to the treatment of the individual clauses that now follow, item by item. Obviously, it is the merit of the ancestors that connects the living Israel to the lives of the patriarchs and matriarchs of old.

While Abraham founded Israel, Isaac and Jacob carried forth the birthright and the blessing. This they did through the process of selection, ending in the assignment of the birthright to Jacob alone. The importance of that fact for the definition of "Israel" hardly requires explication. The lives of all three patriarchs flowed together, each being identified with the other as a single long life. This immediately produced the proposition that the historical life of Israel, the nation, continued the individual lives of the patriarchs. The theory of who is Israel, therefore, is seen once more to have rested on genealogy: Israel is one extended family, all being children of the same fathers and mothers, the patriarchs and matriarchs of Genesis. This theory of Israelite society, and of the Jewish people in the time of the sages of *Genesis Rabbah*, made of the people a family, and of genealogy, a kind of ecclesiology. The importance of that proposition in countering the Christian claim to be a new Israel cannot escape notice. Israel, sages maintained, is Israel after the flesh, and that in a most literal sense.

Jacob's contribution to knowledge of the meaning and end of Israel's history, as sages uncovered it, is exemplified in the following:

1. A. ". . . so that I come again to my father's house in peace, then the Lord shall be my God" (Gen 28:20-22):

   B. R. Joshua of Sikhnin in the name of R. Levi: "The Holy One, blessed be he, took the language used by the patriarchs and turned it into a key to the redemption of their descendants.

   C. "Said the Holy One, blessed be he, to Jacob, 'You have said, "Then the Lord shall be my God." By your life, all of the acts of goodness, blessing, and consolation which I am going to carry out for your descendants I shall bestow only by using the same language:

D. " ' "Then in that day, living waters shall go out from Jerusalem" (Zech 14:8). "Then in that day a man shall rear a young cow and two sheep" (Isa 7:21). "Then, in that day, the Lord will set his hand again the second time to recover the remnant of his people" (Isa 11:11). "Then, in that day, the mountains shall drop down sweet wine" (Joel 4:18). "Then, in that day, a great horn shall be blown and they shall come who were lost in the land of Assyria" (Isa 27:13).' "

Genesis Rabbah LXX:VI

The union of Jacob's biography and Israel's history yields the passage at hand. It is important only because it says once again what we have now heard throughout our survey of *Genesis Rabbah*—but makes the statement as explicit as one can imagine. Now the history of the redemption of Israel is located in the colloquy between Jacob and Laban's sons.

1. A. "Now Laban had two daughters, the name of the older was Leah, and the name of the younger was Rachel" (Gen 29:16):

B. They were like two beams running from one end of the world to the other.

C. This one produced captains and that one produced captains, this one produced kings and that one produced kings, this one produced lion tamers and that one produced lion tamers, this one produced conquerors of nations and that one produced conquerors of nations, this one produced those who divided countries and that one produced dividers of countries.

D. The offering brought by the son of this one overrode the prohibitions of the Sabbath, and the offering brought by the son of that one overrode the prohibitions of the Sabbath.

E. The war fought by this one overrode the prohibitions of the Sabbath, and the war fought by this one overrode the prohibitions of the Sabbath.

F. To this one were given two nights, and to that one were given two nights.

G. The night of Pharaoh and the night of Sennacherib were for Leah, and the night of Gideon for for Rachel, and the night of Mordecai was for Rachel, as it is said, "On that night the king could not sleep" (Esth 6:1).

Genesis Rabbah LXX:XV

The theology encompasses not only "Israel" but also "Rome," to which we shall turn in the next chapter. It makes sense of all the important social entities, for in this theology, "Israel" is consubstantial with other social entities, which relate to "Israel" just as "Israel" as a society relates to itself, present and past. Accordingly, "Rome" is a family just as is "Israel," and, more to the point, "Rome" enters into "Israel's" life in an intelligible way precisely because "Rome" too is a part of that same family that is constituted by "Israel." That is a stunning claim, working itself out time after time so smoothly, with such self-evidence, as to conceal its daring. Again we see how the theology that joins past to present, household to household to "all Israel," in fact encompasses the other noteworthy social entity and takes it into full account—a powerful, successful field-theory indeed. "Non-Israel" accommodates, it classifies, but it does not explain.

Once sages had defined the social entity of Israel by analogy with a family, they naturally imposed upon social entities round about the same metaphor, which, in its nature, is inclusive and not exclusive. That instrument of thought therefore allowed sages to explain within a single, unitary theory what happened to both Israel and everyone else that mattered. If, in *Genesis Rabbah*, Abraham, Isaac, and Jacob stand for Israel later on, then Ishmael, Edom, and Esau represent Rome. Hence whatever sages find out about those figures tells them something about Rome and its character, history, and destiny. God has unconditionally promised to redeem Israel, but if Israel repents, then the redemption will come with greater glory.

The challenge of Christianity from the beginning had come from its spiritualization of "Israel." Here that challenge finds its answer in the opposite and counterpart: the utter and complete "genealogization" of Israel. To state matters negatively, the people could no more conceive that they were not the daughters and sons of their fathers and mothers than that they were not one large family, that is, the family of Abraham, Isaac, and Jacob: Israel after the flesh. That is what "after the flesh" meant. The powerful stress on the enduring merit of the patriarchs and matriarchs, the social theory that treated Israel as one large, extended family, the actual children of Abraham, Isaac, and Jacob— these now-familiar metaphors for the fleshly continuity met head on the contrary position framed by Paul and restated by Christian theologians from his time onward.

"Israel" as family therefore served a powerful polemical purpose in engaging with the new political facts of the age. But the theology did not originate in the fourth century. It originated in Scripture itself. Adopting the metaphor simply formed a stage in the metaphorization of "Israel" in the here and now by appeal to the "Israel" of Scripture. The potential of "Israel" as family existed as soon as thinkers about the social entity, "Israel," realized that they and their contemporaries in the here and now constituted that same "Israel" that Scripture had portrayed. But the family proved remarkably apt for the requirements of the new era, and that is why that definition of "Israel" fully came to realization in just this age. "Family" explained the composition of the household, an economic unit of production. "Family" accounted for the interrelationships of households of a certain sort—the Jewish sort—in a mixed village or in a village made up of only Jewish households. The metaphor of "family" allowed Jews to relate their own social entity to those other entities the political presence of which they chose to take account. In all, the power of the theology lay in its possibility of joining all social entities, whether groups, whether classes, whether of another order altogether, into a single and uniform entity: "the families of humanity," whether of Israel or of Esau. But "family"—whether Israel, whether Esau—left "Israel" different but not at all singular. Sages found self-evident the fact that they—"Israel"—formed a group not at all like other groups. They were not merely the better wing of a common family.

They formed a different type of group altogether from other groups, if a nation, then a singular nation. "Israel" stood for not only family among families, but also people or nation among entities of the same genus. Long before the advent of Christianity, Jews, quite naturally thinking of themselves within the biblical record as embodying, now, the people Scripture had called "Israel," of course had attained consciousness of their singularity among the peoples or nations of the world. In the debate with Christianity sages evoked not only "family" but also "nation," or "people," an altogether political entity. In framing the theology of a social entity like, yet not alike, all other social entities—hence a nation, but a singular nation—sages prepared for their adversaries yet a second, if closely related, point-by-point reply to a critical challenge, in addition to the theology deriving from the family. The reason sages required this second definition of Israel, "Israel" as a nation unlike other nations, is that, for their part, the Christians spoke in political, not only genealogical terms. They too invoked in explaining the social entity constituted by them the theology of people or nation—one of a peculiar order to be sure. Consequently, the polemical task directed attention to the theology built not upon genealogy but upon a different sort of polity.

The Christians from the beginning saw themselves as a people without a past, a no-people, a people gathered from the peoples. Then who they can claim to be hardly derives from who they have been. Identifying with ancient Israel was a perfectly natural and correct initiative, well-founded on the basis of the Christian canon, encompassing the Hebrew Scriptures as "the Old Testament." It admirably accounted for the Christian presence in humanity, provided a past, explained to diverse people what they had in common. One problem from Christians theologians' perspective demanded solution: the existing Israel, the Jewish people, which revered the same Scriptures and claimed descent, after the flesh, from ancient Israel.

These—the Jews—traced their connection to ancient Israel, seeing it as natural, and also, supernatural. The family tie, through Abraham, Isaac, Jacob, as we saw, formed a powerful apologetic indeed. The Jews furthermore pointed to their family record, the Scriptures, to explain whence they come and who they are. So long as the two parties to the debate shared the same subordinated political circumstance, Jewry could quite nicely hold its own in the debate. But with the shift in the politics of the Empire, the terms of debate changed. The parvenu become paramount, the Christian party to the debate invoked its familiar position now with the power of the state in support.

The confrontation with Christianity in sages' thought took the form of a family dispute about who is the legitimate heir to the same ancestor. Judaic sages and

Christian theologians addressed the same issue in pretty much the same terms, with a single mode of argument, appealing to a shared body of facts—the Scriptures—joining the two into a common debate. The several threads of the dispute between Judaism and Christianity draw together into a tight fabric: the shift in the character of politics, marked by the epochal triumph of Christianity in the state, bears profound meaning for the messianic mission of the Church, and, further, imparts a final judgment on the salvific claim of the competing nations of God: the Church and Israel.

What possible answer can sages have proposed to this indictment? Since at the heart of the matter lies the Christians' claim that scriptural "Israel" persists in the salvific heritage that has passed to the Christians, sages reaffirm that scriptural "Israel" persists after the flesh, an unconditional and permanent status. But that consideration formed only part of the matter. Another part concerned the political entity, "Israel," not merely the genealogical entity, "children of Abraham and Sarah." The issue addressed the holiness of "Israel" as political entity, people or nation. That accounts for the joining of two metaphors, the one drawn from genealogy, the other from politics.

A cogent and propositional commentary to the book of Leviticus, *Leviticus Rabbah*, ca. 400–450, reads the laws of the on-going sanctification in nature of the life of Israel as an account of the rules of the one-time salvation in history of the polity of "Israel." To the framers of *Leviticus Rabbah*, one point of emphasis proved critical: "Israel" remains "Israel," the Jewish people, after the flesh, not only because Israel today continues the family begun by Abraham, Isaac, Jacob, Joseph and the other tribal founders, and bears the heritage bequeathed by them. "Israel" is what it is also because of its character as holy nation—not merely family. For salvific issues addressed not solely to individuals but to concerns of history and eschatology frame themselves as political, dealing corporate social entities.

Maintaining, as the Christian theologians did, that Israel would see no future salvation amounted to declaring that Israel, the Jewish people (no longer merely family), pursued no worthwhile purpose in continuing to endure. Indeed, in light of Paul's use of the theology of genealogy, the theology of the family could not serve to convey the proposition that "Israel" (after the flesh) had had its salvation in the return to Zion and would have no future salvation at all. Accordingly, from the perspective of the Christian theologian, the shift from genealogical to political metaphors was necessary. When the argument joined the question, who is Israel? to the question, who enjoys salvation? the theology therefore shifted from family to political entity.

This brings us once more to "Rome" as a state—nation, people—*within the genus of "Israel" as nation or people*. In what is to follow, we see how "Rome" as family shades over into "Rome" as empire and state, comparable to "Israel" as a nation or state—and as the coming empire too. That shading explains why we have called the treatment of Rome a special problem. For while "Rome" stands for "Esau," the comparison of Rome and Israel moves into fresh ground, comparing Rome to animals as well as to the near-family. We have already seen the adumbration of the position that, in *Leviticus Rabbah*, would come to remarkably rich expression. For Rome now stood for much more than merely a place among other places, or even a people or nation among peoples or nations. Rome took up a place in the unfolding of the empires—Babylonia, Media, Greece, then Rome. "Israel" takes its place in that unfolding pattern, and hence is consubstantial with Babylonia, Media, Greece, and Rome. In that context, "Rome" and "Israel" do form counterparts and opposites.

Still more important Rome is the penultimate empire on earth. Israel will constitute the ultimate one. That message, seeing the shifts in world history in a pattern and placing at the apex of the shift Israel itself, directly and precisely takes up the issue made urgent just now: the advent of the Christian emperors. Why do we maintain, as we do, that in the characterization of Rome as the fourth and penultimate empire/animal, sages address issues of their own day? Because Rome, among the successive empires, bears special traits, most of which derive from the distinctively Christian character of Rome. We realize that we have moved very far from the genealogical theology.

Now "Rome" is like "Israel" in a way in which no other state or nation is like "Israel," and, consequently, in the odd metaphors of Rome as an animal unlike other animals or Rome as an empire unlike other empires we have to appeal to a special relationship between "Rome" and "Israel." And that special relationship, already prepared, can only be genealogical. How so? Rome emerges as both like and also not-like "Israel," in ways in which no other nation is ever represented as "like-Israel;" and, it follows, "Israel" is like "Rome" in ways in which "Israel is not like any other people or nation.

The most suggestive disposition of Rome as a matter of fact moved beyond the theory of the family. Esau is compared to a pig. The reason for the aptness of the analogy is simple. The pig exhibits public traits expected of a suitable beast, in that it shows a cloven hoof, such as the laws of acceptable beasts require. But the pig does not exhibit the inner traits of a suitable beast, in that it does not chew the cud. Accordingly, the pig confuses and deceives. The polemic against Esau = Rome is simple. Rome claims to be Israel in that it adheres to the Old Testament, that is, the written Torah of Sinai. Specifically, Rome is represented as only Christian Rome can have been represented: it superficially *looks* kosher but it is unkosher. Pagan Rome cannot ever have looked kosher, but Christian Rome, with its appeal to continuity with ancient Israel, could and did and moreover claimed to. It bore some traits that validate, but lacked others that validate—just as Jerome said of Israel. It would be difficult to find a more direct confrontation between two parties to an argument. Now the issue is the same, who is the true Israel? and the proof-texts are the same, and, moreover, the proof-texts are read in precisely the same way. Only the conclusions differ!

The polemic represented in the Talmud of the Land of Israel, *Genesis Rabbah*, and *Leviticus Rabbah* by the symbolization of Christian Rome makes the simple point, first, that Christians are no different from, and no better than, pagans; they are essentially the same. Christians' claim to form part of Israel then requires no serious attention. Since Christians came to Jews with precisely that claim, the sages' response—they are another Babylonia—bears a powerful polemic charge. But that is not the whole story, as we see. Second, just as Israel had survived Babylonia, Media, Greece, so would they endure to see the end of Rome (whether pagan, whether Christian). But there is a third point. Rome really does differ from the earlier, pagan empires, and that polemic shifts the entire discourse, once we hear its symbolic vocabulary properly. For the new Rome really did differ from the old. Christianity was not merely part of a succession of undifferentiated modes of paganism. The symbols assigned to Rome attributed worse, more dangerous traits than those assigned to the earlier empires. The pig pretends to be clean, just as the Christians give the signs of adherence to the God of Abraham, Isaac, and Jacob. That much the passage concedes. For the pig is not clean, exhibiting some, but not all, of the required indications, and Rome is not Israel, even though it shares Israel's Scripture.

And that brings us to that mixture of metaphors in which genealogy explains relationships between polities. Let us begin with a simple example of how ubiquitous is the shadow of Ishmael/Esau/Edom/Rome. Wherever in *Genesis Rabbah* sages reflect on future history, their minds turn to their own day. They found the hour difficult, because Rome, now Christian, claimed that very birthright and blessing that they understood to be theirs alone. Christian Rome posed a threat without precedent. Now another dominion, besides Israel's, claimed the rights and blessings that sustained Israel. Wherever in Scripture they turned, sages found comfort in the iteration that the birthright, the blessing, the Torah, and the hope—all belonged to them and to none other. Here we see a statement of that view, in the ample and handsomely articulated version of *Leviticus Rabbah*:

9. A. Moses foresaw what the evil kingdoms would do [to Israel].
    B. "The camel, rock badger, and hare" (Deut 14:7). [Compare: "Nevertheless, among those that chew the cud or part the hoof, you shall not eat these: the camel, because it chews the cud but does not part the hoof, is unclean to you. The rock badger, because it chews the cud but does not part the hoof, is unclean to you. And the hare, because it chews the cud but does not part the hoof, is unclean to you, and the pig, because it parts the hoof and is cloven-footed, but does not chew the cud, is unclean to you" (Lev 11:4-8).]

C. The camel (GML) refers to Babylonia, [in line with the following verse of Scripture: "O daughter of Babylonia, you who are to be devastated!] Happy will be he who requites (GML) you, with what you have done to us" (Ps 147:8).
D. "The rock badger" (Deut 14:7)—this refers to Media.
E. Rabbis and R. Judah b. R. Simon.
F. Rabbis say, "Just as the rock badger exhibits traits of uncleanness and traits of cleanness, so the kingdom of Media produced both a righteous man and a wicked one."
G. Said R. Judah b. R. Simon, "The last Darius was Esther's son. He was clean on his mother's side and unclean on his father's side."
H. "The hare" (Deut 14:7)—this refers to Greece. The mother of King Ptolemy was named "Hare" [in Greek: lagos].
I. "The pig" (Deut 14:7)—this refers to Edom [Rome].
J. Moses made mention of the first three in a single verse and the final one in a verse by itself [(Deut 14:7, 8)]. Why so?
K. R. Yohanan and R. Simeon b. Laqish.
L. R. Yohanan said, "It is because [the pig] is equivalent to the other three."
M. And R. Simeon b. Laqish said, "It is because it outweighs them."
N. R. Yohanan objected to R. Simeon b. Laqish, " 'Prophesy, therefore, son of man, clap your hands [and let the sword come down twice, yea thrice]' (Ezek 21:14)."
O. And how does R. Simeon b. Laqish interpret the same passage? He notes that [the threefold sword] is doubled (Ezek 21:14).

Leviticus Rabbah XIII:V

In the apocalypticizing of the animals of Lev 11:4-8/Deut 14:7, the camel, rock badger, hare, and pig, the pig, standing for Rome, again emerges as different from the others and more threatening than the rest. Just as the pig pretends to be a clean beast by showing the cloven hoof, but in fact is an unclean one, so Rome pretends to be just but in fact governs by thuggery. Edom does not pretend to praise God but only blasphemes. It does not exalt the righteous but kills them. These symbols concede nothing to Christian monotheism and veneration of the Torah of Moses (in its written medium). Of greatest importance, while all the other beasts bring further ones in their wake, the pig does not: "It does not bring another kingdom after it." It will restore the crown to the one who will truly deserve it, Israel. Esau will be judged by Zion, so Obadiah 1:21. Now how has the symbolization delivered an implicit message? It is in the treatment of Rome as distinct, but essentially equivalent to the former kingdoms.

This seems to me a stunning way of saying that the now-Christian empire in no way requires differentiation from its pagan predecessors. Nothing has changed, except matters have gotten worse. Beyond Rome, standing in a straight line with the others, lies the true shift in history, the rule of Israel and the cessation of the dominion of the (pagan) nations. Rome in the fourth century became Christian. Sages responded by facing that fact quite squarely and saying, "Indeed, it is as you say, a kind of

Israel, an heir of Abraham as your texts explicitly claim. But we remain the sole legitimate Israel, the bearer of the birthright—we and not you. So you are our brother: Esau, Ishmael, Edom." And the rest follows.

The contrast between Israel and Esau produced the following anguished observation. But here the Rome is not yet Christian, so far as the clear reference is concerned. A further important point was that Esau-Rome ruled now, but Jacob-Israel will follow in due course. This claim is made explicit:

2. A. "And Jacob sent messengers before him:"
B. To this one [Esau] whose time to take hold of sovereignty would come before him [namely, before Jacob, since Esau would rule, then Jacob would govern].
C. R. Joshua b. Levi said, "Jacob took off the purple robe and threw it before Esau, as if to say to him, 'Two flocks of starlings are not going to sleep on a single branch' [so we cannot rule at the same time]."
3. A. ". . . to Esau his brother:"
B. Even though he was Esau, he was still his brother.

Genesis Rabbah LXXV:IV

Nos. 2, 3 make a stunning point. It is that Esau remains Jacob's brother, and that Esau rules before Jacob will. The application to contemporary affairs cannot be missed, both in the recognition of the true character of Esau—a brother!—and in the interpretation of the future of history. This same point is made in another way in the following:

1. A. "These are the kings who reigned in the land of Edom before any king reigned over the Israelites: Bela the son of Beor reigned in Edom, the name of his city being Dinhabah" (Gen 36:31-32):
B. R. Isaac commenced discourse by citing this verse: "Of the oaks of Bashan they have made your oars" (Ezek 27:6).
C. Said R. Isaac, "The nations of the world are to be compared to a ship. Just as a ship has its mast made in one place and its anchor somewhere else, so their kings: 'Samlah of Masrekah' (Gen 36:36), 'Shaul of Rehobot by the river' (Gen 36:27), and: 'These are the kings who reigned in the land of Edom before any king reigned over the Israelites.'"
2. A. ["An estate may be gotten hastily at the beginning, but the end thereof shall not be blessed" (Prov 20:21)]: "An estate may be gotten hastily at the beginning:" "These are the kings who reigned in the land of Edom before any king reigned over the Israelites."
B. ". . . but the end thereof shall not be blessed:" "And saviors shall come up on mount Zion to judge the mount of Esau" (Obad 1:21).

Genesis Rabbah LXXXIII:I

No. 1 contrasts the diverse origin of Roman rulers with the uniform origin of Israel's king in the house of David. No. 2 makes the same point still more forcefully. How so? Freedman makes sense of No. 2 as follows: Though Esau was the first to have kings, his land will eventually be overthrown (Freedman, 766 n. 3). So the point is that Israel will have kings after Esau no longer does, and the verse at hand is made to point to the end of Rome, a striking revision to express the importance in Israel's history to events in the lives of the patriarchs.

1. A. "These are the kings who reigned in the land of Edom before any king reigned over the Israelites: Bela the son of Beor reigned in Edom, the name of his city being Dinhabah" (Gen 36:31-32):
    B. Said R. Aibu, "Before a king arose in Israel, kings existed in Edom: 'These are the kings who reigned in the land of Edom before any king reigned over the Israelites.'" [Freedman, 766 n. 4: "1 Kgs 22:48 states, 'There was no king in Edom, a deputy was king.' This refers to the reign of Jehoshaphat. Subsequently in Jehoram's reign, Edom revolted and 'made a king over themselves' (2 Kgs 8:20). Thus from Saul to Jehoshaphat, in which Israel had eight kings, Edom had no king but was ruled by a governor of Judah. Aibu observes that this was to balance the present period, during which Edom had eight kings while Israel had none. For that reason, Aibu employs the word for deputy when he wishes to say 'existed' thus indicating a reference to the verse in the book of Kings quoted above."]
    C. R. Yosé bar Haninah said, "[Alluding to a mnemonic, with the first Hebrew letter for the word for kings, judges, chiefs, and princes:] When the one party [Edom] was ruled by kings, the other party [Israel] was ruled by judges, when one side was ruled by chiefs, the other side was ruled by princes."
    D. Said R. Joshua b. Levi, "This one set up eight kings and that one set up eight kings. This one set up Bela, Jobab, Husham, Samlah, Shaul, Hadad, Baalhanan, and Hadar. The other side set up Saul, Ishbosheth, David Solomon, Rehoboam, Abijah, Asa, and Jehoshaphat.
    E. "Then Nebuchadnezzar came and overturned both: 'That made the world as a wilderness and destroyed the cities thereof' (Isa 14:17).
    F. "Evil-merodach came and exalted Jehoiakin, Ahasuerus came and exalted Haman."
    Genesis Rabbah LXXXIII:II

The passage once more stresses the correspondence between Israel's and Edom's governments, respectively. The reciprocal character of their histories is then stated in a powerful way, with the further implication that, when the one rules, the other waits. So now Israel waits, but it will rule.

"Israel" beyond all metaphor, unavailable for comparison and contrast, that people "dwelling alone," thus was now the object of intense study on the part of the thoughtful sages, governing from day to day but also gazing beyond the far horizon. Indeed, seeing "Israel" as *sui generis* and not merely an abstraction and instrumentality for classification of entities may well represent a perspective natural to a group within the political class of the population. For, one may suppose, concrete issues in the here and now tended to highlight difference between group and group and to obliterate those points in common that permitted comparison and contrast in the philosophical mode. Portraying themselves as engaged with a real social group on a day to day basis, sages searched within the life of that group for the rules and orderly regulations that governed. Seeking commonalities of pattern, they centered their interest on what they deemed particular.

The definition of "Israel" comes to us not only in what people expressly mean by the word, but also in the implicit terms yielded by how they discuss the social entity. In *Leviticus Rabbah* the conception of "Israel" as *sui generis* reaches expression in an implicit statement that Israel is subject to its own laws, which are distinct from the laws governing all other social entities. These laws may be discerned in the factual, scriptural record of "Israel's" past, and that past, by definition, belonged to "Israel" alone. It followed, therefore, that by discerning the regularities in "Israel's" history, implicitly understood as unique to "Israel," sages recorded the view that "Israel" like God was not subject to analogy or comparison. Accordingly, while not labeled a genus unto itself, Israel is treated in that way.

The vanquished people, the nation that had lost its city and its temple, that had, moreover, produced another nation from its midst to take over its Scripture and much else could not bear too much reality. That defeated people will then have found refuge in a mode of thought that trained vision to see other things otherwise than as the eyes perceived them. Among the diverse ways by which the weak and subordinated accommodate to their circumstance, the one of iron-willed pretense in life is most likely to yield the mode of thought at hand: things never are, because they cannot be, what they seem.

What happens in the writings of Judaism, represented by *Genesis Rabbah* and *Leviticus Rabbah*, is that, reading one thing in terms of something else, the builders of the document systematically adopted for Israel today the reality of the Scripture, its history and doctrines—again with the consequence that "Israel" constituted a social entity that was *sui generis*, now once more by definition. They transformed that unique history from a sequence of one-time events, leading from one place to some other, into an ever-present mythic world. No longer was there one Moses, one David, one set of happenings of a distinctive and never-to-be-repeated character. Now whatever happens, of which the thinkers propose to take account, must enter and be absorbed into that established and ubiquitous pattern and structure founded in the patterns of Scripture's truth. It is not that biblical history repeats itself. Rather, biblical history no longer constitutes history as a story of things that happened once, long ago, and pointed to some one moment in the future. Rather it becomes an account of things that happen every day—hence, an ever-present mythic world. The upshot was that "Israel" now lived on a mythic plane of being, an eternity that happened to be caught up in time, so to speak, but truly, a social entity different in genus, not only in species.

What the sages now proposed was a reconstruction of Israel's social existence along the lines of the ancient design of Scripture as they read it. What that meant was that, from a sequence of one-time and linear events, everything that happened was turned into a repetition of known and already experienced paradigms, hence, once more, a mythic being of a unique social entity. The source and core of the myth, of course, derive from Scripture—Scripture reread, renewed, reconstructed along with the society that revered Scripture. So, to summarize, the mode of thought that dictated the issues and the logic of the document, telling the thinkers to see one thing in terms of something else, addressed Scripture in particular and collectively. And thinking as they did, the framers of the document saw Scripture in a new way, just as they saw their own circumstance afresh, rejecting their world in favor of Scripture's, reliving Scripture's world in their own terms.

The doctrinal substance of the theory of Israel as *sui generis* may be stated in a single paragraph, as follows, using as our source *Leviticus Rabbah* in particular:

God loves Israel (now without its quotation marks), so gave them the Torah, which defines their life and governs their welfare (the position noted above, when God explains God's particular concern for "Israel" by reason of "Israel's" cleaving to God). Israel is alone in its category (*sui generis*), proved by the fact that what is a virtue to Israel is a vice to the nation, life-giving to Israel, poison to the gentiles. True, Israel sins, but God forgives that sin, having punished the nation on account of it. Such a process has yet to come to an end, but it will culminate in Israel's complete regeneration. Meanwhile, Israel's assurance of God's love lies in the many expressions of special concern, for even the humblest and most ordinary aspects of the national life: the food the nation eats, the sexual practices by which it procreates. These life-sustaining, life-transmitting activities draw God's special interest, as a mark of his general love for Israel. Israel then is supposed to achieve its life in conformity with the marks of God's love. These indications moreover signify also the character of Israel's difficulty, namely, subordination to the nations in general, but to the fourth kingdom, Rome, in particular. Both food laws and skin diseases stand for the nations. There is yet another category of sin, also collective and generative of collective punishment, and that is social. The moral character of Israel's life, the treatment of people by one another, the practice of gossip and small-scale thuggery—these too draw down divine penalty. The nation's fate therefore corresponds to its moral condition. The moral condition, however, emerges not only from the current generation. Israel's richest hope lies in the merit of the ancestors, thus in the Scriptural record of the merits attained by the founders of the nation, those who originally brought it into being and gave it life.

If we now ask about further recurring themes or topics, there is one that is utterly commonplace. It is expressed by recurrent lists of events in Israel's (unique) history, meaning, in this context, Israel's history solely in scriptural times, down through the return to Zion. The lists again and again ring the changes on the one-time events of the generation of the flood, Sodom and Gomorrah, the patriarchs and the sojourn in Egypt, the exodus, the revelation of the Torah at Sinai, the golden calf, the Davidic monarchy and the building of the Temple, Sennacherib, Hezekiah, and the destruction of northern Israel, Nebuchadnezzar and the destruction of the Temple in 586, the life of Israel in Babylonian captivity, Daniel and his associates, Mordecai and Haman. These events occur over and over again. They turn out to serve as paradigms of the everyday social reality of the community of Israel, perceived in the here and now: an "as-if"-way of speaking about the social facts of sin and atonement, steadfastness and divine intervention, and equivalent lessons. We find, in fact, a fairly standard repertoire of scriptural heroes or villains, on the one side, and conventional lists of Israel's enemies and their actions and downfall, on the other. The boastful, for instance, include the generation of the flood, Sodom and Gomorrah, Pharaoh, Sisera, Sennacherib, Nebuchadnezzar, the wicked empire (Rome)—contrasted to Israel, "despised and humble in this world." The four kingdoms recur again and again, always ending, of course, with Rome, with the repeated message that after Rome will come Israel. But Israel has to make this happen through its faith and submission to God's will. Lists of enemies ring the changes on Cain, the Sodomites, Pharaoh, Sennacherib, Nebuchadnezzar, Haman.

The catalogues of exemplary heroes and historical events provide a model of how contemporary events are to be absorbed into the biblical paradigm unique to "Israel." Since biblical events exemplify recurrent happenings, sin and redemption, forgiveness and atonement, they lose their one-time character. At the same time and in the same way, current events find a place within the ancient, but eternally present, paradigmatic scheme. So no new historical events, other than exemplary episodes in lives of heroes, demand narration because, through what is said about the past, what was happening in the times of the framers of *Leviticus Rabbah* would also come under consideration. This mode of dealing with biblical history and contemporary events produces two reciprocal effects. The first is the mythicization of biblical stories, their removal from the framework of ongoing, unique patterns of history and sequences of events and their transformation into accounts of things that happen all the time. The second is that contemporary events too lose all of their specificity and enter the paradigmatic framework of established mythic existence. So the Scripture's myth happens every day, and every day produces reenactment of the Scripture's myth. That is, in concrete terms, what it means to state what of a unique entity cannot be said. If we speak of an entity unlike all others, then, by rights, we should not be able to make intelligible statements. But, as we see, sages can and do.

The basic mode of thought—denial of what is at hand in favor of a deeper reality—proves remarkably apt. The substance of thought concerning the unique social entity, beyond all theory, confronts the acute crisis of the present circumstance:

Are we lost for good to the fourth empire, now-Christian Rome? No, we may yet be saved.

Has God rejected us forever? No, aided by the merit of the patriarchs and matriarchs and of the Torah and religious duties, we gain God's love.

What must we do to be saved? We must *do* nothing, we must *be* something: sanctified.

That status we gain through keeping the rules that make Israel holy. So salvation is through sanctification, all embodied in Leviticus read as rules for the holy people.

The Messiah will come not because of what a pagan emperor does, nor, indeed, because of Jewish action either, but because of Israel's own moral condition. When Israel enters the right relationship with God, then God will respond to Israel's condition by restoring things to their proper balance. Israel cannot, but need not, so act as to force the coming of the Messiah. Israel can so attain the condition of sanctification, by forming a moral and holy community, that God's response will follow the established prophecy of Moses and the prophets. And to understand how that takes place, we have only to reflect for a moment about what we learned concerning *zekhut* in Volume Two of this anthology: Israel cannot, and ought not, take the place of God in trying to achieve its own salvation. Study of the Torah, practice of the commandments—these do not coerce God. God will respond to the humility of Israel; when Israel gives up, God gives.

Part One

What Is Israel?

Chapter 2

People of Israel

Alon Goshen-Gottschein

Given the complexity of metaphors invoked by ancient Judaic thinkers to define "Israel," we hardly find it surprising that the definition of who and what is Israel presents difficulty. But the problem is made more parlous still by the secularization of a considerable proportion of the Jews in Europe and America in the nineteenth century, and throughout the Jewish world in the twentieth. Because of that fact, religious, including theological, definitions came to compete with secular and this-worldly ones, and the facts of sociology and politics came to testify to the affirmations of the faith of Judaism, the declarations of the Torah. The definition given here is a theological one: "one who struggled with God," and for this writer, "Israel ... embodies a struggle, a rebirth, and the collective emergence into a higher level of existence." Quite what these words mean is not easy to discern, though the occurrence of the language of "spirituality" signals that a theological, not a racist, intent is present, and this is made explicit. The author's search for appropriate metaphors to express his idea, that "the process of humanity is one of higher and higher evaluation, not only in its cultural achievements but also spiritually, through the formation of spiritual centers within humanity." But this metaphorization and spiritualization of matters sets aside that claim of Israel after the flesh that Scripture, for its part, and the oral Torah, as well, set forth. The components of the theological doctrine of Israel—election, land, covenant, exile and return, suffering and atonement —all figure in any grasp of matters. But, what follows makes equally clear, the concept of "Israel" in all of these dimensions, which forms the center and heart of the Torah's categorical structure alongside God and Torah, presents problems to the Judaic thinker that are not of an altogether theological nature. The exposition of the category, "Israel," carries in its wake a measure of embarrassment; the category is not so much explained as explained away; and the clear and simple standard of Judaic thought of ancient and medieval times, with its unashamed allegation that Israel is made Israel by the covenant of the Torah of Sinai, is compromised. For, viewed by a secular mind, the supernatural categories of God, Torah, and Israel are treated as this-worldly allegations; God becomes an idea, Torah a culture, and Israel a matter of ethnic pride and therefore, as we see, embarrassment.

***

---

*From *Contemporary Jewish Religious Thought*, ed. Arthur A. Cohen and Paul Mendes-Flohr. Copyright 1987 by Charles Scribner's Sons. Reprinted by permission of Macmillan Publishing Company

The patriarch Jacob, after his struggle with the angel, was the first to receive the name *Israel*. This name then became the name of a people known as the people of Israel (*am Yisrael*). The name *Israel* refers, however, not only to the historical people present upon earth, but also to a soul—to an ongoing spiritual work of the people that takes place on planes beyond the visible, mundane order. The work of Israel done here on earth is but an extension of the endeavors of the superior, larger Israel.

The patriarch who was named Israel is the patriarch from whom the people of Israel, and they alone, are born. Unlike his fathers—Abraham and Isaac—Jacob's whole progeny is contained within the fold of the people of Israel. It is for this reason that they bear his name. We can learn something about the meaning of what Israel truly is by looking at the name of the patriarch, shared by his descendants: the one who struggled with God. In Genesis 32:25-32, we read:

> Jacob was left alone, and a man wrestled with him until the break of dawn. When he saw that he had not prevailed against him, he wrenched Jacob's hip at its socket, so that the socket of his hip was strained as he wrestled with him.
>
> Then he said: "Let me go, for dawn is breaking," But he answered, "I will not let you go, unless you bless me." Said the other: "What is your name?" He replied: "Jacob." Said he: "Your name shall no longer be Jacob, but Israel, for you have striven with beings divine and human, and have prevailed." Jacob asked, "Pray tell me your name." But he said, "You must not ask my name!" And he took leave of him there. So Jacob named the place Peniel, meaning, "I have seen a divine being face to face, yet my life has been preserved." The sun rose upon him, as he passed Peniel, limping on his hip.

The primary meaning of *Israel* is thus the one who struggled with God. Through Jacob's struggle is attained rebirth, an elevation to a new level of existence. Born Jacob—the crooked, possibly treacherous one (Gen 27; 36)—his struggle is that of self-transformation of the former self. The crooked here becomes straight, as in the etymology of Israel (*yashar-el*). The struggle also takes its toll—"limping on his hip." The impairment attendant on the struggle is of significance to all future generations. Yet this struggle yielded a blessing, expressed in the new name for the one who has fought with God, overcome, and come to a new life. From this new life proceeds the people of Israel.

From this original act of naming Israel we thus learn something important concerning what Israel truly is. *Israel*, not only the patriarch but the people that flows from him, embodies a struggle, a rebirth, and the collective emergence into a higher level of existence.

Within the context of humanity, we may again view Israel in the same process of struggling to attain this higher spiritual level of existence. The struggle of Israel is not isolated from the struggle of humanity. The very blessing by which the patriarch is given the name *Israel* by God is accompanied by the promise of many nations being born unto him (Gen 35:9-11). There is an intrinsic relation between the struggles of Israel and the struggles of humanity as a whole.

The metaphor through which the relation between Israel and the nations can best be expressed is an organic metaphor, that of the body. As the body has various limbs, so the world has various nations. As the body must work as a whole, so the various nations must work in peace and harmony. As the evolution of the body proceeds to degrees of greater and higher refinement, to degrees of greater cultural and spiritual achievement, so humanity evolves to ever higher levels of ability to recognize God and to give expression to the spiritual aspirations of mankind.

Israel, as suggested, is a dynamic entity, one that relates to struggle and to a dynamic process of growth. In this respect the organic metaphor may be inappropriate, for the body is a defined, closed entity. Yet in the Jewish tradition there is an alternative image of the body that will allow us to incorporate the dynamic element we have related to the concept of Israel. This image, propounded by the kabbalists and upon which we will here elaborate, does not evoke that of the mere physical body.[1] The kabbalah speaks of a supernal body composed of energy centers, of spiritual centers, which are known as the *sefirot* (lit., "spheres").

The *sefirot* are formed in accordance with the structure of the body and they, as a whole, form one organic unity, which enables the divine manifestation through which God as well as all created beings operate. Humanity as a whole may also be viewed as such a body. Within this body are different spiritual centers. Each nation is related to a center or to an aspect of a specific spiritual center, a specific spiritual *sefirah*.

The process of humanity is one of higher and higher evolution, not only in its cultural achievements but also spiritually, through the formation of spiritual centers within humanity. As humanity evolves, it becomes possible for greater and greater aspects of divine perfection to be embodied within humanity. Within this process, we can discern the formation of diverse spiritual centers. A spiritual center that is formed necessitates a specific vehicle or a vessel. The dynamic element that is embodied in the people of Israel is thus the process of the formation of a distinctive spiritual center within humanity, the people of Israel serving as its vessel.

In an altogether different context, we find the structure of the body as a most prominent concept in kabbalistic teaching. The reference is to the supernal divine body of God. Some kabbalistic teachers regard the supernal Israel, as opposed to the manifest historical Israel, as the heart center within the body of God. In one tradition, we even find Israel as the supernal crown (*keter*)—the highest rung in the sefirotic order.

> The supernal crown which is called "primordial Israel.". . .
> The primordial Israel which is the secret of the supernal crown.
> (*Sefer Maraot ha-Zoveot* 82:31; 210:5)

Our presentation of Israel's position within the body of humanity shall proceed from this understanding. Israel is the *keter* within the body of humanity. However, this position is not to be regarded as a source of pride and hubris, for one of the foremost qualities of the *sefirah keter* is its humility. Indeed, one of *keter*'s many names is "nothingness." The rabbis describe God as saying to Israel, "You are the smallest of peoples" (Deut 7:7), and, as the rabbis say, "Even when I bestow greatness upon you, you humble yourselves before me" (*b. Ḥul* 89a). It is this quality of humility that characterizes the work of *keter*.

As the first emanation in the sefirotic order, *keter* is that which takes the divine light and transfers it into others. The quality of *keter* is the quality of the will of God—the will of God being the first divine emanation. When we refer to Israel as *keter*, it is, then an anchor point allowing the will of God to emanate. Through Israel, God's will emanates to humanity.

In kabbalistic teaching the various *sefirot* are divided according to the qualities of openness, constriction, and a quality of mitigation, or balancing of these polar spiritual forces. *keter* is, however, beyond such a division: It is all good, without any constriction, without any limitation. No evil enters *keter*, the quality of which is absolute compassion. In light of all this, therefore, the designation of Israel as *keter* denotes not only an entity but also a purpose; it is a designation of responsibility, of a mission.

In light of our understanding of Israel's position within humanity and the process of the formation of a spiritual center within the body of humanity, we may appreciate the importance of the story of Israel's formation as told in the Bible. The center point of the biblical story of Genesis is the formation of the nation—the formation of a spiritual center. The trials and tribulations of the patriarchs and the story of Israel's Exile in Egypt are all aspects of the process of the formation of the nation. God promises Abraham to form a new nation from him, according to our understanding —a nation that is to bring a new spiritual quality to the world. God's promise to Abraham appertains to humanity as a whole (Gen 12:3). Later, a covenant is made between God and Abraham which defines the special relationship between God and Abraham's seed (Gen 17). God is to be their God, and Abraham's seed is to keep God's covenant. On this occasion, a founding moment of the future Jewish people, the land of Israel is promised to Abraham's seed. It is also noteworthy that on this occasion Abram is renamed Abraham, signifying he is to become the father of many nations. Thus, the founding covenant of the Jewish people is firmly linked with the future of humanity. The covenant made with Abraham focuses on God's promises to Abraham and to the future people of Israel. Israel's commitments to God are also expressed through a covenant, made between God and Israel at Mount Sinai. We may view this covenant—following the Exile in Egypt—as fulfilling the process of the formation of the nation of Israel. Israel's birth takes place between these two covenants. In the latter covenant the specific way of life required of Israel is revealed.

Through the path revealed in this covenant Israel is to grow and to fulfill its mission. This mission is clearly stated as a preparation to the revelation at Sinai:

> Now then, if you will obey me faithfully and keep My covenant, you shall be My treasured possession among the peoples. Indeed, all the earth is Mine, but you shall be to Me a kingdom of priests and a holy nation. (Exod 19:5-6)

The two related aspects depicted in the covenant with Abraham are again to be found here. Israel is to be both—vis-à-vis itself and God—and a "kingdom of priests." One will note that a priest is someone who serves on behalf of others; thus, Israel is to be a nation of priests serving on behalf of all humanity.

Israel's very creation, then, as *keter* is one that endows it with an immense responsibility to be a nation that lives by the will of God, that brings to the world the will of God, and that emanates the will of God. The process by which Israel is to achieve this is through the various covenants it makes with God.

It is noteworthy that, in the covenant made with Abraham, we find the promise for the land of Israel going hand in hand with the promise of the formation of the people of Israel, though both are as yet unknown by these names. Here we touch upon the deeper reason for the common name shared by the land and the people. It is not merely because the land is given to the people of Israel, or vice versa, that those who inhabit the land are called the people of Israel; the connection between land and people is deeper—Israel as a nation represents a spiritual center within the body of humanity. As pointed out, the sefirotic organization, by spiritual energy centers and patterns, is one that is not unique to humanity, but is the organizational pattern determining all that is. Therefore, earth—the land itself—is organized along similar lines. The land of Israel is the center of the earth, representing that which Israel is to represent among people. The connection of Israel the people and Israel the land is therefore vital. It is by dwelling in a place possessing certain qualities and properties that the people of Israel is to partake in these attributes, to fulfill them, and to emanate them. There is an interchange, an interflow between the land of Israel and the people of Israel. The clearest indication of this fact is in Israel's history. When Israel fails to live up to what is expected of it, the land "spews" the people of Israel out (Lev 20:22). Israel is no longer fit to remain in the land.

The Exile from the land of Israel, following Israel's failure to live in accordance with the standards required by the land, brings us to reflect upon one of the most crucial elements in Israel's history—suffering. Jacob became Israel through a struggle with—and toward—God. Though victorious, Jacob was wounded in battle. Jacob prefigures his descendants, who rise and fall in their struggle with and on behalf of God. Their forefather, limping at sunrise, is the source of their strength in the struggle, as well as of their vulnerability to the blows, the falls, and the failures that are their lot until the day of ultimate victory. The history of Israel is the story of

Israel's struggle, of its alternating successes and failures to rise to what had been given it as its task. Thus it is that Israel's formation is brought about through suffering, which is a byproduct of the struggle itself. Accordingly, the suffering of the Exile in Egypt is a constitutive element in the formation of the Jewish people, for only in Egypt is Israel truly formed into a nation. On the other hand, failure to live up to the covenant with God, made so evident in the archetypal story of the Golden Calf, is what brings upon Israel a series of great calamities. This suffering is not merely punishment for Israel's transgressions. It is a means through which Israel is to assume its destiny. As its original formation was brought about by suffering, so its purification from its wrongdoing takes place in the process of suffering. In suffering, the force of *keter* is realized. Through this purification Israel is enabled to maintain its position as a holy nation, to realize its being, and to fulfill its mission.

Essentially, Israel's task is to emanate a spiritual force that has not yet been embodied on earth by a nation. It is the force through which sin is to be eliminated. Historically, Israel has yet to succeed fully in its task. Indeed, one may say it has succumbed to sin. The point is so far-reaching that, on account of Israel's failure in history, other peoples have recurrently come to regard themselves as the true Israel. From the perspective of Judaism such claims are patently false, for Israel is a divine creation. Israel is an entity entrusted with a mission. Just as a foot does not become a head, so someone cannot become someone else. Certainly, when a foot can no longer perform its preordained task the hand may have to take over and assist. When an organ is weak and ailing, other parts of the body may have to put in an extra measure of work to compensate, but in a healthy, functioning body each organ and limb is allotted its own responsibility and position. So it is in the case of Israel. Sin and wrongdoing have played a very important part in the process of Israel's rising to become what God ordained it to be. In light of the prefigurative example of Jacob one may even wonder whether being bruised in the process of the struggle—succumbing and faltering in battle—is an unavoidable, indeed necessary aspect of the battle—a battle against evil and for—and toward—God.

Israel's fulfillment of its ultimate being is thus intrinsically bound up with struggle, suffering, and purification. In all this, however, Israel has never forfeited its true essential being. It has merely failed to reach the height it is destined to reach, and to actualize and realize its ultimate essence within the historical order.

Reflecting upon the process of suffering, cleansing, and purification brings us to the consideration of Israel as a "soul." In speaking of the organization of humanity in the form of a body, we were referring to the manifest earthly reality of humanity. However, this humanity is merely a visible aspect of a much greater entity. Judaism affirms that our life here on earth is merely a preparation for the life on the various higher planes of existence. Our earthly life is merely a school, an arena for education: "This world is like an antechamber before the world to come; prepare yourself in the antechamber so that you may enter the banquet hall" (*m. 'Abot* 4:16). The true life, so to speak, is the life that takes place on planes beyond our own mundane existence. It is, therefore, impossible for us to judge fully what Israel is, what Israel's position is, what Israel's responsibility is, and, conversely, how far-reaching its wrongdoing is and how necessary its purification is. The work of Israel is a work that takes place not only on this plane but also on the planes beyond. When we talk of Israel, the people, we must therefore remember that we are addressing not only their earthly reality but also the people as they belong to a much greater whole.

A statement by Rabbi Akiva may be regarded as an epigraphic summary of the spiritual significance of the people of Israel:

> Beloved is man, for he was created in the image of God. . . . Beloved are the people of Israel, for they are called children of God. . . . Beloved are the people of Israel, for a precious tool was given to them with which the world was created. (*m. 'Abot* 3:14)

In this mishnah we can recognize three distinct stages, the first discussing man, the next two discussing Israel specifically. As we shall later suggest, a continuum exists between the various stages depicted in Rabbi Akiva's words. We should note the expression of God's emotion found in these statements. All three levels are examples of God's love—for mankind and for Israel, manifest in each of the three levels mentioned by Rabbi Akiva.

On the first level, God's love is of man created in his image. Regarding the meaning of the divine image, a further statement made by Rabbi Akiva and his colleagues is instructive. Rabbi Akiva taught: "He who sheds blood is regarded as though he has diminished the *demut* [the divine image]. What is the proof? 'Whosoever sheds the blood of man, By man shall his blood be shed.' What is the reason? 'For in His image did God make man'" [Gen 9:6]. Rabbi Eleazar Ben Azaria taught: "He who refrains from procreation diminishes the *demut*." Ben Azzai taught: "He who refrains from procreation is as though he sheds blood and diminishes the *demut*" (*Gen. Rab.* 34:14).

This passage can possibly shed light on the meaning of the previous statement by Rabbi Akiva describing man's belovedness by virtue of being created in the image of God. What is this *demut* that the second passage mentions? The term *demut* obviously derives from Genesis 1:26: "Let us make man in our image [*z elem*], after our likeness [*demut*]." The use of *demut* here, however, is clearly more far-reaching than the basic notion that man is created in the image of God. The statement teaches us that there is a larger whole to which each individual life belongs. Moreover, each life constitutes an expansion of that whole, and thus the prevention of birth is tantamount to bloodshed as far as it concerns the *demut*. We must note that the biblical verse explicated by the various sages appears as part of the Noachite commandments. Its relevance is, therefore, universal, and the meaning of *demut* derived from it should likewise maintain universal significance.

From the foregoing it can thus be concluded that the concept of *demut* implies that mankind as a whole was created in the image of God. One may then view all of humanity as constituting one organic whole, actually structured in a form said to be that of God. This form or body may be viewed as the body through which God is manifested. Thus the idea of God creating man in his image may be rendered as God manifesting himself through the totality of humanity, presented in a form or image—a *demut*.

From such an understanding several points emerge: It is humanity as a whole that is said to be an embodiment of the divine. This fact is grounded in the order of creation, wherein man—mankind—is so fashioned as to resemble and embody the divine. Mankind is, therefore, to be viewed as a totality, as an organic whole. It is within the context of this organic, divine whole that the position and significance of Israel is to be considered. When we state with Rabbi Akiva, "Beloved is man, for he was created in the image of God," we are hence referring to the totality of the body of humanity.

Within the body of humanity, Israel occupies a special position, which is the progression within the words of Rabbi Akiva from the first to the second statement. The second statement discusses the special position of Israel. Here the people of Israel are called children unto God. It seems, especially in contradistinction with the third statement of Rabbi Akiva, that the idea underlying Israel's being called children is that God's love for them is enduring and everlasting. Even when the son ceases to behave as he ought to and ceases to fulfill his filial obligations, his sonship endures: a son always remains a son. Similarly, Israel's position within humanity is one that will not, or has not, changed in accordance with Israel's behavior. Israel may have failed to fulfill its task fully. Nevertheless, its position as son has not changed. The idea of sonship, then, expresses the immanent value of Israel as a creation, as a being within the body of God.

Israel's sonship underscores God's unconditional love. At this point we should recall, however, that Israel was not only called "children unto God" but was also called God's "firstborn son" (Exod 4:22). The designation of firstborn can be used to describe the relationship between the first son and the other children. It is obviously the responsibility of the firstborn to aid his parents and assist them in rearing his younger brethren. The position of firstborn describes a relation between the older son and his younger brethren as well as a relationship between the firstborn son and his parents.

The people of Israel are firstborn to *keter*. They are the ones who have to take up that energy and disseminate it into the world. Their position and responsibility is that of the older brother in relation to his brethren. In one way, we may say that everyone is firstborn to his own unique quality and capacity. A more specific approach may view *keter*, the first emanation, as firstborn par excellence, for it is the firstborn within the sefirotic order.

Israel is also called the beginning, the first (*Lev. Rab.* 35:4, quoting Jer 2:3). If we return to what we have said concerning the will of God being that which Israel must emanate to the world, we can understand Israel's being first in the following manner. The will of God really is the first: the first stage in the process of creation, the first in the institution of a divine plan. It is from the will that everything else proceeds. Israel, then, as first or firstborn, has the responsibility to emanate this power of the will of God. In this capacity it is firstborn to *keter*.

It is precisely because Israel's position as children is not only one of unconditional love but also one of responsibility that Rabbi Akiva's words proceed to describe the love of Israel as an outcome of the fact that a precious tool has been given to them, with which the world was created. What is this tool? The common understanding views this tool as the Torah, which was instrumental in the process of God's creation of the world: "God looked into the Torah—and created the world" (*Gen. Rab.* 1:1). We may say that the Torah is the way of life—the covenantal statutes—entrusted unto Israel.

The covenant with God ensures his dwelling within Israel. God's dwelling is enabled by means of the presence of a divine force, called the *Shekhinah*, God's dwelling or presence. The presence of this force is a precondition for certain aspects of spiritual life, as well as for life itself. It is the creative force, used in the creative process. It is the power through which direct knowledge of God is rendered possible and through which the presence and reality of God can be known. This force can be said to be the backbone of life itself. All of life's endeavors reach their fuller realization when this power is employed. It is a powerful force—for it is the force of life itself. The immense power associated with this force necessitates strict measures guarding it against abuse. The consequence of misuse of the *Shekhinah* may be detrimental and may bring about destruction—both seen and unseen—affecting a range of existence far greater than one's immediate visible environment. The presence of this force is a special gift of God, to be employed in a manner fitting the divine design. This force has been given by God to Israel. Through its presence Israel's mission is to be fulfilled. This power of God is necessary for the full opening of the spiritual centers, and is thus vital for the full realization of what "Israel" is—for the formation and the opening of *keter* within humanity.

The *Shekhinah*'s presence within Israel is, however, dependent upon Israel's behavior. It is the *Shekhinah* that is given to Israel under the circumstance of the covenant, and it is the *Shekhinah* that is removed from Israel as a result of its sins. As Israel has been in exile, so God's *Shekhinah* has been in exile. Israel's redemption is the process of the return of the *Shekhinah* from its exile.

The catastrophe of Israel's exile is thus not merely a catastrophe for Israel alone. It is a catastrophe for the entire world. One may even say it is a catastrophe for the divine. For, as we have suggested above, Israel exists not merely on the earthly plane but on planes above. God and the divine plan for earth and for humanity are, therefore, affected by and dependent upon Israel's fulfillment of its responsibilities.

Without the return of the *Shekhinah* to Israel, it would be impossible for Israel to become what it must and to emanate to the world what it must. To be sure, a certain measure of Israel's true identity had been maintained in exile. For the last two thousand years, growth in thought and understanding has taken place, alongside a multifaceted contribution in many areas of life. Nevertheless, Israel has not yet risen to its destined height.

This precious tool entrusted to Israel, we may further suggest, is God's *Shekhinah*, the power of God's dwelling. For it is through the *Shekhinah* that the world was created. This is the basis for the portrayal of Israel—or of certain individuals—as partners to God in the creative process. Not merely through the study of Torah as an intellectual exercise, but through the power of the divine present amidst them, Israel can become the partner of God in the creative process. It is thus Israel's position within the body of humanity, emanating the force of *keter* by virtue of the presence of the *Shekhinah*, that finally brings humanity as a whole to perfection.

The three stages described in Rabbi Akiva's statement form a self-contained circle. The first stage is not subservient to the third; rather, we have here a total circle. When Israel assumes its responsibility in full, then the image of God upon earth, manifested through humanity, can reach fulfillment.

We opened our discussion with the struggle and the blessing. The struggle is the struggle of Israel to prevail in its endeavor to be *keter*, to wipe out evil, to emanate the force of the will of God to the world. The growth and rebirth are not for Israel alone; its growth and rebirth is not a blessing for it alone; it is a blessing appropriated for humanity and on behalf of humanity. The dwelling of God, the presence of the *Shekhinah* within Israel, is not of significance for Israel alone, but for mankind as a whole. For "this people I formed Myself, that they shall declare my praise" (Isa 43:21).

References

[1] The organic metaphor has long been employed in Jewish thought, specifically to denote Israel's relation to other peoples, where it, significantly, is used to assign Israel a place of esteem in the body of mankind, and indeed often one of supremacy. Thus Judah Halevi in the *Kuzari* (2:36) likens Israel to the heart within the body. The heart for Halevi, to be sure, is the most vital and significant organ of the body (2:26). One must, however, clearly note that Halevi was cognizant that this was but a metaphor. He employed the imagery of the heart only to underscore what he believed to be Israel's position within humanity. He did not wish to suggest that humanity was actually structured as a body.

Bibliography

Moses Cordovero, *The Palm Tree of Deborah*, trans. Louis Jacobs (1974) esp. 70ff.

Judah Halevi, *The Kuzari*, trans. Hartwig Hirschfeld (1946).

David ben Yehuda he-Ḥasid, *Sefer Marot ha-Ẓoveot*, D. C. Matt, ed. (1982).

Abraham Isaac Kook, *The Lights of Penitence: The Moral Principles, Lights of Holiness, Essays, Letters and Poems* (1978), s.v. "Israel."

Abraham Isaac Kook, "Orot Yisrael," in *Orot* (1923).

Israel ben Gedaliah Lipschutz, *Tiferet Israel* (*Boaz*), ad loc. m. *'Abot* 3:14.

Chapter 3

The Holy Nation

Eliezer Berkovits

As usual, Berkovits can be relied upon for a straight and simple definition of matters in classic terms. He states in so many words, "Israel is not a church but a people, a biological and political entity," and so closes off the spiritualization of matters attempted in the dictionary definition with which we started. But, at the same time, Berkovits cannot treat "people" in terms in which ethnic groups ordinarily find their definition. He denies that "Israel" forms a church, because a church is a spiritual community, "not foremost a community of doers. Because the deed is to be effective in the eternal world of man, the community for which it asks must be a living society in reasonable control of its general order of life." But that, of course, does define a church in the lives of its members. Here once more the complexity and subtlety of the category emerges, when a major theological mind addresses a supernatural category and finds it necessary both to impute to a theological category of Christianity a meaning with little basis and also to define one of Judaism in a way that is profoundly religious while at the same time denying its shared religiosity. Clearly, we have found our way to the central category of the three before us, the one that draws Judaic theologians away from matters of other-worldly theory and toward this-worldly fact. That accounts for the appeal not to Scripture and the Oral Torah, such as is common when we speak of God and Torah, but to categories of social thought instead. And yet, Berkovits does make an important point, which is that the social order forms the focus of the religious life of Judaism, and, it must follow, an entity capable of realizing that social order of sanctification brought about through the mitzvot or commandments must be contemplated. Hence he says, "The full implementation of Judaism requires a society that is prepared to submit its whole life to the ordering will of Judaism. But a society sufficiently free to do so is not a congregation or a church nor a philosophical school or an exclusive club, not even a communion of saints, but a nation—a people in control of, at least, the internal order of its existence." Since, for long centuries, Christianity East and West concurred that it was to form a society defined by Christianity, but making place for Judaism, and Islam throughout the world spoke of the Nation of Islam as well, it is clear that for Berkovits, "Israel" forms a close counterpart to the Church as the body of Christ and Islamic states as the Nation of Islam.

***

From God, Man, and History: A Jewish Interpretation. Copyright 1959 by Eliezer Berkovits. Reprinted by permission of Sali Berkovits.

The concept of Israel is essential for Judaism. Israel is not imaginable without Judaism, nor is Judaism a possibility of faith and living in the world without Israel. All historical evidence proves that Israel is not a church but a people,[1] a biological and political entity.

The questions we wish to pose now are: What need is there for the inclusion of such a national concept in the ideological concept of Judaism? In what way does the meaning of the religious experience require divine revelations to be granted to a people as such and not only to individuals?[2] How does the service of God lead to such a "chosen people" rather than to chosen personalities, elevated through their service? It is to the answer to these—and related—questions that we plan to turn our attention in the next pages.

The Deed Made Effective

From our preceding discussion, it follows that Judaism is not an "idealistic" or a "spiritual" religion, but a human one. It is a religion for the whole of man. It aims at relating life in its entirety to God. It is not, therefore, so much a religion of creed as it is the religion of the deed on earth.[3] The intellect or the soul may be satisfied with the creed; the whole man, however, may serve God only through the deed. The deed, as we saw, is the child of the union of the body and the mind; in the deed alone may body and mind join, complementing each other to mutual advantage.

The deed, however, is essentially social; and in order to be, it must find its place in the external world of man. It is social because it is always expressive of a relationship. Most intimately, it is the relationship between body and soul. The contribution of the body to the deed places it of necessity in the world outside man. The deed, directed to the outside, is always in relationship to "an other." This "other" may be the world, a neighbor, or God. However, in order to be, the deed must be effective; and it must be so in the place where it belongs—in the external world, in history. In fact, the deed is the stuff of which history is made. As the deed of the race so its history.

For the deed to be effective, it must not remain that of an individual but must become that of a community. The deed makes history, if it is the materialization of the desire and the will of a community of people joined together in a common cause. It is obvious that the community of the deed is not a church. A church is the outgrowth of that very dualism which Judaism aims to overcome. A church is essentially a community of believers and worshipers, a spiritual community; it is not foremost a community of doers. Because the deed is to be effective in the external world of man, the community for which it asks must be a living society in reasonable control of its general order of life. This general order must be such that it will not render the deed of Judaism impossible or "unnatural."[4] Even the purely religious aspects of the

Jewish deed are most intimately interwoven with the general matrix of community existence. If, for instance, the Sabbath were a purely spiritual day, to be observed "in the heart" alone by meditation and inner peace, the economic structure of the society in which the Jew lived would have little or no effect on the observance. But since the Sabbath, like any other *Mitsvah*, is a deed, requiring rest for the body as well as for the soul, the economic order is of the utmost relevance even for the purely religious significance of the day. The most conducive habitat for the Sabbath is, therefore, a society whose economic and industrial activities are at a standstill on that day. The Sabbath is more naturally at home in such a society. The Sabbath deed, to be most effective, of necessity strives for the coordination of the material fabric and order of the community with its own intentions. This, however, may be most potently accomplished by a group that possesses sufficient sovereignty to be able to fashion the practical structure of its own life in accordance with its desires.

If one wished to illustrate the point further, the examples from the "ritual laws" alone could be multiplied at will. However, of far greater interest in this connection are the *Mitsvot* concerning inter-human relationships. They cover all the areas of man's life: family and society, law and trade, education and industry, peace and war. Nothing affecting human intercourse is excluded from the scope of these commandments. As always in Judaism, here too decisive is not the entertainment of noble ideals, but their realization in the external world of action and conduct. Therefore, the full implementation of Judaism requires a society that is prepared to submit its whole life to the ordering will of Judaism. But a society sufficiently free to do so is not a congregation or a church, not a philosophical school or an exclusive club, not even a communion of saints, but a nation—a people in control of, at least, the internal order of its existence. The *Mitzvah* is a public deed and not a private one. One cannot be a Jew only "at heart"; one has to be a Jew together with other Jews in history-making action.

A people in control of its own life, capable of implementing Judaism by application to the whole of life, is a people in its own land. Judaism, as the religion of the deed, requires a people in its land. The people alone can realize Judaism; in the land of the people alone it may be fully realized. Abraham was not the founder of a church, but the father of a people. "And I will make of thee a great nation," God promises him at the beginning of his career, and He directs the steps of the patriarch-to-be "unto the land that I will show thee."[5]

What has thus far been put pragmatically may also be expressed ideologically. The deed of the *Mitzvah* aims at oneness in life, at a measure of interpretation between the spiritual and the material, and the transformation of both of these by lending material effectiveness to the spirit and spiritual directedness to the material and biologically vital. The dichotomy of the spiritual and the material is found everywhere in the world of man. The life of the community, as well as that of the individual, is infected through and through with the conflict between what "matters" but is without value and that which is of value but has no power to assert itself on its own. Wherever the dualism is encountered it should be overcome. What has been said of the individual applies also to society: life in its entirety is to be placed in relationship to God. The attempt at "interpenetration" and "transformation" must be pursued on the group as well as the individual level of reality. All the material aspects of society, its complete bio-physical structure are themselves in need of being invested with value and with God-centeredness. But any group of people which is prepared to dedicate its corporate life to such a goal will emerge in history not only as a distinctive spiritual entity, but also as a political and biological unit, i.e., as a distinctive national group. However, since its specific characteristics will be due to its determination to relate all the areas of its group life to God, it will properly be called, a people of God.

The historic mission of Israel has therefore been described by the Bible in the words: ". . . and ye shall be unto Me a kingdom of priests, and a holy nation."[5] This kingdom of priests is not a society in which a priestly caste rules over an unpriestly populace in the name of some god. A holy nation is a realm in which all are priests. But where all are priests, all are servants—and God alone rules. "A kingdom of priests and a holy nation" is not a theocracy, but a God-centered republic.

The Universal Goal

It may now be shown how the concept of Israel as "a holy nation" not only does not conflict with the universalism of Israel's prophets, but actually leads to it as its own logical completion.[6]

The idea of a holy nation is not to be confused with that of nationalism. The goal of nationalism is to serve the nation: a holy nation serves God. The law of nationalism is national self-interest; the law of "a kingdom of priests" is the will of God. From the point of view of a nationalistic ideology, the nation is an end in itself; the "holy nation" is a means to an end. Since, however, the end is the wholeness of life in relationship to God, it obviously points beyond the national frame. The holy nation is the instrument for the realization of a supra-national purpose in history. The nation works toward a universal goal. It does not exclude other nations; on the contrary, the end which it serves seeks the completion of its aspirations by them. The individual does not live alone. Hence, if his deed is to be effective, he must unite with others in the common pursuit of the goal of Judaism. The result is, inevitably, the "holy nation." But a holy nation cannot live in complete isolation. Its deeds will be all the more effective, the more far-reaching the understanding which a people of God achieves with the rest of mankind. The greater the understanding, the wider the area of life that becomes God-oriented. The deed is always public; that of the individual takes place in his immediate society, in the midst of his people; and that of the nation is enacted in the context of the life of the nations. As the individual must make common cause with the community, so the nation, with the community of nations. Realization through the holy people of necessity points to fuller realization through mankind.

The goal of Judaism is accomplished when it is reached by all mankind. Since, however, the goal is not essentially the teaching of noble ideals—which would indeed be rather easy and ineffective—but the realization of the teaching in history, one has to start with the smallest unit of living reality within which the deed of Judaism may become history-making; and such a unit is the nation. Individuals may teach; a people is needed in order to do effectively. However, nationality here is not an ideological requirement but a historical necessity. The gradual realization of the universal purpose in history is unable to dispense with the instrumentality of the holy nation. The universal purpose and its practical implementation in history determine the national characteristics of Israel. The "holy nation" is the only people on earth whose very *raison d'etré* is the pursuit of a universal goal. It is the universalistic idea at the heart of Israel's existence which determines its *national* distinctiveness and uniqueness.

In history, he who wants universalism cannot by-pass the concept of the holy nation. Universalism is only an ideal, perhaps a potentiality; in reality, it has—thus far—never been known to exist. In reality, we have individuals and societies, nations and classes, empires and other concentrations of power and interest—largely at cross-purposes with each other. A universal mankind will come into being only through the reconciliation of all separative interests, ambitions, and aspirations in the world. Reconciliation, however, means awareness of the other and care for the other. This, of course, brings us back to our starting point. The obligation to care we found in the imitation of God; the effectiveness of the caring deed we saw safeguarded through the law of God. The harmony of mankind is the end-result in history of a development which starts with the individual *Mitzvah*, the deed of interpenetration of the spiritual and the material. The God-orientation of the whole of the human being is the beginning of a process that aspires to lead to the creation of universalism or—as it may also be put—to the God-orientation of all life.

What is "last in production may of course be first in thought"; in history, however, one cannot begin with mankind, one must start with man. One builds humanity first within oneself by the establishment of an awareness of "the other," which—implying a measure of reconciliation between body and soul within the individual—leads to the caring deed. But we rended the individual deed effective by building humanity within the nation, by relating the entire scope of a relatively self-contained society to God. And one builds humanity by striving through the people for the final goal: to establish the world in mankind as the Kingdom of God.[8]

The Chosen People

The holy nation is properly called the chosen people. The idea expresses, first of all, the practical necessity for a national instrument for the realization of the supranational goal. This world is established as a kingdom of God when all the nations submit to the will of God. But before all nations will do it, one nation must do it. The "kingdom of priests" is the unavoidable pathfinder and forerunner of the kingdom of God. If the universal goal is to be accomplished in history, there has to be a stage known as "His first-fruits of the increase."[9]

The rise of God's "first-fruits," however, cannot be left altogether to natural growth, as it were. We have seen that the obligation of any law derives not from its rationality, but from the expressed will of a law-giving authority. Therefore, the will of God exists and is obligatory for man only insofar as it has been made known to him.[10] The will of God revealed to individuals is law for them as individuals. While it is correct, as we have maintained, that in order to be effective in history individuals have to join in a common course; nevertheless, should the will of God be proclaimed to them as individuals only, their acting in community of purpose would be logical but it would not be the fulfillment of a divine command. Unless the will of God is directed to the people as such, the dualism between individual obligation and national interest remains unresolved. Religion then becomes the domain of individual souls, whereas the nation as such remains free to be guided by the realism of its self-interest. To submit the entire structure of a people's life to the will of God is a national obligation, if the will of God has in actuality been revealed to the people as a whole. Only because God addressed Himself to the people is the fulfillment of His will a national responsibility for Israel.

It is, however, not altogether irrelevant to ponder on the point that it was not Israel that was chosen, but rather Israel that came into being by having been chosen. God never chose the Jews; but any people whom God chose was bound to become the Jewish people. The choice of God made Israel. Why was it one family that was singled out and not another? Why did God address Himself to one specific tribe and not to all the nations of the earth at once? Was it because among them He first encountered the personalities who were best qualified to become the patriarchs of a proposed holy nation? . . . Who will care to fathom the mind of the Almighty![11] Let it suffice for us to grasp that "a people of God" is a practical requirement for the penetration of the divine purpose into the history of man, that it is needed for the fulfillment of man's destiny on earth as intended by the revealed will of the Creator. As to the rest, Jews can only testify to what has happened to them. They have been called into being by the will of God. They have been fashioned and formed through their "national" encounters with the Divine Presence.

Endnotes

[1] See my essay, The Galut of Judaism, in *Judaism: A Quarterly* (Summer, 1995) where I have argued that any attempt at interpreting Israel as a purely religious association of believers is a distortion, not only of the historic concept of Israel, but also of the ideological contents of Judaism.

[2] The result of "idealistic" religions and philosophies, usually sadly ineffective and often guilt-laden in history, has prompted a great deal of partisan nonsense to be entertained concerning the tribal and national religion of the Jews. Cf. on this the author's *Judaism: Fossil or Ferment?*, the chapters, "The Judaism of the Jews."

[3] Cf. R. Travers Herford's discussion of the overwhelming importance of the creed in Christianity. See his *The Pharisees*. Heresy hunting is the typical affliction of all "idealistic" religions. In Judaism, characteristically, wrong opinions are not punishable, only wrong deeds.

[4] In *Die Religion innerhalb der Grenzen etc.*, Kant has the following to say on the effectiveness of the ideal of the good: "[T]he highest ethical good is not accomplished through the striving of the individual person for his own moral perfection. It is required that such people unite in a whole for this purpose (of accomplishing the highest ethical good), forming a system of well-intentioned men. In such a system, and through its unity alone, may it (the highest good) come into being." 1. Abschnitt, II. The author's somewhat free translation.

[5] Genesis 12:1-2.

[6] Exodus 19:6.

[7] On Jewish Universalism cf. the author's *Judaism: Fossil or Ferment?*, the chapter, "Jewish Universalism and the Chosen People."

[8] See the *Aleynu* prayer in the Daily Prayer Book.

[9] Jeremiah 2:3.

[10] Cf. above, ch. 11, *"Revelation" as the Source of Obligation.*

Chapter 4

The Chosen People

Bernard J. Bamberger

The issue is not the characterization of the society of the faithful formed by the Torah, in reponse to God's commandment, and called "Israel." It is what Judaism—the Torah—has to say about Israel. That is, specifically, that Israel is elect or "chosen," and in modern times, eager to conciliate and gain the good will of their Christian and other gentile neighbors. Jews have wanted not to explain but explain away that critical affirmation of the faith. It is an affirmation that remains when much else in the faith has attenuated, so that, as an acute observer remarked, "The Jews no longer believe in God, but they know for certain that they are the chosen people." This has taken the humble form of a desire for children to marry Jews and so preserve Israel after the flesh, even while all other marks of religious commitment have disappeared. The problem, however, is that, with the doctrine of election, theology is perceived to take up a question of social, not other-worldly interest, and few have grasped the deep thought of a Berkovits in showing the theological meaning of the social question. The result is already apparent to us. Here we have a systematic description of the issue of election, with clear, factual presentation of the components of the concept of the election of Israel.

* * *

The Problem

What theologians call "the election of Israel," is not just a problem for Jews. From the days of Paul to the present, it has been a matter of concern to Christian thinkers; and it has had a place, though a smaller one, in Muslim teaching as well.

For Christians could not evade the facts: Jesus of Nazareth appeared and worked within the framework of Jewish life; Christianity grew out of Judaism and based itself on the Hebrew Scriptures. As a result, Christian thinkers tended to divide into two groups. One held that the Jews had been the chosen people of God, but forfeited their chosenness by making the golden calf, and later by rejecting Jesus. The other group, following Paul, held that the failures of Israel had not completely destroyed their special relation to God. There was a deep mystery here, and ultimately there would be a reconciliation. The outcome of such theories was that the leaders of Christianity never decreed extermination upon the Jews. They tolerated and even indicted

*From *The Search for Jewish Theology*, by Bernard J. Bamberger. Copyright 1978 by Bernard J. Bamberger. Reprinted by permission of Behrman House, Inc.

massacres, persecutions, expulsions, and vilifications; but in the otherwise monolithic Christianity of medieval Europe, some kind of place had to be allotted to Jews and Judaism.

Islam, which drew much of its doctrine and lore from Jewish sources, recognized the Jewish and Christian revelations as basically authentic—as stages on the road to the final and perfect revelation through Muhammad. Jews and Christians, the peoples of the Book, were therefore generally tolerated, but assigned an inferior status.

I am not aware of any serious discussion of these matters in present-day Islam. But Christians have been engaged in considerable rethinking of the subject. The best publicized instance is that of the Second Vatican Council, which led to a cautious (and from the Jewish standpoint, far from adequate) though no doubt well-meant pronouncement. Many Protestants and certain individual Catholics have gone much further; the writings of James Parkes and Reinhold Niebuhr on the subject are outstanding. (Some Christian philo-Semites exceed Jewish writers in their estimate of Jewish virtues and their expectations of Jewish performance.)

But this belief in the special role of the Jewish people within the divine economy, which is firmly held by many Christians, is a source of embarrassment, pain, and perplexity to many Jews.

The Background

The belief had gone unchallenged among Jews throughout the centuries. It is plainly expressed in passage after passage in the Bible, and constantly recurs in the traditional prayerbook. When the scroll of the Torah is read in the synagogue, each person who is called up for the reading praises the God "who has chosen us from among all peoples and given us His law." Closely allied are a series of benedictions containing the formula "who has sanctified us by His commandments and commanded us—followed by a reference to the specific rite to be performed. Without multiplying quotations, to show the presence—indeed the ubiquitousness—of the doctrine in the standard sources, we must take note, however, of the character of the teaching.

First, there is no suggestion that the choice of Israel implies an inherent "racial" superiority. Deuteronomy reminds the Israelites that they were not chosen because they were numerous—"you are the smallest of peoples"—and that they were to receive the promised land for no virtue of their own (Deut 7:7, 9:4-6). Nor are they to regard themselves as specially talented: it will be by observing God's laws, and thus only, that they will gain a reputation for wisdom (Deut 4:16 ff.).

This brings us to a second point. The election of Israel is not for world conquest; it confers no rights and privileges, but rather duties. Israel has been chosen to obey the law. This is the constant burden of the biblical writers; it is also characteristic of traditional prayers and benedictions. The prophet Amos insists that just because of the special care which God has given Israel, He will punish them more severely for disobedience and faithlessness (Amos 3:2).[1]

Third, while one may find chauvinistic utterances in the Bible, as in all national literatures of the past and present, there is a frequent suggestion that the choice of Israel is for the ultimate benefit and blessing of all men. Isaiah's great vision of a warless world—something new and revolutionary in human thought—includes the expectation that divine guidance for all peoples will issue from Zion. Indeed, it is precisely this guidance which will make peace possible (Isa 2:1 ff). The great prophet of the exile depicts the people of Israel as the servant of the Lord, through whose suffering other peoples will be healed, and as a "light of the nations" through whom God will bring His salvation to the ends of the earth (Isa 53:5, 49:6).[2]

Perhaps more impressive than these visionary utterances is the evidence in the Bible itself for a missionary movement which won many new adherents to Judaism. This movement declined after a while, but in the last centuries before the Christian era it revived with tremendous energy, and it continued for centuries until it was brought to a stop by the political power of Christianized Rome.[3]

Shifting Positions

But despite all these considerations, a good many modern Jews have been unhappy about the idea. Some, no doubt, feared Gentile disapproval of what might seem to be Jewish arrogance. Others were genuinely troubled by a concept that seemed to them both irrational and presumptuous. Another factor was the rise of a Zionist movement which was understood by many (though by no means all) of its adherents as completely secular. They were interested in the "normalization" of Jewish life through the establishment of a Jewish state; for, they argued, the Jews are different from other peoples only in that they do not presently have a land and government of their own. And since the Reform movement of the nineteenth century was predominantly anti-Zionist, and this movement had laid great stress on the "mission of Israel" to bring prophetic monotheism to the world, many of the nationalists were all the more disposed to discard the notion of a unique spiritual role for their people. (Yet there were others who argued that the prophetic ideas could be made effective in the world only if they were incorporated in the legal and social order of a Jewish national state).[4]

Today there is a wide variation among thinking and believing Jews on this subject. The orthodox believe without question in the election of the Jewish people, since it is taught unequivocally in the Bible. Many others, not fundamentalists, are still deeply impressed both by the biblical statements and by the character of Jewish history. Most extreme is Will Herberg, with his flat assertion that the Jews are a supernatural people.[5] And Arthur A. Cohen has moved in the same direction with a book entitled *The Natural and the Supernatural Jew*.

Such assertions are almost impossible to discuss. It is extremely difficult, to say the least, to explain what is meant by "a supernatural people." And even were we to agree on a definition, one is at a loss to find a way of proving that any people is or is not supernatural.

At the other extreme, Mordecai M. Kaplan has completely rejected the idea of a chosen people; and this notion has been systematically eliminated from the prayerbook of the Reconstructionist movement, which Dr. Kaplan founded. In contrast with Herberg's position, that of Kaplan can be readily articulated. It regards as impertinence and self-delusion the supposition that the universe is critically concerned about the denizens of a small satellite of one of the lesser stars. Still more unacceptable to Kaplan is the notion that among the inhabitants of that planet, one little people has been singled out by Divinity for a central, perhaps even a cosmic role. Such a claim, he holds, is both foolish and arrogant. It is difficult to answer this criticism in logical terms. But if logic is on Kaplan's side, facts seem to be against him.

Kaplan is prepared to admit that the Jews have a "vocation"; all peoples have their several vocations.[6] But the real issue is not one of terminology: it is the character of the reality to which the terms point. The phenomenon of the Jewish people is the same whether we say that it was "chosen" or just "called."

To speak of the vocation of a people is to use an analogy from the life of individuals. But not every man has a vocation. Some just have a job, others are unemployed. (Of course, in both groups there are some persons who have a vocation which circumstances prevent them from following.) What distinguishes a job from a calling is not, to my mind, the honor and prestige that attach to some kinds of work and are not accorded to others. It is rather to be found in the attitude of the worker toward his work. The most humble task—according to the world's valuation—is a calling if the laborer finds satisfaction in it and feels he is rendering a useful service.

But there are plenty of people, not bad people, who have no special aptitude, no special energy or eagerness; they do what they must, and no more, Either they have no vocation or they have not yet found theirs. Their own work may be useful to society, but they get no particular satisfaction from what they contribute or from the quality of their performance. This is said without condescension or contempt. There are many routine jobs in our world which, though necessary to the smooth running of our economy, are not calculated to fire the imagination of those who perform them. The prevailing standards of "success" do little to reveal the possibilities of vocation in a job that offers neither wealth, power, nor publicity. One of our unsolved problems is to convince ourselves that there is dignity in any useful work honestly performed. But though many of the current distinctions are arbitrary and artificial, there is probably no way to avoid giving special dignity (and perhaps we should not try to avoid it) to those kinds of work that require high degrees of skill, long training, or rare and unusual talent. The same applies to those callings that involve extensive and heavy responsibilities.

As among individuals, so among peoples there is a wide variety. Some have played a prominent role in world history, and some have not. It is not prejudice to say that the roles of the Ammonites, the Afghans, the Paraguayans, and the Montenegrins in human civilization and culture are not comparable to those of the Phoenicians, the Hindus, the Mexicans, and the Greeks. It is also worth noting that many peoples who have made outstanding contributions in past millennia have ceased to exist or have become unproductive; and we do not know when other nations whose historic part has hitherto been modest—or who are just now emerging as nations— will advance to the center of the stage.

Jewish history, however, presents a special complex of problems to the thoughtful student. Here is a people that has played a significant part in world history through thousands of years. Unlike the ancient Egyptians and the ancient and modern Chinese, this people did not owe its continued existence to the possession of a fertile and well-protected country. For most of the past two thousand years they had no territory of their own. Yet despite small numbers, total powerlessness, and dispersion, they have been important in world history both for what they have done and for what has been done to them. Their ordeal and their contribution have been extraordinary. There is literally no parallel or analogue to the history of the Jews. Let the professors of history name one.

To all this the enemies of Israel give eloquent testimony. Without reviewing the ghastly tale of violence, humiliation, oppression, and massacre in earlier centuries, one must be awed at the magnitude and intensity of the obsession which in modern times we call anti-Semitism. Why have both the extreme right and the extreme left been driven to such convulsive efforts to exterminate this one small group? Why did the Nazis have to carry on the "final solution" even to the detriment of their own war effort? What has caused the Soviet leaders to encourage the Arab nations to finish the job in the present? One hardly knows which is more incredible: the persistence of the Jewish people through three thousand difficult years, or the untiring efforts of the Gentile world to liquidate them.

As Jewish existence presents a problem to the outsiders—be he hostile or sympathetic—so it confronts the Jew himself with many perplexities. A great amount of energy has been expended by modern Jews on the attempt to define and classify the Jewish people. Is Jewish identity racial, national, or religious? The facts do not accommodate themselves to any of the usual classifications.

Thus, even if we abandon the language of chosenness, and accept Dr. Kaplan's terminology of vocation, we have not escaped from the predicament that distresses him. Granted that every people has its own vocation—and this assumption is still to be proved—the facts indicate that the Jewish people has a special vocation.

Still Chosen?

But one may ask: Do the considerations thus far advanced lead to any theological conclusion? Or is this all a matter of historical circumstance, even doom? What connection, if any, is there between the biblical Israel and the Jews of today? Are the latter really the lineal heirs of the prophets? Many Christian theologians have argued through the centuries that the Jews, once chosen, are chosen no more; they have forfeited their distinction, and the Church is now the true Israel. Even if we disregard this invidious view, it can still be argued that Israel accomplished its "mission" when it gave the world the Bible with its message of ethical monotheism. Why need the people of Israel continue, and what further claim does it have to being special?

Or the matter might be put thus: As long as Jews believed that the Torah was literally the word of God, and that He had given it to Israel, the idea of a chosen people made sense. And it found expression in the conscientious fulfillment of the commandments by the overwhelming majority of Jews. But today the religious life of the Jewish people is in a state of chaos. A considerable proportion of today's Jews have explicitly or implicitly rejected all positive religion. Of those who maintain a tie with the synagogue and with tradition, not a few do so out of mere habit, out of respect for living or dead parents, out of a desire to identify themselves as Jews, but not necessarily as believers. Within the institutions of Jewish religion, one notes a sad amount of materialism, hedonism, ignorance, prayerlessness, and the exploitation of leadership positions for personal advancement. And those who do take their Jewish religion seriously are in many cases searching, questioning, groping in deep uncertainty. Is such a community the chosen of God?

Yet even this problem is not altogether new. Witness the great prophet who was perhaps the first clearly to articulate the doctrine of the "mission of Israel." This is how he describes the "servant of the Lord":

> My chosen one, in whom I delight,
> I have put My spirit upon him,
> He shall teach the true way to the nations. . . .
> I created you, and appointed you
> A covenant-people, a light of nations. . . . (Isa 42:1, 6)

And yet in the very same chapter, the prophet depicts God as complaining:

> Who is so blind as My servant,
> So deaf as the messenger I send? (Isa 42:19)

There has always been a tragic disparity between what the Jewish people is and what the Jewish people might be—a specific instance of a universal human tragedy.

Still, even in the spiritual chaos of our time there is much of a positive nature to be said about contemporary Jewry. It has manifested enormous creative energy in innumerable fields: industrial, academic, scientific, artistic, literary, and particularly in areas concerned with human welfare. This creative energy was inhibited neither by the horrors of the 1930s nor the affluence of the 1950s and beyond. The Jews have been prominently identified with liberal and progressive causes in North America. In the recent struggle for the rights of black Americans, a disproportionately high percentage of whites who involved themselves were Jewish. (In due course, extremist black leaders got rid of them.) And this happened at a time when Jews had come to feel secure, and did not need the support of liberal forces for their own benefit.

Little short of miraculous is the revival of Jewish consciousness and self-identification among the Jews of the Soviet Union, who for half a century had been denied the opportunity to learn about their own past, and had been cut off from meaningful ties with the Jews of other lands. No one had foreseen that thousands among them would demand, still less obtain, permission to emigrate to Israel. And in the Americas, despite a great increase in the rate of mixed marriage, Jewish self-identification is still high, and the response to Jewish need—especially the plight of the State of Israel—is extraordinary.

In the State of Israel, despite a chronic military and economic crisis, the inequalities of status and opportunity between oriental and European Jews have led not only to deep heart-searching, but to constructive government action. Many Israelis, too, have been troubled by what they considered injustices to Arabs inside and outside their borders. I have not heard of any public protest in Arab countries against the cruelty toward their Jewish citizens, and there have been few voices speaking for moderation and peace.

And indeed, whatever faults may be found with the Jews, individually and collectively, their enemies have made them look good. To list anti-Semitic individuals and societies is to list the enemies of freedom, reason, and humanity. Wherever human liberty and dignity have been denied—whether in the name of blood and soil, dialectic materialism, or law and order—the Jew has been singled out for special attack. He has the unfortunate, but honorable fate to be hated by all tyrants, both of the right and the left.

Thus the unique role of the Jewish people in history is not entirely a matter of choice. Even those Jews who would like to disassociate themselves from the religion and destiny of their ancestors find themselves somehow caught up in both. The prophet Ezekiel put the truth brutally: "What you have in mind shall never come to pass—when you say, 'We will be like the nations, like the families of the lands, worshiping wood and stone.' As I live—declares the Lord God—I will reign over you with a strong hand and with an outstretched arm and with overflowing fury" (Ezek 20:32-33). Of course, this grim warning does not threaten those who embrace their Jewish identity with love.

That the Jewish people have a special role in the divine economy is ultimately a matter of faith, as are all the other affirmations of religion. But the realities of Jewish life in the past and present seem to bolster and justify that faith.

Endnotes

[1] But in 9:7, Amos seems to modify this view: God has indeed shown kindness to Israel, but other peoples have also been guided by His providence.

[2] Some scholars, ancient and modern, have explained the "servant of the Lord" differently—as a prophet of the past, as Deutero-Isaiah himself, or as a messianic figure. But such passages as Isaiah 43:10 and 44:1, which explicitly call Israel "God's servant," seem conclusive.

[3] For the biblical period see, e.g., Isaiah 56:6-8; Zechariah 8:23. For later developments, see Bernard J. Bamberger, *Proselytism in the Talmudic Period*, 2d ed. (New York: Ktav Publishing House, 1968).

[4] See Casper Levias in *Year Book of the Central Conference of American Rabbis* 9 (1899): 180; Abba H. Silver, *ibid.*, 38 (1928): 208ff.

[5] Will Herberg, *Judaism and the Modern Man* (Philadelphia: JPS, 1951) 271. On page 274 he characterizes Israel as "superhistorical."

[6] Mordecai M. Kaplan, "Shall We Retain the Doctrine of Israel as a Chosen People?" *The Reconstructionist*, February 23, 1945. I replied to this article in *The Reconstructionist* of December 28, 1945, and a rejoinder by Dr. Kaplan followed in the subsequent issue.

Chapter 5

The People of the Covenant

Eugene B. Borowitz

The issue of election is only one element in the complex of topics covered by theological "Israel" in Judaism. But chosenness does not determine the whole of matters. Another concerns the definition of who belongs to Israel, how people enter, whether people can leave. In times past, as in our own day, some Jews exercise the right to adopt some other religion, or reject all religion. Do they remain Jews? And throughout history, gentiles, including many Christians, have found their way to the congregation of Israel at Sinai and accepted the Torah, the males undergoing circumcision, males and females alike accepting baptism. How have they found a place for themselves in the community of the faithful that otherwise finds its definition in birth to a Jewish mother? The question is not only religious but also political, since the State of Israel accords citizenship to every Jew who applies, with the consequent issues therefore to be faced: precisely who is a Jew for the purposes of Israeli citizenship? Since the Germans in sentencing every Jew to death defined a Jew as a person with a single Jewish grandparent, considerable opinion would accept as a Jew at the very least the child of a Jewish father and gentile mother as much as one of a Jewish mother and a gentile father, such as the law of the Torah declares to be the rule. And, finally, the very fact that the Jewish state in what was called Palestine and in what the Jews have always called "the land of Israel" calls itself "Israel" or in Hebrew, the State of Israel, further complicates matters. We rely on Eugene Borowitz to sort matters out and to specify the several elements of the issue of who is a Jew and what is Israel. True to his theological vocation, Borowitz finds an entirely rational and well-justified definition: "Israel is the people of the covenant." That for theological thought assuredly solves the problem of atheism joined to Jewishness. At the same time, Borowitz concurs with Berkovits, the former resident in the U.S.A., the latter in the State of Israel at the time of his death, that the State of Israel presents a religious, not only a secular and political, fact to Judaism, since many elements of the Torah's covenant presuppose a nation living in the holy land. But he insists, "Life in the State of Israel is not the only genuine way of expressing the Covenant or of living by it." The facts of history certainly sustain his claim.

***

---

*From *How Can a Jew Speak of Faith Today?* Copyright 1969 by Westminster Press. Reprinted by permission of Westminster/John Knox Press.

Who Is Israel?

On each of his visits to the United States, David Ben-Gurion brought a simple and a single message: "Come to the State of Israel. Those of you who wish to fulfill yourselves as Jews, those of you to whom Jewishness is significant, come and settle in our ancestral land."

What Ben-Gurion offered was quite palpable. He held out to American Jews the possibility of living in a community where almost everyone is a Jew and where Jewish life is culturally predominant. Children learn Hebrew as naturally as they grow. The Bible is a school textbook and a national craze. Schools and factories close not only for the Sabbath and the High Holy Days but in celebration of every Jewish holiday. In short, it is an atmosphere in which by simply living in one's neighborhood and being concerned with issues that confront the community one is already involved in Jewish affairs. Here is normal, natural Jewishness, without the strain, the unnatural tension that characterizes the effort to be a Jew in the Diaspora.

Yet implicit in this call are several critical questions: Who really is "Israel"? What are the Jews? Where may true Jewishness be lived?

It was not by chance that the founders of the Jewish State in what was once called "Palestine" chose as its name "Israel," or, as the proclamation of independence sometimes also terms it, "the State of Israel"—the ambiguity is important. But is Israel primarily that political entity which exists today on the soil of what was once called Palestine? The word "Israel," at least for many centuries, had no political connotations. To this day when Jews rise to say the Shema, "Hear, O Israel"—and that is the point at which the word most impressively comes into their lives—they are not calling to a state. They mean the Jewish people as a whole united by its relationship to God: "Adonai, our God, Adonai is One." Of course, the address is to all Jews wherever they may be, and it in some strange way reaches back to all the generations of Jews who were (who found and bequeathed to them this "our" God) and to all the Jews who will yet be (who must carry on this relationship through history to its Messianic consummation). Still, what binds them together as Israel in this moment is that they are untied in their loyalty to this God and bound together by faithfulness to his service. That, at least, would seem to be the communal implications of the Shema over the centuries.

From Ben-Gurion and the classical Zionist's point of view, Israel is the Jewish people centered around its State, in its land. Jewishness, therefore, is sharing in the life of that people, now happily revivified and restored in the full dimensions of land, language, and political form. The logical deduction from this point of view is indeed Ben-Guiron's invitation. A full Jewish life can be lived only on the land and in the State—and Jews who have merited reaching this happy day in Jewish history should take advantage of an opportunity denied their ancestors for centuries.

But are all Jews prepared to say that the State of Israel is the one authentic representation of the people of Israel? Is the State by virtue of being a state thereby the embodiment of everything the people has wanted to be and thus the State is, in effect, more important than the people?

Jewish history itself would raise these questions even if Diaspora Jews did not. Are, then, the past two thousand years of Jewish struggle and suffering, of creativity and consecration, relatively insignificant? Were the Jews of those years, most of whom did not live in that land and did not speak its language, not authentically Jewish? Should one dismiss as Jewishly stunted and deprived the Golden Age both of Eastern and Western Islam with its giants such as Sasadia and Maimonides? Were Babylonia, Franco-Germany, and Poland not truly Jewish in their varying communal cultural expressions?

Logic would require Ben-Gurion to deprecate these epochs, and he has not flinched from doing so. He has said that the current generation of Israelis has more in common with what the Israelites felt at the time of Joshua than it has with the Jews of the past two thousand years. Although Diaspora Jews can appreciate the new aliveness of the people's ancient entry into the Land, they equally affirm the enduring relevance of a Talmud written in Babylonian Aramaic or Hasidic tales told in Yiddish. It is difficult to believe that as the generations go by, scholars and even ordinary Jews living in the State of Israel will not study the products of Diaspora Jewry and find them not just the archaeological remains of truncated Jewish living but meaningful expressions of Jewishness that still speak to them. The key issue is continuity of spirit. The social setting of Jews has changed radically and with it personal attitudes, but is there no extension of Jewish ideas and values into the modern day? Is the only bond between the generations one of biology, language, and attachment to a land? When the Israelis no longer feel the need to assert their independence against their recent Diaspora past, they will surely recognize that there was an authentic Jewish existence not only outside the Land but in languages other than Hebrew as well.

Two thousand years of Jewish experience have demonstrated to Diaspora Jews the possibility, indeed the desirability, of Jewishness outside the Land. Although today's freedoms pose special problems in Jewish living—yet simultaneously make available unparalleled opportunities—the past indicates to those who do not immigrate to the State of Israel that their position has solid Jewish precedent and legitimacy.

A thoughtful approach to their attitude would be to examine how Jewish tradition itself conceived of the Jews. Of course, the source material is "biased." It is all religious and therefore understands the Jews in this context. But the very word "religious" needs to be understood in its unique Jewish connotation. The tradition depicts the Jews in their beginnings as a people like other peoples. They are described in a way that the modern eye recognizes without hesitation as a Semitic group like so many others in the ancient Near East. As time passes they are subjected to the same vicissitudes as are other peoples and are with equal effect buffeted by the customary forces of history. They have normal difficulties in establishing their monarchy, seeing it break up, being subjugated by larger powers, feeling the impact of economies expanding and contracting. They are surely nothing like a church in this period. They are in terms of their social identity a folk, an ethnic entity, a land-language-literature destiny group like so many others in human history.

One thing, however, is different about them and that difference is decisive, even socially. This people had the good fortune to find God or to be found by him. Not a god, but God—the one and only God was its God. No other people had ever so plainly come to know him. The impact of this new human experience was determinative for the character of this folk and it has been influenced by this discovery/ revelation ever since.

One cannot limit the impact of this experience to Moses and the Hebrews traveling through the wilderness. After Moses a prophetic tradition arose that continued not for a few generations but for centuries. New voices spoke in a fresh way, yet evoking the same original depth of divine understanding found earlier in the Mosaic leadership. Equally incredible, though the voices were often critical, the people accepted their instruction. Thus, over the centuries the life and character of the Jewish people changed. What had begun as a people rather like all other peoples had become different from all other peoples; it was the only people whose peoplehood was determined by its knowledge of God. The tradition says that what gave the Jewish people this unique character was its relationship with God. This it called the *brit*, the Covenant, the promise, the pledge, the pact between God and this people, made at Sinai and renewed in succeeding generations.

For its part, the Hebrew folk pledged itself to remember God and serve him through all of history by making his law the basis of its life. It might do what every other people does in history—work, marry, create, migrate—but in and through and underneath the life of all mankind was its unique folk dedication—the service of God in loyalty to an ancient pledge. Its purpose was to remind all mankind of him until they came to know him too, to acknowledge him as their God and to live by his law. In turn, they knew God would protect and watch over them. Eventually, he would vindicate its service "in the end of days." This was not an all-encompassing guarantee. Individual Jews, families, or even communities might suffer and die, but the people would survive. Its purpose would ultimately be fulfilled in an era of peace, justice, and love; then they and their patient, obedient faithfulness through all history would be fulfilled.

The people of this Covenant is Israel. It is always truly Israel whenever it lives up to its obligations under that Covenant. Israel is simply the people of that Covenant.

That is the traditional sense of the nature of Israel, expressed in modern language to be sure, but with some variation a widely held affirmation even in modern Judaism. This is the special sense of the word "religious" when applied to Jews. It necessarily has a double meaning—folk and faith, community and Covenant, people and pledge. It must not disturb Jews that Protestantism and Catholicism do not know this intimate fusion of people and religion. The history of religions knows many other social forms for organizing religious groups, as for example, the different structures of Buddhism or Hinduism. Jews have no reason in advance to reject their own. Indeed, without it they could not have survived as they did, nor yet hope to fulfill the Covenant in history. For ethnicity is a strong armor against the destructive forces of history. Its multiple bands have bound this people closely together through the ages and thus kept them loyal. Even today, when belief is modest, what exists is reinforced by the folk feelings. Where there is little or no faith, the ethnic ties still keep many true to their people—hopefully until that day when they or their descendants will find their way back to faith in God and their Covenant with him.

Contrast this view with that held by Ben-Gurion. By his standards, strictly interpreted, it would be possible to have an "Israel" which claimed to be the heartland of all the Jewish people and which at the same time might be completely atheistic. This is no idle fancy. The overwhelming majority of Israelis today are not religious in the generally accepted sense of the term. Most feel no particular attachment to the European-style Orthodox Judaism which is almost their only religious option. Since their Jewishness is national, they do not feel any special need to be Jews by faith or religious practice. It is not too farfetched to inquire whether, according to Ben-Gurion, conversions to Christianity would still leave their Jewishness unimpaired. As the case of Brother Daniel made clear, even for a secular Jewish state and its law, conversion to Christianity makes one not fully a Jew. The State of Israel may not identify Jewishness with religiosity, but even it had to admit that a rejection of Jewish faith for another religion makes one somehow less a Jewish national. That clash of sentiment with philosophy was quite revealing.

Clearly, Israel cannot even largely be identified with a particular state. Israel must rather be understood as the community of the Covenant wherever it is and under whatever circumstances, though it becomes most clearly visible when it is living a self-determining existence on its homeland.

The historical origins of the present religious/secular split may help us understand its implications better. The emancipation from the ghetto brought this unique and bewildering division upon Jewish life. Before it, there was no distinction between what it meant to be a member of the people and at the same time to take on its religious commitment. Every Jew was a Jew by relation to God and a member of the Jewish people simultaneously. Since his admittance to the modern world the Jew has faced the problem of identifying himself in some form which is deemed both modern and acceptable in terms of contemporary political and social structures. The Jews of the Western world, living in secular states where religion because of its pluralism was a private matter, identified themselves as another religion. Thus they found a safe social place for themselves which they and their neighbors could accept. So to be a

Jew today in one of the Western democracies is commonly understood to be a member of a religious group.

The Jews of Central and Eastern Europe could not follow this path. Their emancipation had to take a different form because of their states and their religious leadership. Their countries tended toward religious uniformity with a close tie between church and state. Hence, religious change and development was not tolerated. Moreover, their rabbinate was strongly entrenched and opposed to any change. However, there were many nationality groups in these countries, each with its own culture. The Jews therefore began to identify themselves as a distinct nationality, a group united by land, language, and ethos. In a nationality one might be religious if one wanted—a concession to Jewish history and practice but one that limited the power of the rabbis to impede progress to their own, now small, domain. The dominant factor in being a Jew was being born into the Jewish nation-group and participating in its culture. As other nationalities were in the late nineteenth century moving to rebuild their lives on their land, so should the Jewish people. It was a dynamic forward-looking, self-respecting view.

Yet out of these accomplishments was born a deep and unfortunate cleavage of self-understanding among contemporary Jews. It was almost forced upon them by the differing social circumstances in which they found themselves. It determines, in large part, the confusion in communication between the American Jewish community and its Israeli brothers. The one thinks of the Jews largely in religious terms, the other in a secular perspective. Since Ben-Gurion's position has been clarified, let us follow the issue through from the Diaspora point of view.

If the Jews are the Covenant people, how can Jews of that faith understand the Jewish validity and the significance of the political entity called the State of Israel? To begin with, the Covenant belief should provide direct religious motivation to be a Zionist. The oldest, most authentic form of living out the Covenant was to set up one's own community in one's own land, establishing a society that would show God's rule in action and thereby be a model and a sign to the rest of mankind. That, after all, is what the Torah directs the Jews to do.

Today, in the State of Israel, there is a magnificent possibility of living out the Covenant, unequaled by anything Jews have known for nearly two millennia. A Jew who is deeply concerned about his Jewish religious responsibilities might well feel he ought to spend his life participating in the creation of that indigenous Covenant community of which so much of the Bible speaks. Here every aspect of society—its taxes, its education, its welfare, its foreign aid—is "Jewish," and Jewish values are not restricted to a carefully delimited and peripheral realm of life. There is thus not only good reason for building, supporting, and strengthening the State of Israel but there is also motivation for immigration as well. Ben-Guiron is, even from the religious standpoint, not unreasonable. But if the Covenant is the criterion of Jewishness, then much more must be said.

Under the Covenant it may be highly desirable that the Jews build a state, but that is surely not its fulfillment. The Covenant calls the Jews not merely to be a people like all other peoples but one with a messianic task. Ben-Gurion accepts this messianic obligation and often speaks of it. To him it would be in a humanistic demythologization the end result of the fusion of Hebraic ethics with Greek science. Here his nationalism still retains signs of its religious origins. Those who do not share his East European roots in an observant community or are more rigorous in their secular redefinition of Jewish peoplehood do not speak in such terms. Thus no voices rise from other leaders in the State of Israel, most conspicuously not from the younger ones, that messianism is indeed their people's task. With the Covenant as the standard, there is, in a way, less Jewishness to be found in such a "normalized" state of Israel than in an "abnormal" Diaspora existence whose communities accept the religious commitments of the Jewish people. When the State of Israel seeks to be Zion, when nationalism becomes Zionism in the prayer book's centuries-old, hallowed, messianic sense, then it evokes and commands a special sense of Jewish respect and concern.

This is the continuing contribution that the faithful Diaspora Jew can make to his Israeli brother. He can remind him of the religious roots from which they both sprang, of that transcendent other part of their heritage which he may be forgetting. Out of the spiritual experience of the Diaspora communities, both failures and successes, can come a uniquely helpful strength and encouragement to those groups within the State which seek in their own way to develop the religious spirit implicit there.

That hope for the religious development of the State of Israel is rooted in its special national character. How long can a people read and cherish the Bible and remain fully secular? To be vitally concerned with the prophetic imperatives, their standards of righteousness and their demands for justice, means sooner or later coming to wonder why. When a people is willing to sacrifice to bring in its brothers from all over the world, to subject itself to all forms of austerity to feed its hungry, clothe its naked, plead mercy for the refugee widow, seek justice for the displaced orphan, such a people, wittingly or not, is close to the God of the Bible. Is it, then, too much to hope that when the pressures of building and defending the State give way, the grandchildren may reclaim the traditions the parents rejected?

The most important because the most positive point still remains to be made. Life in the State of Israel is not the only genuine way of expressing the Covenant or of living by it.

The last two thousand years of Jewish history, seen in proper focus, testify that there are indeed other and varied modes of being an authentic Jew. In many geographic, political, and social circumstances Jews have found it possible to live by the Covenant and thus to be recognizably and legitimately Jewish. While the emancipation has made it difficult to be truly a Jew, it has not made it impossible.

How extraordinary a prospect would open up if American Jews, now groping for a sense and style of Jewish living, accepted as basic to their life the premise that they are indeed the inheritors of this ancient promise! What if, like other generations in the past, American Jews would pledge themselves in their affluent, secular society to the task that their people have carried on historically? If ever an effective nucleus of American Jews would recognize this as their responsibility, if they would commit their means, their leisure, their intelligence, the power that their talent and industry has won them, could they not build a Jewish community as true to the Covenant as any other the Jewish tradition has yet known? To be sure, it would be expressed in forms somewhat different from those which Jews have used before, for no Jewry has ever been in the open, participating situation of American Jews.

The risks are real and great but so are the possibilities. It is clear that American Jews live in a predominantly Christian culture, and find it necessary to explain, to defend, to reexamine their faith and culture against those of the outside world. This may lead to doubt and to disbelief, even to humanistic dissociation, but it also tends to produce a whole realm of philosophy and willed practice that reveals new dimensions and depths in the old Judaism. Thus, in being part of the most technically advanced civilization known to man, the new Judaism must come to grips with the moral problems that society is creating for man, most notably his dehumanization. The Diaspora Jews are, so to speak, the spiritual advance guard of the people making its way through history and by their wide dispersion another hope for its historic continuity.

So though it is vitally important to have a Jewish state seeking its own roots, building its own culture, and holding high the standard of Jewish self-determination, it is also desirable, perhaps even necessary, to have another pole—Jews who live outside the State of Israel, who establish Jewish outposts in the great cultures and societies, who must therefore ever seek to understand the implications of Israel's Covenant in new terms to meet the new conditions.

The Jews in the small Land of Israel will benefit by the cross-fertilization of ideas and concepts from those Jews who willingly take a precarious stand on the periphery so that they may transmit the lessons learned while participating in the forward-driving movements of human history. As these Diaspora Jews face the danger of being long in their great societies, of bartering away their Jewishness for supposed gains, they can be reminded by that center in the State of Israel of what Jewish knowledge and Jewish self-respect imply.

Is it too much to believe that there are two ways of living out the Covenant, each legitimate, each facing certain risks, each capable of contributing to the other in such a way that Judaism can be fructified?

Jewish optimism born of millennia of transcending historical realism says it is not. If American Jewry can produce the kind of Jew who accepts the Covenant as his own and is willing to help build a community in that understanding, then the most important contribution such a Jew can make to the State of Israel and, more important by far, to the God of Israel, whom they both should serve, is to make Judaism alive and vital and significant right where he is.

Chapter 6

The Election, the Covenant, and the Mission of Israel

Samuel E. Karff

The theological components of the doctrine of Israel, election and covenant, are joined by a third, prominent in Reform Judaic theology but well-founded in the received Torah as well. It is that eternal Israel possesses a mission to perform, a task among the nations. That conception proves attractive to secular Jews, for it links them with two considerable elements in their consciousness: the tradition, on the one side, the fate of the people, on the other. This is expressed through the notion that, while no longer believing in God or the Torah, the child of holy Israel still is subject to the fate, though not the faith, of other Jews, and, moving beyond that point, in the language Karff cites, "accepts responsibility for those who are similarly entangled," at the same time working toward a day of universal "brotherhood," when all of the distinctions that separate people, and, by the way, also mark persons as Jews and therefore different, will be erased. The notion of the mission of Israel provides a this-worldly answer to a question put forth by politics, sociology, and neutral culture: who are you? why are you different? when will you become like the rest of us? This view comes under Karff's examination, and the merit of his presentation lies in his balanced understanding of what is at stake. He finds his way back to the matters of covenant, commandment, and "the transcendent significance of Israel's faithfulness to the covenant." At the same time, on theological grounds, he finds it possible to speak of the Jews' "unique and essential role in the history of redemption," and here he introduces, in a religious framework, the conception of the mission of Israel. Here, in the language of Reform Judaic theology, we find a balanced and authentic statement of the components of theological "Israel."

***

I

During the late Bronze Age a group of Hebrew slaves united under the leadership of Moses and escaped from Egyptian bondage. In the wilderness of Sinai this "mixed multitude" learned the meaning of its liberation. Fate became faith and the people Israel was born.

---

*From *Contemporary Reform Jewish Thought*, ed. Bernard Martin. Copyright 1968 by The Central Conference of American Rabbis. Reprinted by permission.

The Lord called to him from a mountain, saying, Thus shall ye say to the House of Jacob and declare to the children of Israel, "You have seen what I did to the Egyptians, how I bore you on eagles' wings and brought you to Me. Now then if you will obey Me faithfully and keep My covenant, you shall be My treasured possession among all the peoples. Indeed all the earth is Mine, but you shall be to Me a kingdom of priests and a holy nation."[1]

To be a son of the covenant is to remember that mixed multitude's liberation from Egypt as "that which the Lord did for me." It is to share the experience and accept the obligations of that people whom Yahveh, the Nameless One, redeemed and consecrated to His service.

When he asks "What mean *ye* by this service?" the wicked son of the Passover Haggadah is guilty of faithlessness to the covenant. He fails to identify with his people's sacred history. He denies the actuality or, at least, the personal relevance of Israel's escape from bondage and God's redemptive act.

The modern world has created a fifth son. He accepts the enduring relevance of his ancestor's bondage and liberation but is unable to celebrate those events as "that which the Lord did for me." He may feel himself addressed in some special way by the injunction, "you shall not oppress the stranger" and may nod approvingly at the words, "for ye were strangers in the land of Egypt." He shares his people's fate and some of the values forged on the anvil of its common destiny, but he cannot respond to that sacred alchemy by which fate became faith and values became Torah. He acknowledges a covenant with his people, but it is a covenant in which God is at best a silent partner.

For this secular son of Israel Egypt's Pharaoh may be paradigmatic—an ominous portent of Nebuchadnezzar, Antiochus, Titus, Torquemada, Hitler, Stalin. He does not deny that Auschwitz addresses him, a Jew, with special significance. Indeed to be a Jew is to be refused the privilege of forgetting that Egypt may not be too far behind. To be a Jew is to be a member of a particularly vulnerable minority in an imperfect world.

Let two contemporary Jewish writers speak for this fifth son. "Whatever the distance that separates me from a certain part of Jewry in the world," writes Albert Memmi, "I know that we are living a similar experience. What touches them, what affects them, may one day touch and affect me. They must suffer the same apprehension I do, the same expectation, the same ordeals."[2]

Albert Memmi writes out of his experience as an Algerian refugee. Bernard Malamud's vision has been tempered by the placid breeze of a free society. He remains nonetheless Memmi's covenant kinsman. In a fictionalized account of the Mendel Beiliss case, Malamud describes a Jew who learns that he cannot easily escape the "burdens of history." Unable to acknowledge a covenant with God, this Jew makes a "covenant with himself" and accepts "responsibility for those who are similarly entangled" until the day dawns when the Jew will be the truly liberated son of a universal brotherhood.[3]

Is the modern Jew's endurance simply the by-product of the gentile emancipation's broken promises? Is Jewish self-consciousness merely, as Sartre contends, our defensive response to a world which insists that we are Jews?

Monford Harris has convincingly argued that the Zionist movement, even in its most secular form, was impelled by a Jewish will to survive, an inchoate recognition that the Jews qua Jews ought not disappear from the earth.[4] The American Jewish parent who exhorts his marriageable son: "We are not religious, but one thing I expect from you . . ." offers a Diaspora equivalent of this will to endure. To be sure, the world does remind us that we are Jews, but we find in this reminder the confirmation, not the source, of that ill-defined feeling that our Jewish vocation—whatever it may be—has not ended.

According to our sacred history, the Jew's endurance is the by-product of two forces. The first of these is a God whose love and providential purpose will not release this people. He may punish but will not forsake them. For His name's sake, this people must remain His distinct, if not always steadfast, witness until the end of days.[5] The second factor is Israel's faithfulness to its vocation. God's experience with the people is not an uninterrupted series of dismal disappointments. Israel has frequently proved ready to suffer and even die for the covenant. Quoting Psalm 44, the rabbinic sages affirm anew, "because of Thee we are slain the whole day long, we are counted as sheep for the slaughter."[6] And Judah Halevi's Rabbi reminds the Khazar monarch, "think of the thoughtful men among us who could escape this degradation by a word spoken lightly . . . but they do not do so out of allegiance to their faith."[7]

Surely the contemporary American son of the covenant does not suffer for his faith, but he does have the option of escaping through calculated assimilation the still vulnerable status that his Jewishness entails. That many a "nonreligious" Jew eschews this option is not merely a response to lingering gentile exclusivism but the acknowledgement of a claim which he believes ought not to be betrayed.

II

Yet if the fifth son is to recover the depth of his covenant consciousness, he must regain the posture of Jacob-Israel and truly wrestle with his sacred history. He must explore and seek to understand that call-response through which Israel was born.

Jewish theology is the Jew's interpretation of his history. Whether its monotheistic faith came to it decisively during the period of the Exodus or gradually ripened in the prophetic era, a living people emerged which dwelt in an ideological realm far removed from its neighbors. A people was born which acknowledged the sovereignty of a single, universal, imageless, creative, and moral power, unencumbered by mythological counterparts—the sole Ruler of fate, nature, and history. This God demanded exclusive loyalty from His worshippers, and His will was intended to govern every sphere of their lives.

How did Yahveh, the Nameless One, become the God of Israel? How and why was a particular relation (covenant) established between Yahveh and this people? The biblical historian's answer is unequivocal. God took the initiative by revealing Himself to this people as its Redeemer and Lawgiver. God's love was then, at least officially, reciprocated by Israel. The people accepted the sovereignty of the Lord and pledged to serve Him. Thus the covenant was born.

Why this particular people? The traditional answer given in rabbinic literature embodies two diverse strands. The one accentuates the mystery of divine love:

> We would not know whether God chose Israel for His treasure or whether Israel chose the Holy One, Blessed be He. The answer is taught in the following: "And the Lord, your God, chose you." And whence do we know that the Holy One, Blessed be He, chose Jacob? Because it is said, "not like these is the portion of Jacob, for He is the creator of all things and Israel is the tribe of His inheritance. . . ." (Jer 10:16)[8]

The other, seeking a rational ground for the particular destiny of the Jews, explains that God revealed Himself to other peoples as well but Israel alone accepted the demand and promise of the covenant.[9] Only after the people responded "we shall do and we shall hearken" did God refer to Israel as "my people."[10] Rabbi Jose b. Simon has God remind Israel, "Were it not for your acceptance of my Torah, I would not recognize you or regard you any more than the other nations."[11]

Later covenant theologians also sought to rationalize God's love for Israel. Judah Halevi posited a biogenetic endowment which empowered this people to receive God's revelation.[12] And, much later, Kaufmann Kohler was to speak of "hereditary virtues and tendencies of mind and spirit which equip Israel for his calling."[13] But to speak of biogenetic or hereditary endowments is not to dissipate the mystery. Why was Israel so endowed? Ultimately he who seeks to explain the birth of this unique people must invoke such terms as "ripe historical conditions," "chance," "creative genius"—terms no more compelling or explanatory than the claim of revelation and the mystery of divine grace.

III

Jews of today may feel a duty to survive without understanding the meaning of that duty. How did our forebears interpret the significance of their liaison with God? The people of Israel was born by the recognition of God's role in its history and God's claim (the Commandments of the Torah) upon it. This covenant community actually became a missionary people when monolatry ripened into the full blown monotheism of a Second Isaiah; then Israel's faithfulness to Yahveh became a vehicle for His ultimate dominion over all the children of men.[14] The earlier phase of Israel's existence is represented in the declaration, "ye shall be unto me a kingdom of priests and a holy nation";[15] the final phase embraces the promise, "in thee and thy seed shall all the nations of the earth be blessed."[16] But the rabbis knew no historical development: from its very *birth* Israel was a "light unto the nations," and Abraham was the first Jewish missionary.[17]

Whereas the gentile, according to rabbinic teaching, may fulfill his pre-messianic destiny by observing the Noahide laws, the Jew's greater burden of commandments is commensurate with his special divine vocation.[18] By fulfilling the Torah he bears witness to God and hastens the coming of the Kingdom.

By his observance or nonobservance of the *mitzvot*, the Jew either sanctifies or profanes God's Name in the world.[19] When an Israelite observes the Sabbath he bears witness to God as Creator of the world.[20] Indeed, his recitation of the Sabbath prayer renders him, as it were, "a partner with God in the creation."[21] Of the Chanukah *Menorah* the Talmud asks rhetorically, "Does He then require its light? Surely during the entire forty years that the Israelites travelled in the wilderness, they travelled only by His light." To which the following conclusion is given: the light of the *Menorah*, the publication of the miracle, is testimony to mankind that God's presence rests in the midst of Israel.[22]

The transcendent significance of Israel's faithfulness to the covenant is rehearsed in many statements, the boldest of which is attributed to Simeon b. Yochai: "Scripture declares, 'ye are my witnesses and I am God.' This means, so long as you testify to me I am God. If you cease to testify to me, I am no longer God."[23]

Significantly, Israel's vocation was not dependent on an active and successful proselytizing campaign. After Rome's alliance with the Church prohibited Jewish missionary work, Jews still believed that by their very endurance as the *mitzvah*-observing people they were in some direct way hastening the day of redemption.

Jewish existence was, however, not solely the instrument of providence. By covenant faithfulness the individual Jew also attained personal fulfillment. What life has greater meaning than that of the man who believes he is needed by, and has the power to serve or betray, the Source of his being? The Pharisees accentuated this personal dimension of Jewish existence. They elaborated what Ellis Rivkin has called a *"mitzvah* system of salvation," whereby the individual Jew believed that his personal destiny in this world and in the world to come was contingent upon his covenant faithfulness. Under the Pharisaic aegis, Rosh Hashonah was transformed from a ceremony celebrating the enthronement of Yahveh to a day of personal judgment in the presence of the Creator and Ruler of the world.[24]

The motif of personal fulfillment receives its crispest formulation in Rav's rhetorical question, "for what difference does it make to God whether one slaughters [an animal] from the back of the neck or the front of the neck? Hence, the commandments were not given save to purify God's creatures."[25] The Jew, claims Rav, has received a precious path to self-humanization through which he may attain blessing in this world and in the world to come. To the question, "Why should I be a Jew?", the rabbis thus offered a twofold answer: *covenant existence is both the means to my personal fulfillment as a man who was born a Jew and the way I may share my people's unique vocation in the world.*

Later theologians, reflecting on the covenant, have accentuated one or the other of these dual motifs. In his *Guide for the Perplexed*, Maimonides explains that man's "possession of the highest intellectual faculties, the possession of such notions which lead to true metaphysical opinions as regards God . . . gives him immortality, and on its account he is called man."[26] And how does the Jew attain this goal? Maimonides' Commentary on the Mishnah portrays God as declaring: "If you will heed my commandments, I will assist you in their performance, so that you may attain perfection in them . . . the persons who strive to do the commandments will be healthy and secure until they have attained that degree of knowledge through which they will merit the life of the world to come."[27] Even the messianic age itself, Maimonides claims, is but a tranquil state of earthly existence such as would enable the Jew (man) to cultivate his highest intellectual faculties.[28]

If Maimonides conceived the covenant, with its commandments, as a unique and splendid instrument for man's self-realization, Judah Halevi gave priority to Israel's divine vocation in the world. Israel is a prophet people, the bearer of God's truth until the time of the world's redemption. Israel's credentials are certified by its willingness to die for the faith, its steadfast loyalty despite suffering, its very survival, and its unbroken tradition of transmitting the Torah from generation to generation.[29] This people is punished and purified through suffering, but the Torah remains the vehicle for the discharge of its exalted task. Thereby Israel is able to "cleave to the divine quality in prophecy and states of mind that are close to it."[30] Israel, says Halevi, is the "heart of mankind"; as this organ is afflicted by the diseases of the body, so too the health of the heart radiates blessing to the entire body.[31] He speaks also of Israel as a seed "which falls to the ground and apparently is transformed into earth, water and dung without leaving a trace," but in reality this seed "transforms earth and water into its own substance . . . [until] the tree (all mankind) bears fruit like that from which it had been produced."[32]

The distinction between Maimonides and Halevi must not be pressed excessively. Whereas one is especially gripped by the self-fulfilling dimension of Jewish existence and the other by the mission of a living, suffering, and witnessing people, Maimonides surely affirmed that the Jews were also custodians of a unique truth and Halevi regarded the Torah as an avenue to personal salvation as well. But what for them was a matter of emphasis has become in modern times almost a matter of separation.

It may be argued that Jewish liberalism, in its early phase, defined the covenant primarily, if not exclusively, as the vehicle of the world's redemption. To Hermann

Cohen, the Jew was the sole bearer of a truth essential for "the religious progress of mankind." Its elements included the unity and uniqueness of God, man's direct confrontation with his Creator, the freedom and moral responsibility of the individual, and the messianic hope.[33] Cohen's concept of the Jew as a servant of a religious idea became, for Kohler, a people's obligation to a personal God Who consecrated it as "the bearer of the most lofty truth of religion among mankind."[34] Kohler affirmed that past periods of oppression and enforced isolation had caused many a Jew to "lose sight of his sublime mission for the world at large," a mission best expressed in the *Neilah* service of David Einhorn's *High Holyday Prayerbook*: "Endow us, our Guardian, with strength and patience for our holy mission and grant that all the children of Thy people may recognize the goal of our changeful career—one humanity on earth even as there is but one God in heaven."[35] At times, it seems, Jewish religious liberalism was so preoccupied with what the Jew could offer the world that it virtually ignored what living within the covenant could offer the Jew.

This emphasis of classical Reform theology was totally reversed by Mordecai Kaplan's Reconstructionism. "Jewish religion," writes Kaplan, "is that aspect of Judaism which identifies as holy or divine whatever in the cosmos impels and enables the Jewish people, individually and collectively, to make the most of life ethically and spiritually."[36] Whereas Kohler saw Jewish survival as an instrument for the fulfillment of a divine mission among the peoples of the earth, Kaplan has viewed Judaism as an instrument for the survival and self-realization of the Jew.

To be sure, Kohler would not have denied that Judaism humanizes its adherents, and Kaplan, in his later writings, has been drawn to speak of a Jewish vocation in the world. In his book *The Purpose and Meaning of Jewish Existence*, Kaplan contends that "none of the historical religions other than that of the Jewish people is capable of undergoing the reconstruction which is essential to rendering [it] relevant to the urgent needs of contemporary mankind."[37] Thus he who once disdained Reform's concept of a mission for Israel has himself lately assigned a transcendent and unique role to the modern Jew.[38] Whereas Kohler viewed Israel as the bearer of ethical monotheism in its most exalted form, Kaplan's Jew is potentially a unique teacher of the role a desupernaturalized religion ought to play in the life of man. Nevertheless, Kohler saw Israel chiefly as the bearer of God's word, while Kaplan continues to view Judaism primarily as an instrument for the self-realization of the Jewish people.

IV

One who believes that the Jews have a unique and essential role in the history of redemption must still ask: how shall this task be fulfilled? In the pre-emancipation era all Jews would have agreed that the "yoke of commandments" was the way to fulfill the mission of a holy people. However, with the breakdown of the Torah's binding power and the growing self-image of the Jew as a more active shaper of his own destiny (and that of the world about him), the strategy of covenant fulfillment has been reappraised. Let us consider three distinctive answers that have been offered in the modern world.

Negating the Exile, Liberal Judaism in its classical form saw the Jew as a creative catalyst for the messianic redemption within the land of his domicile. Like Hermann Cohen before him, Leo Baeck regarded the Jew as the potential vanguard of the spirit of ethical monotheism which would, in time, become the cornerstone of a just and benevolent society. In his classic volume, *The Essence of Judaism*, Baeck enjoined: "The good that one practices is the best witness of God that one can give . . . the standard of action thus becomes the following test: will it bear witness for Judaism?"[39] The American Reformers found a soil uniquely hospitable to this witness. In response to the query "why be a Jew?" Emil G. Hirsch once replied:

> Our distinction results simply from the keenest sense of responsibility and the consciousness that whether other men may or may not choose to be slow to do the right, we must ever be quick and exemplify the higher life in the eyes of the world. As individuals or by our social institutions, by our public morality, by our deeds and in the secrecy of our closet even, we must so live that indeed through us God's name be sanctified and the families of the earth be blessed through our influence for the good, noble and true.[40]

The Jew, said Hirsch, must fulfill his divine vocation as "sentinel and soldier of righteousness."

At first, one would hardly regard Emil G. Hirsch and Martin Buber as theological kinsmen. Yet each affirmed that it was the Jew's task to serve as God's exemplar. Commenting on Isaiah's messianic vision, Buber declared: "Nations can be led to peace only by a people which has made peace a reality within itself. The realization of the spirit has a magnetic effect on mankind which despairs of the spirit."[41] The "spirit of Israel," Buber maintained, is Israel's understanding that man must initiate the creation of a "true community" and its acceptance of the mandate to lead the way: "There is one nation which once upon a time heard this charge so loudly and clearly that the charge penetrated to the very depth of its soul."[42]

Buber thus shared the vision of the classical Reformers: Israel is commissioned to demonstrate, by word and deed, the goal which God has set for all men. But whereas the Reformers saw the Diaspora Jew as an effective witness for prophetic truth, Buber regarded the rebirth of the Jewish community in Palestine, and particularly the creation of the kibbutz, as the most fertile soil for the cultivation of the Jewish spirit in the contemporary world. In the Diaspora the Jew all too often merely proclaimed his faith in the Messiah without taking seriously the "preparation of the world in readiness for the Kingdom."[43] In the modern Diaspora the "American of Jewish faith" is apt to neglect or even betray his task through lack of any true communal existence. Israel—and here Buber agrees with Ben Guiron—offers the Jew a unique possibility to fulfill his sacred vocation.

> For only an entire nation which comprehends peoples of all kinds can demonstrate a life of unity and peace, of righteousness and justice to the human race as a sort of example and beginning . . . a true history can only commence with a certain definite and true nation . . . the people of Israel was charged to lead the way toward this realization.[44]

To the question of the content of the Jew's divine vocation, Rosenzweig offered still a third answer that is at variance with the more promethean activism of Hermann Cohen, Emil G. Hirsch, and Martin Buber. The Jew, said Rosenzweig, is at once a stranger in the world and at home with God. By his biological endurance and his continuing response to the commanding presence of the God of Abraham, by bearing children, and by observing the precepts of Torah, the Jew simultaneously anticipates the world's redemption and declared that the Messiah has not yet come.[45] Rosenzweig eschewed the role of the Jewish activist. The Jew is already "with God," the God from whom the world remains estranged. His exile is a sign of the world's alienation. In the pre-messianic age, the children of the covenant have no responsibility for God's world save to endure as a faithful community. The Jew need seek no converts, establish no model communities, involve himself in no social movements, to advance God's kingdom. Thus, Rosenzweig could write without fear of misunderstanding: "Insofar as it has reached the goal which it anticipates in hope (for all mankind) . . . its soul . . . grows numb to the concerns, the doing and the struggle of the world."[46]

Two fundamentally distinct modes of Jewish witness have thus been suggested. Hirsch, Buber, Cohen, Baeck, all affirmed that what the Jewish people must offer God is *active engagement in the task of transforming the world in His behalf*, whether as proclaimers of truth, "sentinels of righteousness" in the Diaspora, or builders of a true nation in the land of Israel. For Rosenzweig what the Jewish people offers God is simply its *presence* in the world, a presence which in and of itself proclaims God's sovereignty, casts judgement on all of man's penultimate solutions, and patiently waits for the messianic redemption.

The difference between Rosenzweig and Buber is essentially the distinction between what Sheldon Blank has called the "passive" and "active" mission in biblical prophecy.[47] The "passive mission" is the prophetic claim that God's impending restoration of Israel's glory and Israel's grateful acknowledgment of His grace and power will sanctify God's name and hasten the day of His universal kingdom. *God's* acts are here regarded as the crucial factor. Israel serves Him by receiving and publicly acknowledging *His* benefaction. "I even I am the Lord, and beside Me there is no savior. I have declared and I have saved . . . Therefore ye are My witnesses saith the Lord, and I am God."[48] The "active mission," also embodied in Deutero-Isaiah, commissions this people to speak God's word and to share God's work. "I, the Lord, have called thee in righteousness, and have taken hold of thy hand, and kept thee, and set thee for a covenant of the people, for a light of the nations, to open the blind eyes, to bring out the prisoners from the dungeon and them that sit in darkness out of the prison-house."[49] Rosenzweig offers a modern equivalent of Deutero-Isaiah's concept of the passive mission. Israel's very endurance is a vindication of God's sovereignty, "wordless evidence which gives the lie to the worldly and all-too-worldly sham eternity of the historical moments of the nations."[50] Buber's vision, on the other hand, is more akin to the active mission of a prophetic people whom God has charged to pave the way and begin the work of redemption.

V

"The teachers of Judaism," wrote Abba Hillel Silver, "almost instinctively rejected a formula of either-or in assaying religious values. They avoided all sharp antinomies, all irreconcilables which lead to a spiritual impasse."[51] Let this wisdom guide us as we seek to find the contemporary meaning of the covenant. To the question, why be a Jew? let us answer with the best of normative Judaism: *covenant existence is equally and unequivocally the road to personal fulfillment for a man who is born a Jew and his way of sharing the vocation of a people consecrated to God.*

Each man is the offspring of particular parents. Each man inherits a particular history. When a man or people respond to an event with the words, "this is what the Lord did for me," history becomes revelation. Each man turns to his own "inner history" for the meaning of his individual life. Here, in part, is what continues to separate Christian and Jew. The Christian remembers Bethlehem and Calvary, the Jew remembers Egypt and Sinai.

That sign of God's love which one has found in the Incarnation, the other has received in his liberation from bondage and the gift of the Torah. That standard for piety which the devout Christian finds in the life of Jesus, the Jew obtains from the teachings of Torah. That forgiving grace which one derives from a sacrificial death, the other receives from the God who says, "Am I not like a father unto you, O house of Israel?" That confidence in God's death-transcending, value-conserving power which the Christian affirms through the resurrection, the Jew derives from his covenant relation to Him who is the Author of death and the Renewer of life. That redemptive hope which one finds through him who came and will return, the other finds in him who has been promised and is yet to come. Those categories of meaning which the Christian has found in Father, Son, and Holy Spirit, the Jew has discovered in God, Torah, and Israel.

As a Jew, I need not deny that the mystery of divine love and grace is present in the sacred history of my Christian neighbor, and I disavow the implication—admittedly present in some of my forefather's utterances—that God loves me more than him who dwells outside my covenant. I believe in the mystery of election but reject the concept of special love. Nor must I deny that Christian and Jew each has a role in the work of redemption. But even as the sacred history through which the Christian finds personal salvation is not mine, the truth to which he bears witness subtly and at times not so subtly diverges from my own. Each of us anticipates the coming of God's Kingdom; until then we must wait for the decisive arbitration of our conflicting claims.

The Christian gospel is derived from God's revelation in Jesus Christ, the mission of Israel is grounded in the covenant of Sinai. The key to an understanding of my unique Jewish vocation may be found in *the very structure of the covenant itself, for God's relation to Israel is the paradigm of His covenant with all men*. He whom we have known in our history lifts all men to the dignity of sharing in the work of redemption: "The human world is meant to become a single body through the action of men themselves. We men are challenged to perfect our own portion of the universe."[52]

Man's dignity derives in part from his divinely appointed task, from his power to transform the world in accordance with a divine design. This truth is embodied in the conditional dimension of the covenant. Man is commanded and is accountable. His acts are laden with profound consequences. Through Israel, the Nameless One reveals man to himself as a partner of God. But if one dimension of the covenant affirms man's power, another no less dramatically confirms his finitude. The covenant was born when God's power and unmerited love liberated a band of helpless slaves. The people is called upon to judge itself in terms of a transcendent source of value— a standard given to and not created by man. The people bears witness to a kingdom which God alone must bring to pass.

Israel's life with God uniquely reveals a creative tension in all men's relation to the Source of Being. *We live our lives astride accountability and grace, justice and love, forever poised between an affirmation of our significant power and an acknowledgement of our dependence on divine gifts.*

The Jew is called to proclaim a twofold truth for all men: we mortals stand before God "creaturely and creative." Man both receives life and holds it in custody. He accepts Torah and performs significant deeds. He must wait for the Messiah even as he prepares the way for his coming.

For a covenant-affirming Jew the contemporary theological ferment is a two-edged sword. He will respond to the spirit of the "secular city" with one hand that beckons and another hand that repels. When its prophets call on man to accept a significant measure of responsibility for the work of the world, the Jew will give his gladsome approval. When, however, the "new theology" seeks to deny the transcendent power of a God who creates worlds, redeems the oppressed, and reveals value, the authentic Jew will suspect a new idolatry. The covenant does not call man to glorify God by celebrating his own nothingness, but neither does it permit man to create himself in the divine image.

Twentieth-century man's staggering power lends unprecedented urgency to the prophetic demand for man's acceptance of his human responsibility. An Isaiah reincarnate would hardly counsel reliance on divine love to prevent the nuclear apocalypse. Our prophetic legacy also impels us to see the plague of racial turmoil as warning and judgment upon all who refuse to "let My people go." Man remains, however, God's partner, not His cosmic successor. Man is summoned to share the work of redemption and suffer the consequences of default, but covenant man will deny that he is himself the Redeemer.

The greatest of commandments is the prohibition of idolatry. To serve the Nameless One is to disarm the numberless claimants to His throne. No cult, ideology, social order, or person deserves our uncritical devotion. Indeed, even our *images* of God and Torah are themselves subject of continuing reappraisal. Man's continuing openness to transcendence is his greatest safeguard against worshipping himself or the work of his hands. Such openness is also his deepest ground for hope.

VI

The very structure of the covenant confirms the Jew in a mission at once "active" and "passive." That dimension of his faith which affirms his partnership with the divine summons him to share with all men in the work of the kingdom.

It has been frequently said that we Jews are the "barometer of history." Our fate appears to be inextricably bound up with a nation's response to the issues of justice. When a society in which we dwell fails to build with the plumb line of justice, we who merely *share* in these failures are *singled out* as the most vulnerable victim of the crumbling social order. Is this perhaps the eerie meaning of Amos' prophecy: "You only have I known of all the families of the earth; therefore, I will punish you for all your iniquities"?

When the Jew is tempted to identify with the oppressor or turn a deaf ear to man's cry for freedom, the great weight of covenant responsibility is soon suspended over his head. The Jewish bigot soon discovers that he must ultimately choose between a George Lincoln Rockwell, the neo-Nazi who hated the Jew no less than he did the Negro, and a Martin Luther King.

That individual Jews may betray their heritage, or that many a non-Jew surpasses a son of the covenant as witness for justice, does not compromise, much less invalidate, the primary obligation of a people who first heard the words of the prophets and remain charter witnesses to the divine demand for *tzedek*. That demand addresses the Jew both in the Diaspora and in the land of Israel. If in America we stand especially accountable for the quality and intensity of our involvement in "social action," in Israel we are summoned to build a Jewish state which submits to

The Election, the Covenant, and the Mission of Israel

the judgment of its prophetic legacy. By *tzedek* the prophets meant more than doing justly, but surely nothing less.

What of our "passive" mission? We are history's most illustrious survivors. This in itself lends a unique dimension to our covenant faithfulness. To deny that redemption is here and yet attest that "my Redeemer liveth" is a witness fraught with special significance when borne by history's most time-tested survivor in a world that proclaims "God is dead."

By our Sabbath observance we continue to affirm that life is a purposeful gift, not an accident. The Seder testifies that the tyrants of history do not speak the last word, for man is not alone in his eternal quest for freedom. Our annual observance of the Feast of Revelation and our weekly reading of the Torah confirm that true values are ultimately man's discovery, not his creation. The Jew who "in spite of everything" joyfully brings his children into the covenant of Abraham thereby denies that life is nothing more than a sick joke or a dirty trick, even as the Jew who kindles the *menorah* and pridefully admits that he is a cultural outsider in the Christmas season most poignantly proclaims that the day to which Israel first pointed has not yet arrived.

By all these "ritual" acts which bind him to the covenant of his fathers, the Jew becomes a member of Rosenzweig's "eternal people," affirming that God—the Creator, the Giver of Torah, the Redeemer of the oppressed—is not dead, though his Kingdom has yet to be established upon the earth. By his life as a Jew the son of the covenant "binds creation to redemption while redemption is still to come."[53]

The most formidable task of our time, however, is to develop a generation for whom Jewish history can become once again revelation, a generation able to remember the Exodus as "that which the Lord did for me." Technologically *nouveau riche*, modern man finds it difficult to see beyond his possessions and powers; he feels no compulsion to confess that he is the receiver of divine gifts. Those forces which have corroded modern man's response to transcendence have surely afflicted the Jew with even greater intensity. (After all, is this not what Halevi meant by the price of being "the heart of mankind")

The staggering enormity of demonic evil in our time has compounded man's incapacity to hear by God's failure to speak. The "hiddenness of God" is responsible for the fifth son among us who affirms Jewish fate without faith. His predicament should engage, not the self-righteous scorn, but the empathy of even the most theologically committed Jew. Anyone who takes seriously God's silence at Auschwitz may be forgiven the occasional thought that perhaps Moses was the only hero of the Exodus after all. Yet surely the goal of an authentic covenant existence is a reunion of fate and faith, of history and revelation. The authentic Jew is Yisroel, the one who contends with God but does not deny Him, who argues while he prays, who doubts as he serves, and whose very demands of his Creator betray a primordial trust yearning for confirmation.

Covenant theology speaks of a God Who would much prefer to be honestly challenged than ignored. If in this age of God's eclipse, the Jew remains Yisroel, dare we not hope that in time fate will acknowledge faith and history, revelation? Then the pre-messianic vulnerability of the Jew will be traced once again to Sinai, and his duty to survive will be experienced as an answer to a claim which is at once an inescapable burden and a precious heritage. That heritage will need no longer be transmitted, that burden no longer assumed only "on that day when the Lord shall be One and His name One."

Endnotes

[1] Exodus 19:3-6. [2] Albert Memmi, *Portrait of a Jew* (New York: Orion Press, 1962) 275. [3] Bernard Malamud, *The Fixer* (New York: Farrar, Straus & Giroux, 1966). [4] Monford Harris, in *Rediscovering Judaism*, ed. Arnold J. Wolk (Chicago: Quadrangle Books, 1965). [5] Ezekiel 36:20-24; Sipre 35b, 112a. [6] Sipre 73a; Canticles Rabbah 1:15; b. Gittin 57b. [7] Kuzari, Book IV: 23. [8] Sipre 134b; cf. Deuteronomy Rabbah 5:6. [9] *Mekilta Bahodesh*, Lauterbach Edition, II, 234 ff. [10] Tanhuma B. Vaera 9a. [11] *Exodus Rabbah* 47:4. [12] Kuzari, Book I:95. [13] Kaufmann Kohler, *Jewish Theology* (New York: Macmillan, 1928) 328. [14] Isaiah 42:6; cf. Exodus 20:3. [15] Exodus 19:6. [16] Genesis 12:3. [17] b. So ṭ a 10b; Genesis Rabbah 43:8; cf. Sipre 134b. [18] b. Sandedrin 56a. [19] Mekilta Shirata, II, 28f. [20] Ibid., Shabbata, III, 200. [21] b. Šabbat 119b. [22] Ibid., 22b. [23] Sipre 144a. [24] b. Roš Haššana 16a. [25] *Genesis Rabbah* 44:1. [26] *Guide for the Perplexed*, Book III, chap. 54. [27] Maimonides, Commentary to Tenth Chapter of *Sanhedrin*. [28] Ibid. [29] Kuzari, Book II:30-44. [30] Ibid., I:109. [31] Ibid., II:44. [32] Ibid., IV:23. [33] Hermann Cohen, Lecture to World Congress for Religious Progress (1910), cited in S. Bergman, *Faith and Reason* (Washington DC: B'nai B'rith Hillel Foundation, 1961) 33. [34] Kohler, 323. [35] Ibid., 339ff. [36] Mordecai M. Kaplan, *The Purpose and Meaning of Jewish Existence* (Philadelphia: Jewish Publication Society, 1964) 55. [37] Ibid., 310. [38] Compare above with Kaplan, *Judaism as a Civilization* (New York: Reconstructionist Press, 1957) chap. 10. [39] Leo Baeck, *The Essence of Judaism,* trans. Victor Grubehwieser and Leonard Pearl (New York: Schocken Books, 1948) 271. [40] Emil G. Hirsch, "Why Am I a Jew?" in *My Religion* (New York: Macmillan, 1925) 30. [41] Martin Buber, "Plato and Isaiah," in *Israel and the World* (New York: Schocken Books, 1948) 110f. [42] Martin Buber, "The Spirit of Israel and the World Today," 186. [43] Ibid., 188. [44] Ibid., 187. [45] Selections from "The Star of Redemption" in Rosenzweig, *Franz Rosenzweig: His Life and Thought*, ed. Nahum Glatzer (New York: Farrar, Straus & Young, 1953) 292 f. [46] Ibid., 339. [47] Sheldon H. Blank, *Prophetic Faith in Isaiah* (New York: Harper, 1958) 143-60. [48] Isaiah 43:11f. [49] Isaiah 42:6f. [50] Rosenzweig, 340. [51] A. H. Silver, *Where Judaism Differed* (New York: Macmillan, 1957) 108. [52] Martin Buber, "The Spirit of Israel and the World Today," 186. [53] Rosenzweig, 340.

Chapter 7

A Religion or a Nation

Jonathan Sacks

Gentiles rightly wonder, given the prominence of "Israel" and its definition in secular and not only theological terms, whether the Jews are a religion or a nation. Here the Chief Rabbi of Great Britain answers that question. It bears within itself the ambiguities of the secular and the religious, the political, cultural, and social and the theological, with which we have contended to this point. It is not a theoretical question, but one that was formulated to deal with practical issues of public policy. For theology responds not only to the received tradition and contemporary philosophical modes of thought, but also to the interplay between the received tradition and urgent issues of the social order. It is, in a very precise sense, a social science, addressing as it does issues of society from the perspective of revealed truth. For, as we have already noted, revelation—Torah for Judaism—raises more questions than it settles, and, in raising them, presents issues of immediate and pressing consequence to the intellectuals among the faithful. Sacks here spells out in a forthright way the ambiguity of a religion that brings into being a distinct people, rather than a Church. We have already observed, in the doctrine of Israel put forth by the oral Torah, that "people" no less than "church" or "body of Christ" constitutes a supernatural category. But in modern and contemporary terms, the word "people" does not bear the same religious sense that "church" does, and when we consider the fact that among the Jews are many who by their own word in no way are religious, it is not without reason that "people" is found a secular, and church a religious, category. The advent of the Jewish state in the Land of Israel, of course, intensifies the dilemma, since, in the West, the joining of "holy" to "nation" rather than "church" is hardly comprehended; and no one claims that the State of Israel, a this-worldly fact bearing (for part of eternal Israel) otherworldly significance to be sure, in itself is the kingdom of Heaven. To sort matters out, readers will now find themselves reviewing the entire intellectual history of the Jews and Judaism in Western Europe from the seventeenth century forward.

***

More than two hundred years ago, in 1789, the Count of Clermont-Tonnerre rose to make a speech in the French National Assembly. It was a fateful moment in the

---

*From *Arguments for the Sake of Heaven: Emerging Trends in Traditional Judaism*. Copyright 1991 by Jonathan Sacks. Reprinted by permission of Jason Aronson, Inc.

history of Western Europe and it was to have repercussions for Jewish identity that have lasted to this day.

The French Revolution had ushered in, earlier that summer, the modern democratic state. The National Assembly had made its momentous declaration of the rights of man: "All men are born, and remain, free, and equal in rights. . . . No person shall be molested for his opinions, even such as are religious, provided that the manifestations of these opinions does not disturb the public order established by the law."

The question was: did these rights apply to Jews? In theory, yes. But theory was at variance with public sentiment. There was powerful antagonism to Jews, particularly in Alsace where the local peasantry, in a wave of revolutionary fervor, rioted against the Jewish population. Jews were seen, and to some extent saw themselves, as outsiders: not so much Frenchmen as a section of the Jewish nation in temporary exile.

It was in response to the reports of the riots that the count rose to make his speech. He defended the idea of the separation of church and state. The law, he reaffirmed, has no concern with a person's beliefs. It is interested only in his actions. Jews therefore were entitled to equal rights within the state. But he made one promise: if Jews were to be part of the French nation, they could not at the same time be members of the Jewish nation. "The Jews should be denied everything as a nation, but granted everything as individuals. . . . It is intolerable that the Jews should become a separate political formation or class in the country. Every one of them must individually become a citizen; if they do not want this, they must inform us and we shall then be compelled to expel them."

Were Jews adherents of a religion or were they members of a people with its own distinctive laws, governance, and homeland? This was the choice the count called on Jews to make, and it was to determine the course of emancipation for Jews throughout Europe during the course of the nineteenth century. The question demanded, in effect, a revolutionary transformation of Jewish identity. It led, as we shall see, to radical and divergent ideas of what it was to be a Jew. Ultimately, it was to divide Jews to such an extent that Martin Buber was to say later that emancipation had led to the end of *knesset Yisrael*, the idea of the Jewish people as a single entity standing before God.

A People Apart

The choice was, of course, impossible. Judaism is a *religion* with its distinctive beliefs and practices. But it is the religion of a *people*. To be sure, there are conversions and apostasies, entrances and exits, but for the most part Jewishness is a matter of birth. The concept of an unbelieving Christian is self-contradictory; that of an unbelieving Jew is not. And it is a religion tied to a particular *land*, the land of Israel. During their long dispersal, Jews saw themselves in but not of their geographical and cultural environment. They were not merely scattered, they were in *galut*, exile. They had a homeland, which they had left not voluntarily but "because of our sins" and to which they believed they would eventually return. It was toward Jerusalem that they prayed; Jerusalem that they remembered at the heights of religious emotion; nowhere outside Israel was ultimately home.

In a real sense, then, prior to modernity, Jews constituted a single if scattered nation. They were divided by country, language, culture, and custom. But they were united by a common history, beliefs and hopes, and above all, by the shared discipline of conduct spelled out in *halakhah* or Jewish law. They were a people apart. To a certain extent, this was a matter of belief. Jews were a singular and chosen people, the children of the covenant. They were linked together as the family of Jacob, bound by the sense that "All Israel are responsible for one another."

In part, too, it was a matter of conduct. Jewish law maintained a code of difference. In the book of Esther, Haman describes Jews as "a certain people, dispersed and scattered among the peoples . . . whose laws are different from those of all other peoples," and this distinctiveness was not accidental. It had been one of the dominant motifs of biblical law that Jews and Judaism should be kept apart from the pagan practices of surrounding nations. Intermarriage with idolaters was forbidden, and Ezra and Nehemiah waged a successful campaign against it. Rabbinic law extended some of the biblical fences against intermarriage and too close a social interaction between Jews and non-Jews.

These internal safeguards were reinforced by the external reality of the Middle Ages in which Jews were usually minorities in an Islamic or Christian culture. Their participation in society, in terms of the occupations they could engage in and the areas they could live in, was limited. For the most part they had little access to the main avenues of political power. There were times in which they were made to wear distinctive clothing; others in which they were confined to specific and enclosed locations, the ghettos. They were subjected to suspicion, sporadic attacks, and arbitrary and restrictive decrees. They suffered periodic expulsions. The biblical concept of exile precisely matched the historic reality.

Their apartness from the central institutions of the majority culture had another consequence. Throughout the Middle Ages, Jewish communities exercised a degree of autonomy, governing their own educational, welfare, and judicial functions. The *kehillah*, or self-governing community, imposed both Jewish law and local legislation and had at its disposal the coercive sanction of fines and excommunication. Since, for the most part, a Jew could only leave the Jewish community at the cost of conversion to another faith—something to which Judaism embodies a profound aversion —the power of the community to impose its will on individuals was considerable.

A New History

The premodern Jewish world, then, was one in which much else was problematic but Jewish identity was not. To be a Jew was to be born into a society, history, destiny, and way of life whose content was coherent and shared by other Jews across space and time. But that identity did not fit into the abstract conception of the modern state as embodied in the French Revolution. Jews were no longer to be members of the Jewish nation who were temporarily located in France. They were to be French citizens first, and only secondarily Jews.

The Count of Clermont-Tonnerre did not spell out specifically what this might mean. But it became clear in the questions directed by Napoleon a generation later to the assembly of Jewish notables and to the specially convened group of rabbis, the Napoleonic "Sanhedrin." Did Jews, Napoleon wished to know, practice their own laws of divorce distinct from those enforced by civil courts? What judicial powers did rabbinic courts possess and what sanctions were available in enforcing their decisions? Were Jews allowed to marry non-Jews? Did they consider non-Jewish Frenchmen as "brothers" or as "strangers"? Did French-born Jews consider France their country?

These questions, untroubling now, went to the heart of the new situation. A social order that had dominated Jewish existence since the destruction of the Second Temple was coming to an end. Jews were to be fully integrated in the secular state. They were no longer to be outsiders. This meant opportunity but also sacrifice. The conditions were unstated but implied. Jewish self-government would have to cease. Jews would no longer have the power to fine or excommunicate individuals who disobeyed community ordinances. In addition, Jews would have to demonstrate that in their language, dress, and etiquette they were fully part of the majority culture.

The implications for Jewish identity were profound in two respects. Firstly, Judaism was henceforth to be a voluntary commitment. To be sure, Jewish law was not directly affected. One who was born a Jew was still bound by the commandments and prohibitions. But existentially, there were choices available to a Jew in the new situation that had not existed before. If he chose to ignore Jewish law, the community could not compel him to do otherwise. Moreover, the secularization of the state meant that one could cease to be a Jew without becoming a Christian. When Benjamin Disraeli was asked what his religion was, he took an English Bible and pointed to the blank page between the Old Testament and the New. "I," he said, "am that blank page." That "neutral space" had not existed before.

Secondly, to be a Jew was now only one aspect of personal identity, not its totality. Emancipated Jews were expected to work and mix socially with non-Jews and to become fully conversant with European culture. Their Jewishness, it was tacitly agreed, should not be too obtrusive. Jews had to pass through what one writer has called "the ordeal of civility." This meant a new double identity, one that the poet

Judah Leib Gordon described as being "a Jew at home and a person in the street." Sigmund Freud, for example, spoke of the "dissimulation [which] I practice every day." The art was to be Jewish without seeming to be. This was sharply at odds with the integrated identity of traditional Jewish societies. How far was the new order compatible with Jewish tradition itself?

Moses Mendelssohn

Moses Mendelssohn (1729–1786), the first Jewish philosopher of emancipation, argued that it was. In 1783 he published *Jerusalem*, his plea for freedom of religious conscience. The laws of the state and the commands of religion are, he insisted, two entirely separate realms. Religion uses education and persuasion, not power, to secure the loyalty of its followers. Excommunication is "diametrically opposed to the spirit of religion." What then of the fact that the Bible prescribes punishments for sins? That, he argues, was only as long as Jews were a nation in their own land, when an offense against the law of God was also a crime against the state. Since then, Judaism "knows of no punishment, no other penalty than the one which the remorseful sinner *voluntarily* imposes on himself."

Already, then, we see in Mendelssohn an argument for the voluntariness of Judaism and an attempt to persuade the Jewish community to renounce its self-regulating powers and embrace the new terms of emancipation. What is more, he suggests, Judaism is a model of rationality and tolerance. "It boasts of *no exclusive* revelation of eternal truths that are indispensable to salvation." What was revealed at Sinai were not truths like the Divine creation of the world. These are arrived at by reason, and are thus available to any rational human being. They constitute the "universal religion of mankind." The revelation at Sinai disclosed only "revealed legislation," the commands that are peculiar to Jews. Here, in philosophical terms, is the distinction crucial to the Jewish response to emancipation, between the "Jew at home" practicing his particular religious heritage, and the "man in the street" engaged in the pursuit of universal truth and the general welfare.

Mendelssohn was a traditional Jew, who proposed no halakhic or intellectual reforms. But already we sense the strain to which Judaism would be put in this new environment. Why, we ask ourselves reading *Jerusalem*, should Jews continue to practice their ancestral faith when a new and glittering secular culture was beckoning? To this question Mendelssohn can give only the most negative of answers. "Adapt yourself to the morals and constitution of the land to which you have been removed; but hold fast to the religion of your fathers, too. Bear both burdens as well as you can! It is true that on the one hand, the burden of civil life is made heavier for you on account of the religion to which you remain faithful, and on the other hand, the climate and the times make the observance of your religious laws in some respects more irksome than they are. Nevertheless, persevere; remain unflinchingly at the post which Providence has assigned you. . . ." This is not an argument calculated to inspire.

Nonetheless, it provided the basis on which Jews in England, France, and Italy came to terms with their new situation. Jews could indeed be both loyal and active citizens and remain within the classic terms of the Jewish tradition. To be sure, they prayed for a return to Zion. But that was in the messianic future, not the immediate present. Within their countries of birth they heeded Jeremiah's words to "seek the peace and welfare of the city to which I have carried you in exile; pray to the Lord for it, because in its prosperity you shall prosper." In France, a semblance of the old *kehillah* was recreated, the *Consistoire*, under state supervision. In England, it took the form of voluntary but governmentally recognized institutions: the Board of Deputies, the Chief Rabbinate, and the United Synagogue.

In England, in particular, the course of political equality ran slowly but smoothly. There were no preconditions asked, no religious reforms or declarations. Victorian society was both liberal and traditional, and Jews of all social classes acculturated without seeking religious legitimation for their new behavior patterns. The institutions of Judaism, for their part, adapted to the new environment through merely cosmetic changes: grand synagogues, ministers who wore canonicals with more than a passing resemblance to those of the church, sermons in the vernacular, choirs, and an insistence on decorum during services. The style was eminently English; the substances remained within the boundaries of Judaism.

But it was in Germany that Jews encountered the greatest hostility to emancipation. It seemed that as Jews they remained suspect and unacceptable. There was, in the last decades of the eighteenth century, a wave of conversions to Christianity, especially among the most affluent and cultured. They counted among their number several of Moses Mendelssohn's own children. Heinrich Heine famously described Judaism as not a religion but a misfortune, and called the baptismal certificate "the ticket of admission to Western culture."

One of Mendelssohn's disciples, David Friedländer, proposed a form of general conversion to Christianity that he believed might find favor among Jews and Christians alike. Mendelssohn had, after all, described a universal religion of reason. What was distinctively Jewish about Judaism was its rituals, and these could be abandoned in favor of their Christian equivalents. The church should invite Jews into its ranks without insisting that they believe in Christian dogma. Jews then would merely be exchanging one set of practices for another. Within sixteen years of Mendelssohn's defense of Judaism, therefore, his own arguments were being employed to argue for its total dissolution.

The Legacy of Spinoza

Friedländer's proposal outraged both sides, but it is a measure of the traumatic impact of the new situation in which Jews found themselves, especially when the equality they sought was being actively and politically resisted. The nineteenth century saw a retreat from this conversionary brink. But it was in Germany that two radical Jewish proposals emerged. Their inspiration came, not from Mendelssohn but from an earlier and more disturbing figure, Baruch Spinoza (1632–1677), who in his early twenties had been excommunicated by the Amsterdam Jewish community for propagating heretical views.

Spinoza was the first of a series of intellectuals of Jewish origins—Marx, Freud, and Durkheim were others—who not merely rejected Judaism and religion generally but sought to explain and thus exorcise it. For Spinoza, God was not supernatural but was nature itself under a different aspect. It followed that there were no supernatural events and therefore no revelation. The Torah was the work of human beings (Spinoza was a forerunner of "biblical criticism") and the commandments were a system of national legislation. It followed that, with the destruction of the Second Temple and the loss of national autonomy, the commandments no longer applied and Jews themselves had ceased to be the chosen people. They had continued to exist as a separate people only because anti-Semitism blocked the way to assimilation. Where tolerance reigned, Jews would and should merely abandon Judaism, though, in an aside, Spinoza conjectured that "if the foundations of religion have not emasculated their minds" they might yet rebuild their nation in Israel and "God may a second time elect them."

These views are, by any standard, radically destructive of Judaism but they were to exercise a powerful influence over Jews grappling with the phenomenon of German anti-Semitism, and they were to lead eventually in two diametrically opposed directions.

The first was Reform. To understand the development of the Reform movement in Germany, it is necessary to remember two things. The first was that enlightened defenders of Jewish emancipation like Clermont-Tonnerre did not demand that Jews renounce their Jewishness completely. But they did assume that Judaism was, or could be turned into, a religion in the "Protestant" sense of a private faith of individuals. The second is that opponents of Jewish emancipation seized on just those aspects of Judaism that did not conform to this definition, but instead seemed to mark Jews as a people apart, a group who were incapable of being fully integrated into society.

Some of these features had little to do with Judaism as such. Jews spoke a distinctive language, Yiddish, and were concentrated in trading and financial services. These facts, their critics argued, showed that Jews kept themselves apart and were naturally exploitative. But there were other objections that had everything to do with Judaism. Jews believed that they would one day leave Europe and return to Zion.

Johann David Michaelis, in 1782, accordingly argued that "The Jews will always see the state as a temporary home, which they will leave in the hour of their greatest happiness to return to Palestine." Their dietary laws kept them from fully mixing in Gentile society. Michaelis drew the conclusion that "As long as they observe the laws about kosher and nonkosher food it will be almost impossible to integrate them into our ranks." The laws of *Shabbat*, too, Michaelis argued, prevented Jews from accepting the full responsibilities of citizenship. The "Jews will not fight on the Sabbath, for they are forbidden to do so if not attacked." They would not provide reliable soldiers for the German army and would not therefore contribute fully to the state.

Nineteenth-Century Reform

Was it possible to construct a Judaism that met these objections? In 1817 a Reform "Temple" was opened in Hamburg. Its major innovation was the elimination from the prayer book of all references of the ingathering of exiles and the return to Zion. The name Temple itself signaled its founders' intentions. They no longer yearned for Jerusalem. A temple could be built in Hamburg as well. It was, its constitution declared, a "church," a purely religious institution without the political-national motifs hitherto associated with Judaism. Many of the prayers would be said not in Hebrew but German. The *Shabbat* services would be accompanied by an order and choir. It was a significant breach with Jewish tradition, and was denounced, a little over a year later, by a group of distinguished rabbis. The breach between Reform and the classic terms of rabbinic Judaism—or Orthodoxy as its opponents now named it—had begun.

It was to widen. Opposition to Jewish emancipation, often couched in brutally hostile terms, continued. German Jews were making their own compromises with a non-Jewish world and were rapidly abandoning religious observance. The early efforts at the "Germanization" of Judaism, represented by the Hamburg Temple, were seen by some to be inadequate. A fresh wave of radical reform took place in the 1840s. There were those who advocated an abandonment of the laws of *kashrut*; others who promised a curtailment of the laws of *Shabbat*; there were even those who proposed the transfer of *Shabbat* to Sunday. Some argued for the abolition of circumcision; others for the abandonment of the Jewish laws of divorce in favor of recognition of civil divorce as an adequate termination of Jewish marriage. These became the hallmarks of radical reform as it developed in Germany and America.

These were violent assaults on the substance and spirit of Jewish life as hitherto conceived, and they produced strong reactions. In 1845 a previous sympathizer, Zechariah Frankel, broke with the Reform movement and proposed in its place a more traditional, evolutionary form of Judaism. This he called "positive historical," and it eventually became known in America as Conservative Judaism. A Galician rabbinic authority, R. Zvi Hirsch Chajes, who was deeply impressed with the Enlightenment and contemporary secular culture, nonetheless proposed, in his 1849 pamphlet *Minchat Kena'ot*, a formal ban declaring Reform leaders total Gentiles in Jewish law. The most modern of Orthodox leaders in Germany, R. Samson Raphael Hirsch, devoted a significant part of his energies to a ceaseless campaign against Reform. The discontinuities between Reform and tradition were obvious. What were the continuities? By what logic did the radical reformers defend their innovations as lying within the parameters of Judaism?

There were two dominant schools of thought. One, advocated by Abraham Geiger (1810–1874), argued for a historical understanding of Judaism that would see both its biblical and rabbinic forms as not a fixed orthodoxy but a process of constant development and adaptation. In Geiger we see the influence of Spinoza's "biblical criticism" allied to a Hegelian idea of history as evolution. What was fundamental to Judaism was its monotheism and morality. Ritual could and should change as Judaism developed from its early particularism to a more universal mission to humanity. Judaism was not fixed for all time at Sinai. Instead, it was an expression of "Progressive Revelation."

More radical still was his contemporary, Samuel Holdheim (1806–1860). Holdheim argued that there were two elements in biblical Judaism: religious and ceremonial. The religious element—with Geiger, he saw this as monotheism and morality—was eternally valid, but the ceremonial law applied only as part of the constitution of a Jewish state. Since the state had ceased to exist with the Roman destruction in 70 C.E., it was now null and void. "Now that Jews have become integral elements of other peoples and states. . . all laws and institutions of Judaism which were based on the election of a particular Jewish people—yes, of a particular Jewish state—and hence by their very nature implied exclusiveness and particularism . . . have lost all religious significance and obligation and have given way to the national laws and institutions of such lands and peoples to which the Jews belong by birth and civic relationship."

This was a restatement of Spinoza's argument in the *Tractatus Theologico-Politicus*. Emancipation heralded a new messianic age of universal brotherhood, and all laws which tended to keep Jews as a separate people were irrelevant at best; at worst, they impeded the progress of civilization. Holdheim's revolutionary stance was adopted as the ideology of the American Reform movement in its Pittsburgh Platform of 1885. Thus, Spinoza had inspired radical reform.

The Birth of Secular Zionism

But German Reform showed how extreme were the implications of Clermont-Tonnerre's either/or. Was Judaism a religion of individuals or was it the national expression of a people? Holdheim's Reform carried to its logical conclusion a positive answer to the first alternative and a rejection of the second. Judaism, to be turned into a religion in a sense acceptable to German opinion, had to be a religion in a sense acceptable to German opinion, had to be stripped of its most fundamental laws, those of *Shabbat*, *kashrut*, circumcision, and divorce. They represented a dimension of nationhood in Judaism that Holdheim and others felt was inappropriate to the new age. Emancipation proposed to recognize Jews as individuals, not as members of a collective people. German Reform was a Jewish response to this unprecedented dichotomy.

But, as was already evident in the France of 1789, theory was one thing, public emotion another. Throughout the Middle Ages, Jews had suffered from a Christian anti-Judaism that at times—during the Crusades, fifteenth-century Spain, and the periodic blood libels—exploded into persecution and violence. The Enlightenment promised an era of rationality, religious freedom, and tolerance. It did not happen. Already in the writings of Voltaire (1694–1778), one of the most powerful advocates of Enlightenment, we sense that Jews were to be the exception to the rule of universal toleration. We find in Jews, he wrote, "only an ignorant and barbarous people, who have long united the most sordid avarice with the most detestable superstition and the most invincible hatred for every people by whom they are tolerated and enriched." He made one concession. "Still," he added, "we ought not to burn them."

A new phenomenon was making its appearance: hostility to Jews without a theological framework to justify it. An emotion that had had a specific place within an ordered religious world view was in the process of being secularized. Christian anti-Judaism was being transformed into racial anti-Semitism. Anti-Semitism as such—the hatred of Jews not for what they believe and do but for what they are, because of their supposedly indelible racial characteristics—is, properly speaking, a phenomenon of the nineteenth century. And it led one perceptive Jewish thinker to conclude that the entire project of European emancipation would fail. Jews would never be accepted within German society, however they adapted their dress, language, mores, and religion. For they were now experiencing a hatred that was directed not at externals of behavior but at their very birth and being. Clermont-Tonnerre's choice still stood before them. But Jews must see that their future lay in the opposite direction to that taken by Reform. They were a nation, not a religion. And they must seek their future not in Europe, where anti-Semitism was ineradicable, but in a rebuilt land of Israel. Individual emancipation in the diaspora would fail. The only alternative was collective emancipation in a land of their own. It was in this series of perceptions that secular Zionism was born.

Moses Hess

The author of these ideas was Moses Hess (1812–1875). Hess had been deeply influenced in his youth by the work of Spinoza. His first book had been entitled *The Holy History of Mankind, by a Young Spinozist*. From there he moved on to the cause of international socialism, in which role he became a friend and collaborator of Karl

Marx. In this vision Judaism had no place. To the contrary, he believed, as Isaiah Berlin put it, that "The people chosen by God must disappear forever, that out of its death might spring a new, more precious life."

Three phenomena, however, influenced Hess in a new direction. The first was the rise of European nationalist movements in the 1840s. Nationalism rather than internationalism was the order of the day. The second was the profound shock he and other European Jews experienced at the revival of the medieval blood libel in the Damascus Affair of 1840. This shook Hess's assumption of a new era of tolerance in which Jews would benignly assimilate, much as the Dreyfus Affair a half century later was to radicalize another alienated Jew, Theodor Herzl. The third was the escalating anti-Semitism Hess detected in Germany. Nothing Jews could do to reform their religion would have the slightest effect on this animosity since, he wrote, the Germans, "hate the peculiar faith of the Jews less than their peculiar noses."

These slowly maturing observations came to expression in Hess's brief but powerful book *Rome and Jerusalem*, published in 1862. It was prefaced by a personal declaration of *teshuvah*, spiritual homecoming: "Here I stand once more, after twenty years of estrangement, in the midst of my people. . . . A thought which I had stifled forever in my heart is again vividly present with me; the thought of my nationality, inseparable, from the inheritance of my ancestors, the Holy Land and the eternal city." Hess's argument was simple. "That which Jews were not able to obtain as individuals, the people can secure as a nation." Instead of emancipation, Jews should seek self-emancipation as a people in their own right. Jewish nationalism was, after all, far more ancient than European nationalism, and if the French could establish and create their own revolutionary state, so could the Jews. With the French Revolution began the rebirth of the nations who owe their national historic religion to Judaism.

Reform Judaism, he argued, was utterly misconceived. "Danger threatens Jewry only from those reformers of its religion who, with their newly invented ceremonies and stale rhetoric, have sucked the last marrow out of Judaism and have allowed nothing to remain of this sublime phenomenon of history but the shadow of a skeleton." The reformers believed that anti-Semitism could be deflected by a change of conduct on the part of Jews. But it cannot be done. Firstly, "even baptism itself" does not protect the Jew from "the nightmare of German Jew-hatred." Second, Jews are a primary race whose distinguishing features cannot be disguised. Third, the denial of the national components of Judaism is ethically unacceptable. The Jew who argues that Judaism is a religion only is "a traitor to his people and to his family."

The Jewish tradition had always seen religion, peoplehood, and nationalism as inseparable. The biblical and rabbinic literature sprang from a "deep national fountain of life." Jews felt bound to one another as members of a single family: "All Israel are responsible for one another." Jewish identity went deeper than religious identity: "The Jew who sins remains a Jew." Judaism, through its holy deeds and days, preserved the memory of its national past. On the ninth of Av, Jews sat in mourning for the ruins of Jerusalem. In their messianic hope they longed for the reconstruction of the nation in its own and promised land.

Never, prior to the nineteenth century, had it been thought possible to separate Jewish religion from nationalism. Enlightened European Jews felt a sense of inferiority to Christians, but they were wrong. Christianity was purely a religion; therefore it was threatened by the decline of religion in a secular age. Judaism was more than a religion; therefore it would be lifted on the rising tide of nationalism. "Only from the national rebirth will the religious genius of the Jews draw new powers, like that giant who touched the mother earth, and be again animated by the sacred spirit of the prophets."

Spinoza and the Secularization of Zionism

Hess was not the first Zionist. In one sense he was only a precursor. It was to take another generation before the Russian pogroms of the 1880s and the Dreyfus Affair of the 1890s energized Pinsker and Herzl to set the movement into motion. In another sense he was only a follower. It had been two Orthodox rabbis, Zvi Hersch Kalischer (1795–1874) and Yehudah Alkalia (1798–1878) who first argued for a new program to settle the land of Israel, set up agricultural colonies, revitalize the Hebrew language, and create a land-purchasing scheme under the leadership of Jews of international stature like Sir Moses Montefiore and the Rothschilds. Hess acknowledged Kalischer as an influence and inspiration.

But Hess's seminal significance is that he was the first secular Zionist. Alkalai and Kalischer spoke within the classic religious vocabulary. The return to Zion was part of the Divine process of redemption, even though, they argued, the first steps must be taken by man. Hess, by contrast, spoke in terms of national spirit and the processes of history in which "race struggle is primary, class struggle is secondary." His work is punctuated by a secular messianism that owes more to Marx than to Moses. His greatest mentor, whom he constantly acknowledges, was Spinoza. Reading *Rome and Jerusalem* for the first time, in 1901, Theodor Herzl remarked, "Since Spinoza, Jewry has brought forth no greater spirit than this forgotten Moses Hess."

To be sure, Jews had always longed for the return to Zion. At the twin peaks of the religious year, on Pesach and Yom Kippur, they had said with deep feeling, "Next year in Jerusalem." But, as Yehoshafat Harkabi has pointed out, "Zionism is not an idea; it is the realization of an intention, a political program." A certain secularization is implicit in the translation of the longing for Zion into a practical and political movement. Throughout the Middle Ages, Jews like Judah Halevi, Maimonides, and Nachmanides had traveled to Israel. At the threshold of modernity, figures like the Vilna Gaon, R. Moses Sofer, and a number of chasidic leaders, had encouraged settlement there as an antidote to the corrosive forces of a secularizing Europe; perhaps even as a mystical means of hastening the messianic age.

The first *yishuv*, the settlement of Jews who had arrived in the land between 1840 and 1880, was composed primarily of deeply religious Ashkenazi Jews who sought to create a religious community on Eastern European lines. But their vision did not extend to creating the infrastructures of an economy, a defense force, and a government, nor did it envisage political action to generate international support for the Zionist cause. To the contrary, such action would have seemed heretical, "forcing the end" by seeking redemption through secular channels.

In Jewish mystical thought, the idea of Israel had become deeply spiritualized. R. Nachman of Bratslav (1772–1811), chasidic leader and great-grandson of the Baal Shem Tov, shortly before his own visit to the land, reported on a conversation he had had with some other *chasidim* who had just returned. Before they had gone, they told him, they could not visualize the land of Israel as actually existing in this world. They had imagined that the holy land was located outside time and space.

Nor was this the primary obstacle to religious Zionism. Since the failure of the Bar Kochba rebellion in the early second century, Judaism had encouraged a stance of quietism and political passivity. In 1770 a German nobleman suggested the idea of a Jewish state in Palestine to Moses Mendelssohn. Mendelssohn replied that the idea was quite implausible. The Jewish people, he lamented, was "not adequately equipped to undertake anything great." The long exile had sapped its spirit. "It is not our fault; but we cannot deny that the natural urge to freedom has completely ceased to be active in us. It has transformed itself into a monkish virtue and expresses itself in prayer and patience, not in action."

It was here that Hess found Spinoza liberating. For it was Spinoza who had "demythologized" the land of Israel, describing it not as a land possessed of intrinsic holiness but as a "certain strip of territory" on which Jews "could live peaceably and at ease." It was Spinoza who had reconceived Jewish history in naturalistic terms, without Divine intervention. It was Spinoza who had stressed the national component of biblical Judaism. And it was Spinoza who, as Hess wrote, "believed that the restoration of the Jewish state depended merely on the courage of the Jewish people." All these effectively secularized the ideas of the Jewish people, Israel, and the connection between them. They allowed them to be translated into the emerging European vocabulary of nationalism. They turned the return to Zion from a religious hope into a political program.

Discontinuities

Spinoza, a thinker who had actually argued the dissolution of Judaism, thus ironically became the inspiration of two radically opposed conceptions of Jewish identity, each of them a revolutionary break with the past: German Reform Judaism and secular Zionism. The Enlightenment, and its political expression in the French Revolution, embodied a sharp dichotomy between religion and state. The state itself was neutral and secular. Religion was to be the private persuasion of individuals.

For a Christian Europe this was a gradual and internal development. For Jews it came as a sharp external demand, stated with unavoidable clarity by Clermont-Tonnerre at the very threshold of emancipation. Was Judaism a religion or the framework of a nation? It could not be both. Holdheim's Reform took the first alternative to its limits, Hess's Zionism took the second. The former denationalized Judaism, the latter secularized it. Each involved a fundamental rewriting of Jewish history and tradition. Thus were born the two major alternatives to Orthodoxy that have persisted into the late twentieth century.

There were other revolutionary Jewish identities, particularly in Eastern Europe: Jewish socialism, culturalism, and a movement for diaspora Jewish autonomy. None proved durable. We will, in a later chapter, encounter a peculiarly twentieth-century alternative, neither religious nor national though mixing elements of both: the phenomenon of Jewish ethnicity. But this chapter has shown how the French Revolution set in motion a questioning and redefinition of Jewish identify that had no precedent in the previous seventeen centuries of exile. It led—in two opposite directions—to a dramatic break with tradition. Was this inevitable, or were there ways of preserving Jewish continuity within the classic terms of faith and practice? What were the traditional responses to the challenges of modernity?

Part Two
Israel in the Here and Now

Chapter 8

On the Theology of Jewish Survival

Steven S. Schwarzchild

The power of the Holocaust in attesting the vitality of Judaism finds full force in the decision of the survivors to be, remain, endure as "Israel," the Jewish people. Schwarzchild begins with that fact, showing the full meaning of the nearly unanimous affirmation of the survivors of Hell on earth and also of those in Britain, North America, Africa, and what was then called "Palestine," to rebuild and go forward. Only a handful opted out, converting to the local form of Christianity in Europe, for example; most did the opposite. For it was a collective and universal decision, brought to concrete form by the Palestinian Jews' decision to create the State of Israel, and by the diaspora Jews' decision to build a strong and vital community, one with a range of ethnically-distinctive traits, on the one side, and with a considerable institutional basis for Judaism, the religion, on the other. Schwarzchild links that affirmation beyond the Holocaust to the theology of Israel as the covenanted people, finding the religious foundations for the national (for the Israelis) and ethnic (for the diaspora) renaissance of the past half-century. Issues of demography, intermarriage between Jews and unconverted gentiles (gentile converts are fully part of Israel), concern for the future of the distinctive people—these settle no questions. Schwarzchild asks, "What can we learn about how we are to survive from how we did survive?" But he finds as his answer not the triumphalism that was rampant in the later 1960s and earlier 1970s, but rather in the ancient, enduring faith: "the survival of the Jewish people is guaranteed by God."

***

Into the first blessing of the prayer, *Shmoneh Esreh*, liberal Judaism has introduced one change which is linguistically minor but doctrinally major. The traditional formulation—He "brings a Redeemer"—now reads, He "brings redemption." This changed liturgical formula persists in practically all authorized liberal prayer books to this day (including the "Conservative" version of Reconstructionism), although the theological reasons which induced the change were among the very earliest issues raised against Orthodoxy at the beginning of the nineteenth century.

Much, if not most, of the liberal Jewish platform has been modified in these one hundred fifty years, and the trend of such modifications has almost unexceptionally been in the direction of a gradual and limited return to the original, traditional

---

*From *Arguments and Doctrines: A Reader of Jewish Thinking in the Aftermath of the Holocaust.* Copyright 1970 by Arthur A. Cohen. Reprinted by permission of Harper & Row, Publishers.

position of Judaism. The doctrine of the peoplehood of Israel and the concomitant significance of the earthly Jerusalem for Jewish hopes have long been restored to non-Orthodox religious thinking; the meaningfulness of ritual and ceremonial has been emphatically reasserted; even the validity of the continuous authoritativeness of Jewish law, if not actually re-established, is certainly increasingly becoming a matter of major concern to Reform Jews. It is, therefore, a little surprising that almost the only basic claim of pristine Jewish liberalism which has not been subjected to this process of reevaluation in the course of time, should be the doctrine of the Messiah.[1]

The reason for this comparative neglect may well be that the doctrine of the Messiah superficially appears to be merely a matter of theory. The question whether the Messianic fulfillment is to be brought about by the instrumentality of a single, individual person or through the collective progress of mankind seems of little moment when put side by side with such pressing, concrete problems as Zionism, the homogeneity of the Jewish community, the observance of Jewish practice and obedience to Jewish law. If this assumption were correct, it would be perfectly proper to relegate so theoretical a question to the background. And yet, it is very easy to demonstrate that the Messianic doctrine is not academic at all but, on the contrary, exceedingly "practical"; perhaps it can even be proved that it, too, requires reinvestigation within the framework of contemporary, non-Orthodox Jewish thinking and life.

There were basically three reasons why liberal Judaism in the first half of the nineteenth century was moved to transform the doctrine of the personal Messiah into the doctrine of the Messianic age—or, to use the phraseology of the *Shmoneh Esreh* prayer, the doctrine of the Redeemer into the doctrine of redemption. These three reasons can be described respectively as antinationalistic, antimiraculous, and optimistic.

In the minds of early reformers, lay as well as rabbinical, the foremost consideration in favor of the depersonalization of the Messiah certainly seems to have been the fact that they regarded the personal Messiah as inextricably interwoven with the hope of the eventual restoration of the people of Israel from the lands of the Diaspora to Palestine, the re-establishment of the Temple and the sacrificial cult. For the present, it implied the foreign character of Jews in the countries of their domicile. These promises, or implications, of the belief in the personal Messiah they rejected most strenuously. They had begun to receive civil rights in Germany and throughout Western Europe, where Reform had its origin; together with nonJewish liberals, they continued to agitate for expansion and completion of their citizenship rights; and they confidently looked forward to an early consummation of these aspirations. To declare, at this juncture of history, that they were still awaiting a person who would lead them from their present homes and reconstitute them as a separate nation in a distant land struck them as aiding and abetting their antagonists who insisted on refusing them their civil rights on the grounds that they neither were nor wished to be members of their host-nations. Thus, in his report of the pertinent discussions at the Rabbinical Conferences of 1844-46, Philipson relates that Dr. Mendel Hess identified the personal with the "political" Messiah.² Even earlier, the Frankfort Society of the Friends of Reform, in the single substantive statement of its beliefs, had announced: "A Messiah who is to lead back the Israelites to the land of Palestine is neither expected nor desired by us. The nonexpectation is understandable and, in this context, logical; the undesirability evokes the ironical picture of the Messiah appearing in Frankfort and being received at the city gates by a delegation of respectable Jewish citizens with the urgent request kindly to remove himself since his presence was likely to obstruct current attempts at the complete emancipation of German Jews. We know no fatherland except that to which we belong by birth or citizenship." And, in another hemisphere as well, many years later, K. Kohler still says: "A complete change in the religious aspiration of the Jew was brought about by the transformation of his political status and hopes in the nineteenth century. The new era witnessed his admission in many lands to full citizenship on a equality with his fellow citizens of other faiths. . . . He therefore necessarily identified himself completely with the nation whose language and literature had nurtured his mind, and whose political and social destinies he shared with true patriotic fervor. He stood apart from the rest only by virtue of his religion. . . . Consequently the hope voiced in the Synagogal liturgy for a return to Palestine, the formation of a Jewish State under a king of the house of David, and the restoration of the sacrificial cult, no longer expressed the views of the Jew in Western civilization. The prayer for the rebuilding of Jerusalem and the restoration of the Temple with its priestly cult could no longer voice his religious hope. Thus the leaders of Reform Judaism in the middle of the nineteenth century declared themselves unanimously opposed to retaining the belief in a personal messiah. . . . They accentuated all the more strongly Israel's hope for a Messianic age, a time of universal knowledge of God and love of man, so intimately interwoven with the religious mission of the Jewish people."³

It may be taken for granted that this particular reason for the abolition of the doctrine of the personal Messiah in liberal Judaism need no longer be taken seriously in the middle of the twentieth century. In the further pursuit of the argument quoted above, Kohler explains that Eastern European Jewry, still subject to disenfranchisement and persecution, continues to adhere to the Orthodox longing for a Jewish political restoration—that for this reason Zionism was born there as an answer to anti-Semitism—and that both of these situations are inapplicable to Western Europe in the first place, and must, in the second place, be made superfluous everywhere else by social progress. The irreconcilability of Zionism with liberal Judaism has long been given the lie in theory as well as in practice and need no longer be argued. But one additional observation must still be made in this connection before we proceed to the next point. It is surely an ironical paradox that Reform Judaism eliminated the personal Messiah because it was held that belief in him was inevitably accompanied by Jewish nationalism, while extreme right-wing orthodoxy of the *Aggudat Yisrael* brand rejected Jewish nationalism because it awaited the advent of this very Messiah! The

Aggudah argued exactly the other way around: the personal Messiah will redeem the Jewish people; therefore, we must not attempt to anticipate by human action what he will do on divine instruction. Reform remained aloof from Zionism because it did not believe in the personal Messiah, the *Aggudah* remained aloof because it did.

This ironical paradox conclusively illustrates the essential *non sequitur* of Reform reasoning on this point: whether one believes in the personal Messiah or not has nothing whatever to do with Jewish nationalism. Theoretically, there is no reason why the personal Messiah must mean Jewish nationalism and the Messianic age must mean "universalism." It is just as possible, logically, to believe that the Messianic person will bring universal redemption rather than the ingathering of the Jewish people, and that the Messianic stage in human history will bring with it the national restoration of Israel rather than its complete absorption among the converted nations of the world.[4] Practically speaking, the outstanding Reform Jews who, during the last half century, were also Zionist leaders do not seem to have been inhibited in their Jewish nationalism by their rejection of the belief in the personal Messiah.

In short, not only has the antinationalistic argument against the doctrine of the personal Messiah been refuted in theory and in fact, but it can be shown never to have been a cogent argument in the first place.

A logically more tenable approach against the personal Messiah was the belief that to await him implied in fact expectation of a miracle. Traditionally, in Bible, Talmud, and post-Talmudic Jewish literature, the functions which the Messiah would fulfill were regarded as being indeed miraculous: nature itself would be transformed to accord with moral requirements, human life would be rid of all natural or moral deficiencies, Israel and Judaism would be established in their proper place of spiritual primacy.[5] But such a doctrine ran counter, of course, to the positivistic, scientific outlook of nineteenth-century liberals. As Kohler put it straight-forwardly: "Our entire mode of thinking demands the complete recognition of the empire of law throughout the universe, manifesting the all-pervasive will of God. The whole cosmic order is one miracle. No room is left for single or exceptional miracles. Only a primitive age could think of God as altering the order of nature which He had fixed, so as to let iron float on water like wood to please one person."[6]

On closer analysis, however, even on its own premises, this objection to the doctrine of the personal Messiah on "scientific" anti-miraculous grounds cannot long be maintained. In the first place, it is very difficult to understand why the achievement of the Messianic aims by many ordinary men—which is, after all, what the concept of the Messianic age boils down to—is any less miraculous than their achievement by one extraordinary person. Even if it be considered a miracle from our perspective, a notion which, as we shall see immediately, is not necessary to the doctrine as such, it presumably will be miraculous regardless of the agency through which it is brought about. In one sense, therefore, the transformation of the doctrine does not accomplish this declared aim of rationalization. In the second place, however, it is not at all certain that miraculousness is necessarily one of the ingredients of the Messianic state. Long before the nineteenth-century reformers came along, the medieval Jewish scholastic rationalists, at their head, Maimonides himself, on occasion objected to a supernatural interpretation of this tenet: "Let it not occur to anyone that in the days of the Messiah a single thing will be changed in the natural course of the world or that there will be any kind of innovation in nature. Rather, the world will continue to exist as it always has. . . . The Messiah will come exclusively in order to bring peace to the world. . . . How all these things will come about none can know until they have actually come about."[7] And yet they certainly anticipated the arrival of the person of the Messiah "though he may tarry, at any time." Therefore, as in the case of the antinationalistic objection to the doctrine of the personal Messiah, here, too, a complete *non sequitur* in the liberal argumentation must be noted: in fact, people, and often "better people than we," have believed in him without subscribing to his miraculous advent. In theory, Messianism is bound up with miraculousness either in both of its variants, the personal and the collective, or in neither. Thus, miraculousness cannot decide the issue between them.

We have stated that miraculousness is inherent in the Messianic doctrine even when it is reformulated in liberalistic, collective terms. Apart from the commonsensical argument already adduced to that effect, no better evidence can perhaps be added than that of Hermann Cohen, the man who was rightly described by Klatzkin as "a spiritual giant who guarded the inheritance of an impoverished generation."[8]—the liberal generation. In him, liberal theology, including the depersonalization of the Messiah, reached its grand consummation—and if it failed here it must be regarded as having failed *in toto*.

History was for Cohen the infinite human process of striving for the ideal, and Messianism is the term designating the completion of this infinite process. But how can infinity be completed? If, to use an analogy of which Cohen was fond, the ideal state of the future lies on an axis which the curve of human history approaches even more closely but cannot actually touch, like an asymptote, then perfection is not an ideal whose reality is guaranteed at some point however far removed but a mathematical impossibility—and there is no guarantee of success at all; to the contrary, there is only a guarantee of relative failure.[9] The conception of the Messiah as an age leaves man swimming desperately in the ocean of history without a shore where he might eventually reach safety. Julius Guttman had pointed out that Cohen's depersonalization of the concept of God had deprived it of the ability to perform the real, historical, and ontological function which Cohen himself had ascribed to it.[10] The same must be said of his view of messianism.[11] In fact, the rational picture presents itself in this manner: that there may be such a thing as history at all, progress must be possible; for progress to be possible there must be a logical guarantee of the eventual attainability of the goal of progress; by Cohen's own admission the goal of progress, perfection, is unattainable through human endeavor. If, therefore, the goal is to be reached at all, it can be reached only by a divine intercession at the end-point of history. And once the theological, even the philosophical necessity of divine, i.e., miraculous intercession is established, it becomes absurd and arrogant to declare the concept of the miraculous, personal Messiah out-of-bounds. To say that the Messianic state must be miraculously brought about, if at all, but not through the miraculous agency of a person, is clearly a purely arbitrary assertion.

Another, usually unexpressed, reason may have contributed to the hostility which the reformers of the last century felt toward the concept of the individual Messiah. Maimonides had stipulated the belief in the bodily Messiah as a fundamental doctrine of Judaism and declared the denier thereof to be a heretic.[12] Taenzer has convincingly demonstrated that the medieval philosopher, Joseph Albo, relegated this doctrine to a very much lower level of Jewish obligatoriness. On this level, belief or disbelief in the personal Messiah by the individual Jew would be without effect on his full religious status.[13] In effect, Albo proclaimed not only that a Jew need not necessarily believe in the Messiah but actually, by implication, recommended against such belief. The historical conditions under which he lived explain his attitude. By his time, the doctrine had become a serious obstacle to Jewish theological self-assertion, for it was used to good effect by Christians in formal as well as informal religious disputations. "Also the others (!) make out of it [the messianic doctrine] a basic principle with which to refute the Torah of Moses."[14] Once the principle of an individual Messiah was accepted, and with the narratives of the New Testament difficult to refute in an age bereft of historical or literary criticism, the crucial issue between Jews and Christians seemed to become one of picking the right person to fit the messianic prerequisites—an unproductive quarrel at best. By eliminating the Messianic doctrine, Albo hoped to prevent further unconstructive controversies and even to strengthen the Jewish position which could then actually turn the argument around: the Messiah having been declared to be irrelevant to true religion, a religion which made him the central test of faith demonstrated its own unauthenticity.

From the Jewish point of view, the phenomenon of Christological Christianity is, of course, only one of many pseudo-Messianisms. By the nineteenth century there had been many such movements in Jewish history; some of them extremely unsettling. If enlightened, rationalistic, liberal Christians of that era were embarrassed by the traditional claims of Christianity regarding the historical Jesus, as indeed they were, how much more eager must liberal Jews have been to rid themselves of all the theological preconditions which might again lead, as they had done so often in the past, to the recurrence of enthusiastic messianic claims. One recalls Graetz's immoderate observations on the subject.[15] How much easier to answer the claims of traditional Christianity, than to dissociate oneself from Jewish pseudo-Messianisms and the entire Jewish Messianic doctrine, and thus prove the rationality of Judaism. In short, this was Joseph Albo in nineteenth century disguise.

Perhaps it is no longer necessary to show both the uselessness and the invalidity of this procedure. It is truly a case of throwing out the true gods together with the false ones. If a doctrine is to be rejected because it can be or even has been abused, the very belief in God must be dispensed with, since men have also often represented themselves as God and created havoc by the falsehoods announced in his name. Furthermore, Buber quotes the pointed Chassidic story which compares the pseudo-Messianic movements to wet compresses that keep the patient awake until the doctor comes: "When God saw that the soul of Israel had fallen sick, he covered it with the painful shawl of the *Galut*. So that it could bear the pains, however, He bestowed upon it the sleep of numbness. Again, so that it would not be destroyed, He awakens it each hour with a false Messianic hope and then lulls it to sleep again until the night will have passed and the real Messiah will appear. For the sake of this work, the eyes of the wise are occasionally blinded."[16] Franz Rosenzweig made the same point in a less anecdotal, more theological and poetic fashion: "The expectation of the coming of the Messiah, by which and because of which Judaism lives, would be a meaningless theologumenon, a mere 'idea' in the philosophical sense, empty babble, if the appearance again and again of a 'false Messiah' did not render it reality and unreality, illusion and disillusion. The false Messiah is as old as the hope for the true Messiah. He is the changing form of this changeless hope. He separates every Jewish generation into those whose faith is strong enough to give themselves up to an illusion, and those whose hope is so strong that they do not allow themselves to be deluded. The former are the better, the latter the stronger. The former bleed as victims on the altar of the eternity of the people, the latter are the priests who perform the service at this altar. And this goes on until the day when all will be reversed, when the belief of the believers will become truth, and the hope of the hoping a lie. Then—and no one knows whether this "then" will not be this very day—the task of the hoping will come to an end and, when the morning of that day breaks, everyone who still belongs among those who hope and not among those who believe will run the risk of being rejected. This danger hovers over the apparently less endangered life of the hopeful."[17] Herein also lies the answer to those who will always worry: if the belief in the personal Messiah as such is granted, why not Jesus?

Underlying all these motivations for the depersonalization of the Messiah-concept lay an optimism about the future of the Jewish people and of mankind as a whole. This optimism resulted in the belief that, as already indicated, the redeemer had become not only impossible and undesirable, but also unnecessary. After all, the Messiah was logically and historically a product of need. In the former sense, the anticipation of his coming implied consciously and unconsciously that man by himself could not master his destiny or reach his goal. Instead, a divine agent would either have to bring about or at least complete the messianic, i.e., perfect human society. And historically it is true that, as Israel's historic situation became increasingly hopeless, the concept of the Messiah became increasingly supernatural, for the greater the need the more powerful had to be the person who would triumph over it. "The burden of exile narrowed their horizon. They could see no other way of redemption from their abject position than by supernatural events."[18] Or as Baeck put it impressively: "It was especially true in the centuries of despair: only by seeing before him a mirage was many a man able to procure the strength with which to keep on marching through the desert which life had become for him.[19] Now, in the nineteenth century, it was believed that such pessimism about the nature of man and the prospects of history had once and for all been refuted.

Certainly, the political development of the times seemed to indicate that the Jewish despair which had so largely formed the concept of the Messiah had become a thing of the past. Everywhere and increasingly Jews were being enfranchised and at least promised, often also given, equal rights with their fellow citizens. Physical persecution, except in some God-forsaken corners of Russia, had almost completely ceased. Liberal democracy was making headway everywhere in the West; material and technological developments were fast progressing. And even culturally, the mellowing of Christianity as evidenced by the new liberal theology, Unitarianism, ethical humanism and similar phenomena, persuaded the usually sober I. M. Wise that America would be Jewish within the foreseeable future. Thus Samuel Hirsch declared: "Everywhere the emancipation of mankind is being striven for so that a morally pure and holy life may be possible of being lived by man on this earth."[20] Auerbach agreed with him: "In our days the ideals of justice and the brotherhood of men have been so strengthened through the laws and institutions of modern states that they can never again be shattered; we are witnessing an ever nearer approach of the establishment of the Kingdom of God on earth through the strivings of mankind."[21] Herzfeld chimed in: "The conference must declare what it means by redemption; yes, it should state that we are now entering upon the period of redemption. Freedom and virtue are spreading, the world is growing better."[22] And, of course, the famous Pittsburgh Platform announced: "We recognize, in the modern era of universal culture of heart and intellect, the approaching the realization of Israel's greatest Messianic hope for the establishment of the kingdom of truth, justice, and peace among all men."[23] In this respect, Wiener summarizes the spirit of the time trenchantly and convincingly: "The new generation was dominated by an almost too gay optimism. . . . Transcendent, eschatological ideas receded in the face of the confidence that this world would soon be the scene of divine justice within the moral life of humanity. By the latter was meant above all the completion of equality of civil rights in all countries—which was an understandable preoccupation, though it became embarrassing by being constantly overemphasized." He recalls that for Moritz Lazarus the outcome of the Dreyfus Affair was positively "a Messianic event." Wiener indicts this entire generation of shallowly optimistic, self-centered and self-deceiving leaders when he states: "If it is ever true that religious beliefs are the ideological superstructure of the economic-political conditions of society, then it was certainly true of this class. It interpreted and accommodated religious doctrines in conformity with its enthusiastic attitude toward civil society which it regarded as final, eternal, and divine."[24]

This outlook no longer deserves a reply. The neoexistentialists, Jewish, Christian, and nonreligious, have effectively knocked down this straw man to build up a case for themselves. Rosenzweig, for example, reports the famous incident in which Hermann Cohen is supposed to have pleaded with him that he must expect the Messiah within no more than fifty years.[25] Thus, he wanted to reveal this vapid optimism for the self-deceiving hallucination that it was—and as a symbol his story serves well enough; although we must add that as a truthful report of Cohen's mind it is a thoroughly incredible tale. It belies everything that Cohen stood for in his affirmation of the infinite Messianic process, his violent rejection of all forms of eudaemonism, and even his definition of the Messiah itself. Nonetheless, that the contemporary pessimists have completely and justifiably deflated this hallucination cannot be disputed. We have learned for a fact that the nineteenth century was profoundly wrong in its vast overestimation of the social abilities of man. If persecution, pogroms and oppression are indeed the rationale for Messianism, then our age is, and by rights ought to be, the most Messianic age of all in the history of Israel.

If, then, we must discard the third main reason which the liberals of the nineteenth century proffered for the abolition of the concept of the personal Messiah, literally not one of their arguments has been found to withstand critical examination. Their antinationalism has been repudiated by Jewish history; their antimiraculousness has been refuted by the necessities of their own position, not to speak of the views of others; their optimism has been repudiated by general history. Furthermore, it turns out that at least two of their reasons were not logically constructed in the first place. In short but brutal fact, their case against the personal Messiah crumbles at the first touch.

We could end the argument at this point. Religious tradition must always be regarded as valid until, and unless, invincible reasons are brought forth against it. The reasons militating against the traditional doctrine under consideration have been shown to be anything but invincible, and we may, therefore, with good and calm conscience return to the original position. Ours is not necessarily the task to prove the doctrine positively; to refute its refutation ought to suffice. Nevertheless, without venturing to prove its tenability, there are a few hints which may be given toward the construction of the positive case.

The first is a mere technicality. The liberal prayer books of the last century have abounded, and still abound, with phrases which must, if they are to be intellectually acceptable, be interpreted very broadly by the Jews who use them. "The Torah of Moses" is as clear-cut an example as any, although there are many others. Do liberal Jews believe that "the" Torah was given to, by, or from Moses? As a matter of fact, the very ritual reading from the Torah has become a metaphoric act for most of them. A very high percentage, certainly well over half, of everything read from it, if it is to be acceptable at all, must be homiletically decontaminated of its original historical, theological, moral, or social intent. And nonetheless these things are retained—reinterpreted but retained. Yet the phrase "Who brings a redeemer" cannot be so treated; it must be changed!? All that was required to bring the traditional text into conformity with liberal belief was the interchange of a single letter of the Hebrew alphabet, an *Heh* at the end for a *Vav* in the middle of the word. But this had to be done through a surgical operation on the prayer book, when much more serious problems were solved with exegetical palliatives. We may assuredly draw two conclusions from this observation: (1) There was more to this than meets the eye; more fundamental interests were involved than those that were expressed; (2) A return to the original phrase is justified if only because it will violate no one's conscience; completely free exegesis will still be offered to anyone who wishes to take advantage of it.

In analyzing the views of Hermann Cohen, we pointed out the intimate connection between the belief in the personality of the Messiah and the belief in the personality of God. For him, as for the liberal mentality in general, the entire concept of personality as such was a terrible stumbling block. As Kierkegaard and existentialism never tire of pointing out, the existence of the individual personality defies all the universal and theoretical laws of science as well as of idealism. They, therefore, try to dissolve it into general propositions. God as an idea, the Messiah as an age—these are entities with which theoretical reason can deal. The persons of God and of the Messiah, on the other hand, are hard, stubborn, even—as it were—empiric realities that defy classification. But then, so does every individual. And thus, the depersonalization process does not stop with God or the Messiah so far as liberalism was concerned.

A change was likewise introduced into the second benediction of the *Amidah*. "Praised be Thou, O Lord, who bringest to life the dead" seemed to be a liturgical formulation of the doctrine of resurrection, and this doctrine was regarded as outmoded as the reference to the personal Messiah. Do we not know that the body decomposes in the grave? Where would physical resurrection take place in the spiritual world of God? Does not the belief in the eternity of the body imply a vast overemphasis on the material aspect of life? And so the modernistic arguments ran. Therefore, again the liturgical formulation was changed, and so remains to this day: "Praised be Thou, who hast implanted within us eternal life." In this manner, belief in the immortality of the soul was substituted for the concept of resurrection of the body.

The rejection of the belief in resurrection is closely connected with the rejection of the personal Messiah—not only because they both found expression at the very beginning of the *Amidah*. Ever since Ezekiel pictured the messianic rebirth of Israel in terms of the famous revived bones, one of the traditional marks of the advent of the Messiah in Jewish thought has been the resurrection of the dead.[26] "May the All-merciful make us worthy of the days of the Messiah and of the life of the world-to-come."[27] And at the Conference of American Reform rabbis in Philadelphia in 1869, the rejection of the one doctrine was immediately and logically followed up with the rejection of the other.[28] Thus, the depersonalization process has gone one step further: God is not a person but an idea or a force; the Messiah is not a person but an age; and man is not a person but a universal reason confined in an individualizing and debasing body—a state of affairs fortunately remedied in the hereafter!

Herein also lies the most important reason for our time for a return to the personalism of the Messiah. Not only have we reacknowledged the unitary character of the human person: if scientific conclusions have any bearing on this discussion, they tend to assert the indivisibility, even the indistinguishability of "body" and "soul." Martin Buber's philosophy of dialogue is premised on the recognition of persons, human and divine, as the carriers of life. The outlook of the Bible which deals with "the whole man" is reasserting itself in the form of what is called "personalism." Baeck[29] describes this outlook in these words: "It is particularly true of prophetic thinking that it is far removed from abstract descriptions and instead envisages the figure of a real human being with its views and deeds. The prophets speak less of a future time than of a future person. The ideal of the future becomes for them an ideal personality. . . . The son of David is the future man. As a man of flesh and blood he makes real and vivid what the ideal man ought to be and will be." As Tillich puts it: "Ontology generalizes, while Biblical religions individualizes."[30] And specifically with regard to the Messiah, the "liberal" Wiener puts the case clearly: "It is always the great miracle, the emergence into overpowering visibility of the deeds of God Himself, which characterize the days of the Messiah—the expression of the personal shaping of world-history by the personal God. For this reason so much emphasis is put on the personality of the Messiah. . . . It is precisely in the belief in the Messiah that one can recognize the full vitality of a religiosity for which God is personality and His revelation the tangible guidance by means of miracle. One is inclined to say that at this point piety is most distantly removed from everything abstract, from conceptual ideology—and that it rather becomes faith in the true sense of the word, believing confidence in the revelation of concrete facts."[31] We have learned from religious as well as nonreligious existentialism, that all moral reality, as distinguished from nature or mathematics, is the reality of persons. Man, the person, is the *locus* of ethics, not ages, ideas, or forces. The Messianic age is a Utopia; the Messiah is a concrete, though future, reality.

Let us consider one last objection which will be raised against this view. It will be said again, as it has often been said in the past, that reliance on the Messianic fulfillment will lead to moral quietism and passivism. If men expect a divine agent to bring about perfection, they will sit back, relax their own efforts toward the good, and leave to him the work they themselves ought to do. This has, indeed, often happened. Was it not a delegation of Orthodox rabbis of the *Aggudah* type who requested the British mandatory governor not to withdraw his troops since Zionism was human supererogation anyway, and the Messiah was to come in 1999? But the drawing of an improper conclusion does not mean that the doctrine ought be abolished. It ought rather be protected against false interpreters.

"Perish all those who calculate the end,"[32] was the motto of the Talmudic rabbis who opposed the view that the Messianic time was fixed mechanically without regard to the human contribution to its hastening. They taught emphatically that the arrival of the Messiah was dependent upon man's actions: if they were good it would be sooner, if evil—later. "God said: everything depends on you. Just as the rose grows with its heart toward heaven, so do you repent before Me and turn your hearts heavenward, and I will thereupon cause your redeemer to appear."[33] There is even the view, which commends itself on ethical grounds, that the Messiah will appear after the Messianic state has been established, leaving its attainment to humanity but guaranteeing its maintenance thereafter. Even Mendelsohn seems to have held this view.[34] The nineteenth-century proto-Zionist, R. Hirsch Kalischer stipulated the return to Zion as a prerequisite, not consequence, of the Messianic advent.[35] And even the man who was later to become one of the foremost and most radical leaders of American Reform, Samuel Hirsch, in the days before he went to greater extremes, advanced this same thought. "It is up to us to turn to God, for the Messiah cannot come before we have become completely good. . . . No, it is not the duty of the Messiah but that of the entire household of the vanguard against evil, the entire house of Jacob, to wage this battle on behalf of all the inhabitants of world, and the root of Jesse cannot shoot forth out of its midst until it has fulfilled this duty and carried out its task."[36]

Therefore, not only is it untrue that the doctrine of the personal Messiah must necessarily lead to quietism. On the contrary, it can help in suppressing the peculiar modern variant of pseudo-Messianism. One of the most horrible and disastrous illusions to which modern men have fallen prey is that they have actually achieved the Messianic state. It is on the basis of the self-deception that our contemporary dictatorships have ruthlessly eliminated all dissent, for they maintain that dissent from perfection is, by definition, falsehood. Whereas in the Middle Ages pseudo-Messianisms operated around a central, individual pseudo-Messianic person, in our time it is characteristic of our collectivist and societally minded frame of references that pseudo-Messianisms take the form of national movements. More than ever, therefore, the absence of the person of the redeemer should constitute a constant warning against such blasphemous exaggerations. This warning is, furthermore, not without its applicability to the present Jewish world-situation. The Messianic undercurrent in the history of modern Zionism has in turn led to the far-reaching secularization of "the Messianic thought in Israel," as a result of which, as Leon Roth has pointed out, we no longer ask in the words of the Bible: "Who will recount the mighty deeds of God?" but rather in the words of the Israeli song: "Who will recount the mighty deeds of Israel?" What is even much more dangerous is the hazy notion floating through the minds of a not inconsiderable number of super-Zionists that the establishment of the State itself constitutes the Messianic fulfillment. Here lies the road to certain disaster! When Rabbi Kurt Wilhelm, formerly of Jerusalem and now chief rabbi of Sweden, and this writer dared point out in a series of articles that Jewishly there is a vast difference between *yeshuah*, historical salvaging, and *ge'ulah*, redemption, an Israeli newspaper attacked us vehemently as new *retestrabbiner!*"[37] If this journalist had only been waiting for the Messiah!

Endnotes

[1] The only theologian who seems to have concerned himself with the problem, and he with his customary perspicacity and ardor, is the much neglected Max Wiener, *Der Messiasgedanke in der Tradition und seine Umbiegung im modernen Liberalismus*, in *Festgabe für Claude G. Montefiore*, 151-56.

[2] *The Reform Movement in Judaism*, 5, 122, 173-80.

[3] *Jewish Theology*, 388f.

[4] The identification of the personal Messiah with nationalism was based on the traditional identity of the Messiah as a descendant of David the King. Thus, the Jewish monarchy was believed to be involved and with it all the features of a reconstituted state.

[5] Cf. J. Klausner, *The Messianic Concept in Israel* (Jerusalem, 5710) 138f.

[6] Ibid., 165. [7] *Mishneh Torah*, Laws of the Kings, 12.1.

[8] *Hermann Cohen* (Berlin, 1921) 11.

[9] Cf. Rosenzweig, Glatzer, 358: "According to the words of a philosopher whom I regard as an authority even greater than Hermann Cohen, what is not to come save in eternity will not come in all eternity."

[10] *Die Philosophie des Judentums*, 351.

[11] Cf. Cohen, *Religion der Vernunft*, 276-313. I have discussed this point somewhat more lengthily in "The Democratic Socialism of Hermann Cohen," *Hebrew Union College Annual* 27, "Conclusion."

[12] Cf. Thirteen Principles, last no.; *Mishneh Torah*, Laws of Repentance, 3:6.

[13] *Die Religionsphilosophie Josef Albo's*, 34-37.

[14] Albo, *Ikarim*, 1, 4.

[15] Cf. *History*, 10: 190f., 312f., 387f. The Zohar, the source of much late Jewish messianism he never refers to other than as "the book of lies."

[16] Quoted in *Israel-Volk und Land*, 31.

[17] Glatzer, *Rosenzweig—His Life and Thought*, 350f.; cf. Rosenzweig, *Jehudah Halevi*, 239.

[18] Greenstone, *The Messiah Idea in Jewish History*, 264f.

[19] *The Essence of Judaism*, 4th ed., 273f.

[20] Ibid., 178. [21] Ibid. [22] Ibid. [23] Ibid, 356.

[24] *Juedische Religion in Zeitalter der Emancipation*, 172f.; *Der Messiasgedanke*, ibid., 153.

[25] Glatzer, loc. cit.; *Jehudah HaLevy*, loc. cit.

[26] Cf. Greenstone, ibid., 57-60. Elbogen, *Judaica, Cohen Eestschrift*, 671, indicates that resurrection precedes the advent of the Messiah.
[27] Grace after the meal. [28] Phillipsohn, ibid., 263. [29] Ibid., 269f.
[30] *Biblical Religion and the Search for Ultimate Reality*, 39.
[31] *Der Messiasgedanke*, ibid., 154f. [32] *Sanh*, 97b.
[33] *m. Tehillim* 45:3; cf. generally, A. H. Silver, *Messianic Speculation in Israel*, "Opposition to Messianic Speculation," 195-206.
[34] Cf. Wiener, ibid., 170. [35] Cf. Greenstone, ibid., 267.
[36] *Die Messiaslehre der Juden*, 402, 404. [37] *Yedi'ot Chadashot*, 3 October, 1950.

Chapter 9

The Link between People, Land, and Religion in the Structure-of-Faith of Judaism

Menfred H. Vogel

Three quintessentially-theological issues flow together: election of Israel, the holiness of the Land, and the coming of the Messiah. The covenant between Israel and God takes place in the setting of Israel's relationship to the Land of Israel. Violate the covenant, lose the Land, keep the covenant, endure securely in the land—that is the condition specified in the written Torah. Having lost the Land, Israel yearned to return, and the classical theological position identified return to the Land with the coming of the Messiah, who would gather the exiles and bring them home. So exile and redemption, Israel and Land, the coming of the Messiah—these issues are intertwined and scarcely to be considered in isolation from one another. In this and the next chapters we turn to the concrete, specific, this-worldly formulations of the supernatural doctrine of election as set forth in Scripture and the oral Torah as well, and we conclude with the matter of Zionism and its relationship to Judaism. The first issue proves the most difficult: the enlandisement, or land-centered-ness, of Judaism's Israel. Scripture itself defined matters in such a way, its narratives leaving no doubt on the matter. Vogel reviews Peoplehood and Land, spelling out the religious dimensions of both, and showing their relationship, with Peoplehood primary, Land contingent and subordinate.

***

Our purpose in this essay is to determine the status and role which are assigned respectively to the category of peoplehood and the category of land in the structure-of-faith of Judaism. To help us carry out this task we propose to turn first to modern Jewish thought to see how various figures in this domain perceived and understood these categories in the context of Judaism. The rationale and justification for first undertaking such a review lie in the simple fact that in modernity these two categories have come to occupy an especially central and prominent place in Jewish consciousness and as a result (not surprisingly) modern Jewish thought has come to greatly occupy itself with these themes which, in turn, resulted in the fact that most of the possible formulations (and sometimes even the not-so-possible formulations)

---

*From *A Quest for a Theology of Judaism*, by Manfred H. Vogel. Copyright © 1987 by University Press of America. Reprinted by permission of SIDIC © 1975.

regarding these categories have at one time or another found expression in it. As such, a review of this literature (albeit somewhat cursory and haphazard as this review is) should prove most helpful as it will present us with the central options, the main alternatives, that are available with regard to these categories on the basis of which we can then attempt to pursue our own analysis and draw from it some conclusions and observations of our own. Thus, this essay divides itself in the main into two parts—the first part being a brief review of some of the formulations propounded in modern Jewish thought regarding the category of peoplehood and that of land, while the second part is a summary of our conclusions regarding these categories.

Formulations of Peoplehood and Land in Modern Jewish Thought

We would suggest that in attempting to encompass the distinctive and central expressions of modern Jewish thought one encounters in the main five major trends. These trends are: (1) The philosophical-theological trend, by which we mean those writings which are systematically philosophic-theological in nature rather than publicistic or ideological. This trend expresses itself primarily within German Jewry (e.g., Lazarus, Hirsch, Steinheim, Formstecher, Cohen, Rosenzweig). (2) The Zionist ideological trend. The literature in this trend actually divides itself into two subdivisions: (a) the writings of political Zionism (e.g., Herzl, Nordau, Zangwill) and (b) the writings of cultural Zionism (e.g., Ahad Ha-Am). This is the main fork in the road within Zionist literature and the distinction between the two subdivisions is usually characterized by the observation that the question for political Zionism is the problem of the Jews while for cultural Zionism it is the problem of Judaism. This is a catchy formulation and up to a point valid but it may not be the most fundamental. For the problem of Judaism and the problem of the Jews are ultimately linked, the problem of one being ultimately the problem of the other. A more basic distinction may lie, as we would try to suggest below, in the scope of ethnicity accorded to the Jewish people in these two alternatives. (3) The culturalist-autonomist trend (e.g., Dubnow). This trend is, in a way, but the other side of the coin of the cultural Zionist trend. The two trends grasp the phenomenon of Judaism in essentially the same way. The fundamental difference between them is that the former affirms exclusive diaspora-existence while the latter sees a need for a settlement in the land of Israel. (4) The socialist trend, namely, the literature concerned with the socialist question, where the Jewish question enters the picture within this underlying context. This trend divides itself, in turn, between those socialist formulations that are Zionist (e.g., M. Hess) and those which are virulently anti-Zionist and diaspora-affirming (e.g., the Bund). (5) Lastly, we have the mystical trend. Namely, we would like to examine some expressions in modern Jewish thought that may be legitimately characterized as mystical formulations of

Judaism. Here again, a further subdivision may be introduced between religious and non-religious expressions. Of course, a case can be made that in a certain sense all mystical formulations are religious. But if one is to take specifically rabbinic Judaism, i.e., Orthodoxy, as the criterion for religiousness, a subdivision may be introduced between those formulations that adhere to Orthodoxy (e.g., Rav Kook) and those formulations which vis-à-vis Orthodoxy must be characterized as non-religious (e.g., A. D. Gordon, M. Buber.)[1]

Now, it would seem to us that all authentic expressions of Judaism will incorporate the category of Jewish peoplehood, at least in the minimal sense of being a distinct collectivity. This, of course, is not to say that there were no formulations by Jews that denied the category of Jewish peoplehood altogether; but in doing this, such formulations denied equally the general category of peoplehood as such, affirming only one indivisible unitary category, i.e., the category of mankind. Such formulations were entertained, for example, by certain Jews in the Communist camp. But such formulations cannot, by any stretch of the imagination, be taken as authentic expression of Judaism. At best, they can be taken as the expressions of the pathology of modern Judaism. Formulations that can be taken as authentic expressions of Judaism must, no matter how minimally, affirm the reality of the phenomenon of Judaism. And such affirmation necessitates, in turn, the affirmation of the category of Jewish peoplehood, at least in the minimal sense that it constitutes a distinct collectivity. For without a collective human carrier the phenomenon of Judaism could not manifest itself in reality, indeed, could not have a reality. Judaism as a body of tenets or a body of beliefs or a pattern of behavior or whatever else one may want to describe it as, cannot have reality unless it is carried by a human collectivity. Thus, for any affirmation of Judaism, and therefore for any expression of Judaism, the category of Jewish peoplehood must in some sense be affirmed also.

Indeed, the problem before us is not whether or not the category of Jewish peoplehood is affirmed in the various formulations of modern Judaism; rather, it is to determine how the category of Jewish peoplehood is conceived and understood. Here, three possible formulations suggest themselves. First, Jewish peoplehood can be conceived as a purely religious community, a "church," completely devoid of any national character. Secondly, Jewish peoplehood can be understood as an ethnic entity, namely, as a national entity, in the full sense of the term, thus including not only the cultural and spiritual but also the social, economic and political dimensions. Third and lastly, Jewish peoplehood can be understood as an ethnic entity in a restricted sense of being limited only to the cultural and spiritual dimension.

With regard to the second and third possibilities it should be noted further that they can be formulated either within a religious context or within a secularized context. Namely, the category of Jewish peoplehood either in the full or in the restricted sense of ethnicity can be seen as an instrument within the religious scheme of things, i.e., as an agent in the working of redemption; as such, the nation is seen integrally and by its very essence, as a holy nation. Or the category of Jewish peoplehood can be seen in purely naturalistic, humanistic terms as a nation like all the other nations without a religious vocation that constitutes its very essence. Although the battle between the religious and the secularized view was severe and is of great significance, we cannot enter it here in detail. Indeed, for our immediate concern it carries no importance since both the religious and secularist views agree as regards the centrality of the category of Jewish peoplehood in the phenomenon of Judaism (and this is the question that concerns us here). Where they disagree is with regard to the question of the status of this category within the whole scheme of things (whether ethnicity is to be taken in a full or in a restricted sense). Suffice it here perhaps to say that for the religious view the category of peoplehood is taken as a means, as an instrument in the realization of the religious vocation and therefore the category receives its meaning and significance, its rationale, from the religious end which it serves, whereas in the secularized view the category of peoplehood is taken as the end in itself, as the primary datum, and therefore the justification and rationale for the category are derived from the primary biological urge and right of every nation's desire to go on perpetuating itself. We may add that while in the last analysis either formulation may be theoretically acceptable as a vantage point from which to understand the phenomenon of Judaism, accepting the secularist formulation may raise for many of us a serious existential problem in justifying Jewish history; namely, it may be very difficult for many of us to justify the perseverance of the people in the past in maintaining their Jewish identify, seeing what a high cost in suffering this entailed, if such perseverance was merely for the sake of maintaining yet another secularized ethnic entity, or merely the result of satisfying the biological urge for self-perpetuation. And even more poignantly, such a secularized formulation could not provide us with the rationale and justification for our on-going determination of our progeny to remain within Jewish ethnicity.

Likewise with regard to the category of the land, there are in principle three possible stances that can be taken vis-à-vis this question. One stance would maintain that the category of the land is not required for the survival or functioning of Judaism. Judaism is a purely spiritual entity, a religious or a cultural phenomenon that can function and survive without attachment to the land, any land. A second stance would maintain that Judaism does indeed require the category of the land but that there is no specific geographical location that is required. Any land, any geographic location, will satisfy the requirements of the phenomenon of Judaism. The third and last stance would maintain that the phenomenon of Judaism requires a specific land, a specific geographic location, namely the land of Israel. The full, optimal functioning of the phenomenon of Judaism requires the specific geographic location known as the land of Israel.

All of these possible formulations (the three, or, rather, five relating to Jewish peoplehood and the three relating to the land) find expression within modern Jewish thought. Let us proceed, then, according to the formulations relating to the category of Jewish peoplehood and corresponding to this deal with the formulations relating to the category of the land.

Peoplehood as a Religious Community

The first formulations, i.e., the formulation perceiving Jewish peoplehood as purely a religious community, is reflected in the maximal assimilationist trend within Judaism and although it might well have been quite widespread and popular among emancipated, assimilated Western Jewry, it is not really a serious option either in terms of the structure of Judaism or in terms of its reality in the world. Indeed, it does not find significant expression within the more serious, thoughtful literature. We shall, therefore, not dwell upon it here. Of course, with such an understanding of Jewish peoplehood it is clear that the only formulation regarding the category of the land that is feasible here is a formulation that radically negates the need of Judaism for land. Jewish peoplehood as a pure, spiritualized religious community (often the religion here is nothing else than idealized, utopian but commonplace individualistic ethics) clearly needs no land. It should be clear that such formulations serve nicely the desire for full assimilation by removing all factors that may be obstacles to such full assimilation.

But if we were afterall to present this formulation in some greater length, we would be well advised to do it with regard to an expression that while preserving the essential view of this formulation nonetheless argues passionately for the reality and preservation of Jewish nationhood. What we have in mind, for example, is the position of the early Smolensky (prior to his conversion to *Hibbat Zion*). The early Smolensky is the father of the notion that the Jewish people is a "spiritual nation." Jewish peoplehood is seen as carrying a special spiritual teaching, we might even say a religious teaching, and its vocation is to spread this teaching among the nations of the world. It is by virtue of this special religious, spiritual teaching that the distinctiveness of the Jewish nation is constituted and maintained. This distinctiveness is seen as long-lasting, indeed, for all intents and purposes, as a permanent distinctiveness. For the distinctiveness of the Jewish people will be maintained as long as the world at large has not appropriated this teaching, and the occurrence of this event, if it takes place at all, is placed in the remote future. Conceived in this way, i.e., as a completely spiritual, religious entity, the Jewish people have no need for a land or a state or even a national language. As such, of course, Smolensky wants to argue that the distinctiveness of the Jewish people should not constitute an obstacle for their full emancipation, i.e, participation in the social, political, and economic life of the host nation. Since the distinctiveness is constituted exclusively by a spiritual factor and the concrete factors of distinction like land, language, and state are not applicable, there is no reason for the Jews not to adopt the concrete dimensions of national life like language, land, etc., of their host nation. The Jews are a nation but a spiritual nation, a nation not of this world. Thus, in terms of this world the factor of nationhood does not enter the picture. In terms of a this-worldly emancipation, the Jews can be fully emancipated. Yet this emancipation would not obliterate their distinctiveness which comes about by virtue of their being a distinct spiritual entity. Whether this formulation is valid is a different question. What is interesting and most important, however, is that although the formulation here conceives of the Jewish people as a religious, spiritual community, and therefore it should really be understood as a collectivity of individuals sharing the same vocation, Smolensky insists on the ethnic, national nature of the entity. Namely, it is a biological group that is entrusted with this vocation, in turn imparting this vocation to its individual members. Smolensky attacks viciously the Jewish enlightenment precisely on the point that it abrogated and canceled out the dimension of peoplehood in its understanding of Judaism. The giving up of the category of nationhood by the Jewish enlightenment (Mendelssohn) signaled the death-knell for Jewish survival. And quite evidently, as it is clearly implicated by his view of the nature of Jewish peoplehood, for the early Smolensky Judaism has no need or requirement for land.

Peoplehood as an Ethnic Entity

In contra-distinction to the previous formulation, this formulation, i.e., the formulation perceiving Jewish peoplehood as an ethnic entity in the full sense of the term, is a most significant and important expression. Still, its expression is primarily limited to certain quarters of the Zionist ideological trend, specifically, to the trend of political Zionism. But, although numerically this formulation may not find a wide expression, it is an extremely important formulation in terms of the practical destiny of the Jewish people in our time and, indeed, in terms of the very structure of the phenomenon of Judaism, because it captures and represents (as we shall try to show below) an essential aspect of this structure. So, clearly, the importance of such formulations cannot be decided on a quantitative basis.

A good example of this formulation can be encountered in the view of Leon Pinsker as he expressed it in his *Autoemancipation* (a view which, though by no means identical, is very similar in many respects to the view put forth by Herzl in his *Judenstaat*). True to the orientation of political Zionism, the concern of Pinsker is with the problem of the Jewish people rather than of Judaism. The problem is the problem of anti-Semitism, which for him, in contradistinction to Herzl, is not a modern problem but a problem as old as Jewish diaspora-existence. In his analysis, such factors as economic competition and social incompatibility do not constitute the essence of the problem of anti-Semitism. They are secondary factors aggravating the problem, but not its source. The primary, essential factor which brings about anti-Semitism is the fact that the Jewish nation is perceived as a "ghost-nation." In its diaspora-existence it is perceived as a separate distinct entity, as a nation, and yet it is unlike any other nation known to mankind. It is not concretely a nation, merely a ghost of a nation. And deeply seated within the soul of man there is a primal fear of ghosts, of anything that is ghost-like. Such fear easily links itself with feelings of hatred and mockery, and the constellation of such emotions constitutes the phenomenon of anti-Semitism. Now, the Jewish nation in its diaspora-existence is ghost-like because it does not have its homeland. Many other people dwell as strangers in other lands, but their condition is not the same as that of the Jews because they have a homeland some place. The Jew, therefore, is not merely a stranger in other lands, but a ghost creature roaming the world. Emancipation, therefore, will not work; it is bound to fail. The only solution is for the Jews to regain a homeland for themselves. Auto-emancipation in the sense of regaining national sovereignty is the solution.

Clearly, the understanding of Jewish peoplehood reflected in this analysis is that of an ethnic group in the full sense of the term. The Jews are ghost-like because their ethnicity is not expressed in this-worldly terms. They are strange and unlike any other nation because they do not possess their own land and as such allow their ethnicity to express itself in the political dimension.

Given this understanding of Jewish peoplehood as an ethnic entity in the full sense of the term, it is clear that the formulation which rejects the need for land will be inapplicable here. Such a formulation of Jewish peoplehood can be consistently combined only with a formulation that requires the appropriation of land for that people. If the Jewish people is to express itself in the political dimension, it must have political sovereignty. The expression of political sovereignty, however, is the possession of statehood. And statehood can be established only with reference to a specific geographic location. Thus the realization of the political dimension requires of necessity the possession of some land. The inner logic of the formulation which perceives Jewish peoplehood as an ethnic entity in the full sense of the term requires the formulation that argues for the need of the Jewish people to have a land of their own. But the inner logic of this formulation does not require that this land be specifically the land of Israel. What is needed is some land so that statehood can be established and it is the establishment of statehood that is vitally needed by the Jewish people. In principle, in theory, any land can serve that purpose. As such, the "Territorialists" or the "Ugandists" were indeed consistent. In real life, however, their position could not be maintained, and most of them veered towards the requirement that the land be specifically the land of Israel. That is, not just any geographic location would do but only, specifically, the geographic location that is the land of Israel. However, the reasons for this requirement did not follow from the inner logic of the formulation but rather from extraneous considerations such as the historical connection or the emotional attachment of the people to the land of Israel and from various other pragmatic considerations. Because of these considerations (and these considerations, though extraneous in terms of the inner logic, are of utmost importance in terms of the realities of life), the preponderance of the formulations that perceived Jewish peoplehood as an ethnic entity in the full sense of the term linked themselves to the requirement for a specific geographic location, i.e., the requirement for the land of Israel.

The above understanding of Jewish peoplehood in its full ethnicity, and commensurate to it, therefore, the need for a land, clearly arose out of the problematic of Jewish existence. A similar understanding of Jewish peoplehood and the need for a land can also arise, however, in the context of socialism. That is, the fulfillment of the socialist program, seen in connection with the question of Judaism and the Jewish people, leads to an understanding of Jewish peoplehood in its full ethnicity and to the need for a land. Thus, within the Zionist trend there was an important expression that derived its stance from considerations emanating from the socialist orientation. But the most interesting illustration of this position may be found perhaps in a thinker who is really a precursor of the Zionist movement. This is Moses Hess. In Hess we find a most intriguing philosophic expression for this stance.

Moses Hess in his *Rome and Jerusalem* clearly grasped the significance of the category of Jewish peoplehood within the context of socialist thought. He had the genius to perceive that the category of peoplehood is the necessary and inescapable matrix for the expression of social relations; and even more penetrating was his insight that the maximal expression of social relations requires the category of peoplehood in the sense of full ethnicity, i.e., the category of peoplehood that implies not only the cultural and spiritual dimensions, but equally the economic and political dimensions. Seeing the Jewish people as being charged by its very vocation to fulfill the socialist ideal, he grasped that the Jewish people had to be taken as a full, all-encompassing ethnic group. And being taken as an ethnic group in the full sense of the term, the Jewish people in order to fulfill its vocation, i.e., to fulfill the socialist ideal, requires sovereignty, i.e., it requires the machinery of a state. And this, in turn, requires that the Jewish people be concentrated in a certain geographic location. The inner logic of his stance should have been satisfied with any particular geographic location, for a geographic location is required solely for the establishment of a state, i.e., for the establishment of sovereignty, so that the ethnic group should be able to express itself in the economic and political dimensions. And any geographic location would lend itself for this purpose. But it is at this point that the romantic side of Hess enters the picture and historical memory and emotional attachment exercise their influence leading Hess to require the restoration of the Jewish people to its ancient homeland in the land of Israel. Thus, he requires specifically the return of the Jewish people to the land of Israel rather than requiring that they establish a state in whatever geographic location is available.

Ethnic Entity in a Restricted Sense

The third formulation, namely, the formulation that views Judaism within a limited ethnic context, i.e., a context which excludes the political dimension, is the most widespread formulation. This is understandable on extraneous grounds. That is, this formulation is the formulation that would be the most congenial to emancipated Jewry in diaspora. For, on the one hand, the formulation does not run head-on against the reality of the Jewish phenomenon in the past, a reality whereby the Jewish people always understood itself and was understood by others as a distinct separate group of an ethnic nature. Nor does it fly in the face of the present reality where the Jewish entity continues to be distinct not only as a religious community bus as an ethnic entity (although in the present many Jews might not want to accept this reality). This formulation, therefore (in contradistinction to the formulation which sees the Jewish people as merely a "church"), precludes the necessity of making the preposterous claim that ethnically the Jewish people are one and the same as the host-nation. This formulation does grasp the distinction as being of an ethnic nature and as such it grasps the distinction authentically, i.e., in accordance with reality. At the same time, however, it does not radicalize this distinction by including the political dimension within the ethnic formulation. Indeed, by leaving out the political dimension it allows an ethnically distinct Jewish people to go on living within a political context which belongs to another ethnic group. Thus, it can serve very conveniently as a rationale for the half-way existence of emancipated diaspora Jewry, an existence which wants to be both separate and distinct from the host-nation and at the same time included within its social, economic, and political life (but whether such a situation as envisioned by this formulation is feasible is, of course, another question.)

But to return to the main line of our discourse, this formulation, as said, finds wide expression in modern Jewish thought. Indeed, this wide expression reflects itself in the fact that this formulation articulates itself both in the religious and in the secular context. Namely, it articulates itself in terms of a Jewish peoplehood which is defined both in a religious and in a secular context.

(a) Jewish Peoplehood as Defined in a Religious Context

In this form the formulation mainly finds its expression in the philosophical-theological literature created by German Jewry in the last two centuries (of course the religious understanding involved here is by no means the same as the rabbinic, halachic understanding, but then we surely would not want to limit the religious understanding of Judaism and Jewish peoplehood in so restrictive a manner that only the rabbinic, halachic understanding would qualify as religious). Jewish peoplehood is grasped here as the carrier of the religious vocation and in this capacity it is grasped as being of limited ethnicity. And it can be so grasped, i.e., grasped as being of limited ethnicity, because the religious vocation of which it is the carrier is, in turn, formulated here in one of two contexts neither of which is understood as implicating the political dimension.

Thus, the first of these contexts is the ethical context (a context which was shaped under the marked influence of Kant's philosophy). The vocation of the religion of Judaism is essentially constituted here by the realization of the ethical. This ethical refers, of course, to the relations between man and man and, as such, it is understandable that Jewish peoplehood be the carrier of a vocation so understood, in as much as it is precisely the category of peoplehood which provides the matrix for the relations between man and man. But it is important to note that the ethical here is essentially confined to the relations between individuals and is not extended to cover the political dimension, i.e., to cover the relations between collectivities of individuals; political ethics is not available here. As such, the category of Jewish peoplehood which is the carrier of this non-political ethical vocation need not be ethnic in the full sense of the term, but can be ethnic in a limited sense (of course, whether with such a vocation of individualized ethics the category of peoplehood rather than a mere association of individuals is, in the last analysis, really required, is a different question). Hermann Cohen and Leo Baeck may serve as good examples of this kind of formulation.

The second context is the metaphysical context. Here, the religious vocation is perceived in terms of the realization of another realm of existence, and the category of Jewish peoplehood is seen as an instrument in the realization of this vocation. A good example may be Franz Rosenzweig. For in Rosenzweig's formulation the religious vocation consists, in the last analysis, in realizing an existence which is outside the flux of time and history—an existence in eternity. The vocation of the Jewish people is to carry the presentiment of such an existence while still existing within the flux of history.

Now, clearly for such a task the category of Jewish peoplehood does not have to be taken as ethnic in the full sense of the term. Indeed, Jewish peoplehood in the full sense of the term would not do. For the political dimension is part and parcel of the flux of time and history. Possessing the political dimension thus means being involved, in a positive and affirmative sense, in the flux of history. And this, in turn, means that being ethnic in the full sense would necessarily imply an affirmation and a furthering of the flux. But the vocation here is precisely to ultimately negate the flux. True, one exists passively for the time being within the flux, but the pointing, the vocation, is to that which negates it. The category of ethnicity which implicates the political dimension must, therefore, be rejected. It is only the category of ethnicity in the limited sense that can be used in such a scheme of things (though here too it is questionable whether even ethnicity in the limited sense is really required in terms of the inner logic of the formulation, whether such a scheme of things is not really, in the last analysis, individualistic, requiring at best an association of individuals, a "church," rather than the category of ethnic peoplehood).

In view of this it should not be surprising that most of the formulations within this trend, both in the ethical context and in the metaphysical context, consciously reject the political dimension in their formulation of Jewish ethnicity. Thus, most of them are strongly opposed to political Zionism. They see in the inclusion of the political dimension a secularization of the vocation of Jewish peoplehood. By including the political dimension, so the logic runs, the Jewish people would become like all the other nations and the purity and uniqueness of its religious vocation would be undermined. Now, while it is true that such a danger exists, it is by no means true, as these formulations nevertheless imply, that such a danger will of necessity be actualized.

Commensurate with this understanding of the category of Jewish peoplehood, the various formulations of the philosophical-theological trend do not express any appreciation for the requirement of the category of land; indeed, they expressly reject it. Most of the representative figures in this trend, people such as Steinheim, Formstecher, Hirsch, Lazarus, Cohen, Rosenzweig, and others reject the category of land. Within their respective representations of the structure of Judaism the category of land is for all intents and purposes not present. And this is in clear contradistinction to the central place given to the category of history. Actually this is quite understandable, seeing that this trend grasps the essence of Judaism as lying either in the ethical (though let us hasten to note in the non-political ethical) or in the metaphysical domain. In either case the category of land would not be significant in such a scheme of things. The domain of ethics does not require space but time. Ethical relations are realized in time and not in space. Thus, if the essential vocation of Judaism is the realization of the ethical, the working towards the bringing about of this realization would require history but not land. And since we are dealing here with non-political ethics, a requirement for statehood is not implied and, therefore, there is also no possibility here of getting a requirement for land through, so to speak, a once-removed process, i.e., through the agency of statehood (for clearly a requirement for statehood would have, in turn, implied a requirement for land). In any event, even political ethics does not imply a requirement for any *specific* land. The domain of the ethical is by its very essence universal and cannot recognize nor appreciate any particularity. And similarly with the metaphysical domain, it too can in no way imply a requirement for land. If anything, just the opposite is the case. For clearly, formulations that articulate themselves in the metaphysical domain will perceive the essential vocation of Judaism in terms of the metaphysical domain and this, in turn, means that for them the essential vocation of Judaism lies in transcending the spacial-temporal flux of this world. Judaism deals with the realm of the beyond but this means that it deals with a realm in which the category of land has no role to play.

(b) Jewish Peoplehood as Defined in a Secular Context

The restricted ethnic formulation can also be found formulated in a non-religious context, i.e., in a secularized context. Here, Jewish peoplehood is seen as the carrier of a national cultural heritage like any other nation. This cultural heritage may, of course, have its special contribution to make, but the existence of the Jewish people, its special contribution, its *raison d'etré* are conceived with no reference to a divine cosmic working of salvation. The religious grounding is removed. It is conceived purely in horizontal terms with no vertical reference. Now, this formulation can be encountered in the context of socialism. Here, the vocation of the Jewish people and the significance of its heritage are seen to lie in the bringing about of secularized social justice. The Jewish people becomes the instrument in the realization of secularized socialism.

But the Jewish people is taken here (and this in contradistinction to the instance above exemplified by Hess) in a restricted ethnic sense which means that it does not possess its own political dimension. Rather, it contributes its ideals of social justice to the political dimension of the host-nation. It participates in the political dimension of the host-nation. As such, it is a view of Jewish peoplehood in a socialist context which affirms diaspora existence. We find it expressed, for example, in the Bundist formulation. Thus, within the context of socialism we get not only a formulation that grasps Jewish peoplehood in its full ethnicity, and that correspondingly requires the category of land, but also a formulation that grasps Jewish peoplehood in a limited ethnic sense and which correspondingly denies the category of land.

Another secularized formulation within this context of restricted ethnicity is known by the name of Autonomism and is associated with the name of the famous Jewish historian Dubnow. It has links with the socialist context though it is not essentially formulated within this context. Rather, it can be seen as an outgrowth of Smolensky's formulation given above. What we have here is a reduction of the extremely spiritualized conception of Judaism encountered in the early Smolensky. The extreme abstractness of Judaism is concretized. The religious is secularized. While in Smolensky Judaism is essentially but a system of abstract tenets and teaching, Judaism here is a system of concrete cultural patterns and values; it is much less of an other-worldly entity. Indeed, it is very much within the horizontal, this-worldly context.

As such, it is not possible for this formulation to take the position that Smolensky takes regarding the possibility, and indeed the desirability, of the complete assimilation of the Jew in his host-nation. Smolensky could take this position inasmuch as for him Judaism was completely spiritualized and otherworldly and consequently could not constitute an obstacle to an assimilation that is completely within a this-worldly context; nor was there any objection to such an assimilation since it could not impinge upon, i.e., weaken, the allegiance to Judaism. But in the Autonomist formulation, Judaism being grasped here in a this-worldly context, such an assimilation would not only be deterred by the interests of Judaism but would also impinge in a detrimental way upon these interests. Consequently, the Autonomist formulation envisions Jewish existence in diaspora in the form of ethnic islands with internal autonomy lodged within the host-nations. Not grasping the category of Jewish peoplehood in its full ethnicity, i.e., as including the political dimension, it does not require a specific national homeland and the full sovereignty of the state for the Jewish nation. Instead, it affirms diaspora-existence. But to protest the cultural distinctiveness of the Jewish people it wants to introduce not a political, territorial division but a cultural, spiritual division. The result of this is that it proposes an internal cultural autonomy for the Jewish people which, however, is to be exercised on the land, and within the political framework, of other nations.

It is also to this context of viewing Jewish peoplehood as a restricted ethnic entity that the formulation of a most important and influential thinker, namely, the formulation of Ahad Ha-Am, belongs. For to Ahad Ha-Am Judaism is a cultural rather than a political entity. It is a system of values and patterns of living, essentially a system of ethical values and teachings. As such, the entity that is its human carrier, i.e., the category of Jewish peoplehood, is commensurately perceived as an ethnic group that is ethnic in the limited sense of being cultural. Perceiving the category of Jewish peoplehood in this restricted ethnic sense, Ahad Ha-Am can and indeed does affirm, in the last analysis, diaspora existence. Granted, such an existence is problematic in our time, given the circumstances of emancipation affecting the Jewish people. The problem for Ahad Ha-Am, however, is not the possibility of the survival of the Jews *qua* human beings, but rather the possibility of the survival of Judaism under these circumstances. And in this connection it is important to note that his diagnosis and solution do not negate the possibility and desirability of the ongoing existence of the Jewish people and of Judaism in diaspora. Indeed, diaspora-existence is for him an inescapable fact of Jewish reality. For the possibility of redeeming the entirety or even the majority of the Jewish people from diaspora existence and constituting them in their own homeland does not seem realistic to him. If the Jewish people, therefore, and thus Judaism, are to survive, a solution for their ongoing, continued existence in diaspora must be found. Thus, in the last analysis Ahad Ha-Am too remains an affirmer of diaspora-existence. He differs, however, from the formulation of Autonomism in that he does not believe that under the circumstances envisioned by the formulation of Autonomism Judaism could have enough strength and vitality to withstand the influence of the foreign culture of the host-nations and thus succeed in preserving the Jewish people in their distinctiveness. His formulation calls, therefore, for a concentration of part of the Jewish people in their own homeland where they would constitute a majority and where, therefore, danger of foreign influence would be greatly reduced. In such a homeland the strength and vitality of Judaism can be revived and then "exported," so to speak, to the bulk of the Jewish people living in diaspora, thus strengthening their Judaism and insuring their survival and even prosperity in the circumstances of diaspora existence.

The geographic location for constituting such a center, such a national home, for a part of the Jewish people is for Ahad Ha-Am the land of Israel. In this sense he is a Zionist. Now, there is no denying that the inner logic of his formulation does, indeed, require a specific geographic location, a land, for the survival of Judaism and the Jewish people in the circumstances of the Emancipation. For Judaism and the Jewish people to survive in these circumstances, part of the people must be concentrated as a majority in a national home. And such a concentration in a national home requires a specific geographic location. But why specifically the land of Israel as the geographic location? Why should one geographic location have any advantage over another? After all, is it not the case that in terms of the inner logic of Ahad Ha-Am's formulation what is essential is that the Jewish people constitute a majority in a certain geographic location rather than which geographic location it is to be? It would see, therefore, that choosing specifically the land of Israel is determined here not by the inner logic of the formulation but rather by extraneous considerations such as historical memory and emotional attachment. In terms of the inner logic of the formulation, the concentration of a part of the Jewish people as a majority in some place like Argentina, Africa or any place else in the world should be as satisfactory and efficacious as its concentration in the land of Israel.

The Mystical Trend

So far we did not include the mystical trend. The reason is that the mystical trend is really separate from the other trends. All the other trends are formulations of Judaism in a mainly this-worldly context. They are essentially horizontally oriented (the one exception is the metaphysical formulation in the philosophical-theological trend, e.g., Rosenzweig, which indeed is in many respects similar to the mystical trend). Not so the mystical trend; it is otherworldly and vertically oriented. As such, we thought that it might be more convenient to consider it by itself. This we propose to do covering both the mystical trend's religious and non-religious orientation, the former being expressed most prominently by Rav Kook while the latter finds a most impressive expression in A. D. Gordon.

It is most interesting, however, for us to note that, notwithstanding the various differences between them, both orientations, the religious and non-religious, affirm the category of Jewish peoplehood and the category of land, specifically, the land of Israel. Even more interesting is the further observation that this affirmation follows from the inner logic operating in these orientations. It is interesting because one would not have expected it, seeing that within the mystical formulation there is really no room for the particularity of peoplehood or of land. Rather, one expects the mystical formulation to operate in terms of the individual (and thus in the context of the universalism which this implies). For after all, the very essence of mysticism lies in its striving to overcome the flux of this world and to transcend all division and separation into an all-encompassing unity. And these are clearly acts which implicate the individual and not the collectivity, certainly not ethnic collectivity. Yet we have mystical formulations both in the religious and non-religious orientation which do precisely this, namely, implicate the category of Jewish peoplehood and that of the land of Israel (thus implicating collectivity and particularism). But how is this possible? What is the possible rationale that these formulations resort to?

(a) The Implication of Peoplehood and Land in the Religious Orientation

There is one possibility where the ethnic entity may be required by the inner logic of the mystical formulation. This is when the mechanism of bringing about the mystical salvation, i.e., the union with the One, devolves on some special powers or attributes which are determined genetically and which as such inhere in the redemptive agent. That is, some people may be endowed with special "mystical talent" while other people are not (on the analogy of some people being endowed with musical talent or with certain physical characteristics). On this basis a case can be made that the mystical vocation may devolve on a certain people by virtue of blood kinship, i.e., by virtue of the genetic common pool which characterizes the ethnic entity. This, of course, introduces the biological-racial dimension into the category of ethnicity, thus transforming the nature of the category from its original constitution within mainstream Judaism where it is constituted as a historical and not as a racial category. Still, such a transformation is possible and we do encounter it in the tradition, as, for example, in Yehuda Halevi, Maharal and perhaps Rav Kook. In this connection it is interesting to note that in Rav Kook's thought the status of Jewish peoplehood is determined not solely or even mainly by election *(behira)* but by an inherent special quality *(segula)*. The Jewish people are endowed with a quality whereby the yearning for God and thus the power of transforming the profane into the sacred is more clearly expressed.

Thus, the Jewish people by virtue of an innate quality is the redemptive agent in a universal, cosmic redemption. And since the redemption is envisaged here not as the separation of the holy from the profane, but rather as the transformation of the profane in its entirely into the holy, thus inclusive of the profane political dimension, the category of Jewish peoplehood is grasped here in its full ethnicity (we thus have here an instance of a full political Zionist stance derived from a rabbinic, albeit mystical, orientation.)

Likewise with the category of the land, because the redemptive agency is determined by an innate quality *(segula)*, the rationale is provided for particularly. The category of land in general is introduced because redemption includes the domain of nature. Redemption is not merely an event on the human social level, it is an event on the cosmic level. And the specific portion of land that is the land of Israel is endowed with special redemptive power, or rather, the redemptive power flows through it in a concentrated form, thus making it a redemptive agent in contradistinction to other lands.

(b) The Implication of Peoplehood and Land in the Non-Religious Orientation

In A.D. Gordon the category of the land plays a central role, seeing that it is the shaper of nationhood (in contradistinction to society), and that nationhood, in turn, is the agency that mediates between man and nature, between man's soul and the cosmic soul. The spirit of a nation, however, is created through contact with the cosmic spirit in a specific place, and the spirit of a nation, in turn, determines the spirit of the individual by virtue of his membership within the nation. Indeed, the link between a nation and its land is permanent and essential. Thus, not only is the category of land and the category of peoplehood essential and inextricable in this scheme of things, but also the particularization of land and people is provided for. For the individual Jew, redemption, in the sense of establishing full communion with the cosmic spirit, necessitates the Jewish people which, in turn, necessitates the land of Israel.

One could not ask for a tighter inner logic establishing the category of peoplehood and the category of land than is given in the thought of Rav Kook and Gordon. But it is established on certain premises which are taken as facts, as given data, and for which no rationale is provided. Thus for Rav Kook the particularity of Jewish peoplehood and of the land of Israel is established on the fact that a special *segula* is inherent in them. For Gordon it is established on the one-to-one relationship between land and nation, and the role of the nation as mediator of the cosmic spirit to the individual. If a critique is to be lodged against these formulations, then it must be lodged at this point, i.e., questioning the validity of these premises. And these premises can be questioned seriously, both as to whether they are really required by their respective scheme of things and whether they authentically reflect the distinctive phenomenon of Judaism.

Overview and Conclusions
The Inner Logic of the Various Formulations

Let us briefly recapitulate the picture that emerges from our short and selective description of the various formulations in modern Jewish thought regarding the categories of peoplehood and land. We have seen that all formulations affirmed the category of peoplehood. The preponderance of formulations, however, understood the category of peoplehood in terms of limited ethnicity, i.e., ethnicity exclusively in terms of ethos and culture; only some formulations understood the category of peoplehood in terms of full ethnicity, i.e., ethnicity that encompasses the social, economic and political dimensions. With regard to the category of land the consensus is not so clear. There were some formulations (and they are significant formulations that cannot be dismissed out of hand as idiosyncratic) that did not affirm the category of land. Still, the preponderance of formulations did affirm the category of land. However, with regard to the affirmation of the specific geographic location that is known as the land of Israel there was no unanimity. Many formulations did indeed affirm the specific geographic location that was the land of Israel. But there were also formulations for which the specific geographic location where the category of land was to be affirmed was of no consequence; any geographic location would do.

A much more intriguing but difficult task was to ascertain the consistency of the particular affirmations of peoplehood and land with the inner logic of the respective formulations. Still, we believe that we have shown that the category of peoplehood is not only necessary in terms of the inner logic of the various formulations but that it is established as a primary category; the only exception was the case of the formulations in the mystical context where some question could be raised as to the legitimacy and necessity of affirming the category of peoplehood (at least as a historical category rather than a biological-racial category). With regard to the affirmation of the category of land the situation was much more complicated and difficult. Our conclusion was, nevertheless, that when the category of land is affirmed, it can be affirmed in terms of the inner logic only as a secondary category, i.e., a category whose affirmation is required by virtue of the needs of the category of peoplehood, the primary category, and not on its own terms. Furthermore, the affirmation of the category of land led in terms of the inner logic only as far as requiring some geographic location but not the specific geographic location that is known as the land of Israel (the need for the affirmation of the land of Israel came from historical, emotional and pragmatic considerations but not from considerations of the pure inner logic of the formulations concerned). Here again, however, formulations in the mystical context presented an exception. In terms of their inner logic the category of land and specifically the land of Israel was required, and indeed required as a primary category. For these formulations it is a holy land not just in name but in reality, not derivatively but directly.

Thus, if the formulations in the mystical context are left out, we can say that the inner logic operative in the remaining formulations clearly places the category of peoplehood as a primary, essential and necessary category within the structure of the phenomenon of Judaism; that, on the other hand, it allows the entry of the category of land within this structure only as a secondary, derivative category; and that, strictly in terms of the requirements of the inner logic as such (thus excluding such considerations as historical association, emotional attachment, and pragmatic feasibility, considerations which are very significant and not to be dismissed lightly but which, nonetheless, are extraneous as far as the inner logic as such is concerned), there can be no specification of the category of land, namely, preference cannot be given to any one particular geographic location, e.g., the land of Israel, over another.

Now, we would want to maintain that this inner logic in its delineation of the status of the categories of peoplehood and land authentically reflects the inner logic that characterizes the distinctive religious structure that constitutes the mainstream expression of the phenomenon of Judaism. Of course, as an historical phenomenon Judaism is not monolithic; it encompasses a number of different expressions implicating different structures of faith and consequently different kinds of inner logic. Still, we would want to maintain that among these various structures there is a structure which establishes, in contradistinction to the rest, the distinctiveness of Judaism within the general phenomenology of religion, that can explain its history and characteristics most adequately, that indeed, historically speaking, found widespread expression within Judaism and that, therefore, can be seen as constituting the mainstream expression of the phenomenon of Judaism. At any event, the crux of the point made here is that the inner logic of this structure delineates the same status respectively for the category of peoplehood and for the category of land that we have encountered in the non-mystical formulations of modern Jewish thought. Namely, in the structure of faith characterizing the distinctive, mainstream expression of Judaism the category of peoplehood is a primary category—essential and inextricable as far as the very existence of the phenomenon is concerned; on the other hand, the category of land can enter the structure only as a secondary, derivative category—a category which certainly carries significance for the optimal, full realization of the phenomenon but which, nevertheless, is not essential and inextricable for its very existence (indeed, the fact that Judaism could survive in diaspora is clear proof for this assertion).

(a) Primacy of Peoplehood but not of Land

It is evidently not feasible for us to fully argue and demonstrate this claim here. But if it be granted that the substance of the redemptive vocation as constituted in the distinctive, mainstream expression of Judaism is the establishment in a this-worldly context of the righteous community, then we can attempt to trace quickly the workings of the inner logic operative here as it impinges upon the categories of peoplehood and land, showing that it delineates them in the way suggested above. Thus, with regard to the category of peoplehood, it can indeed be shown that it is of necessity delineated here as a primary category that is essential and irremovable. For quite clearly vis-à-vis a redemptive vocation that is constituted in terms of the establishment of the righteous community, the category which can function both as the principal agent in the working towards its realization and as the sole matrix in which such realization can take place must be the category of peoplehood. The righteous community cannot be established except in the context of the category of peoplehood, and likewise the striving towards its realization can be carried out only in those terms. The establishment of the righteous community cannot be carried out in terms of the individual *qua* individual, nor in terms of a collectivity that is but an association, a sum total, of individuals with a common denominator; it necessarily requires a collectivity that ontologically, if not chronologically, precedes the individual. Namely, it requires the ethnic-national collectivity, the collectivity that in its very constitution provides the social, economic and political dimensions, the dimensions in whose terms only the righteous community can be established; in short, it necessarily requires the category of peoplehood.

But as such, the category of peoplehood is a category of history and not of nature, and its workings towards redemption, as indeed the consummation of such redemption, is in the dimension of time and not of space. The category of land, on the other hand, is a category of space, of nature. As such, it is understandable that the category of land, unlike the category of peoplehood, would not be implicated by the inner logic that is operative here, i.e., an inner logic that flows from the requirements of a redemptive vocation whose substance is the establishment of the righteous community. For the workings of the inner logic here, as traced so far, are exclusively in the temporal-historical dimension, while the category of land subsists in the spacio-natural dimension. Thus, the redemptive vocation implicates directly the category of peoplehood but not the category of land.

The category of land enters the structure of faith of Judaism secondarily and derivatively, through the category of peoplehood implicating it. That is, the category of peoplehood in order to be able to strive for the realization of the redemptive vocation and, indeed, to consummate this striving in a fulfilled realization of the redemptive vocation, needs sovereignty—it needs power to regulate its life both internally and externally. Without the possession of sovereignty, the freedom to decide and direct the life of the community, the category of peoplehood cannot possibly carry out the redemptive task assigned to it. But sovereignty, in turn, implicates the category of land. For sovereignty can be attained only by a people that possesses a land. The possession of a land is the condition *sine qua non* for the exercise of sovereignty (although in itself it may not be a sufficient condition, it is certainly a necessary one). Thus, the thrust of the inner logic operative here is as follows: the redemptive vocation being the establishment of the righteous community, it of necessity requires sovereignty; and sovereignty, in turn, of necessity implicates the category of land.

(b) Land Secondary but Essential

Now, we must be clear and precise as to what this presentation actually says with regard to the categories of peoplehood and land. First, although the category of land is secondary and derived (and will always be so in the distinctive structure of faith of Judaism), it should be clear that as far as the redemptive vocation, i.e., the specific task of realizing redemption, is concerned the category of land is no less essential than the category of peoplehood. Without a land to allow the exercise of sovereignty, the fulfillment (and even the very workings) of the redemptive vocation is simply not possible. Where the category of land, in contradistinction to the category of peoplehood, is not essential is with regard to the question of the capacity of the religious phenomenon of Judaism to maintain itself, i.e., to go on enduring in existence. While without the category of peoplehood the phenomenon of Judaism collapses and cannot possibly go on existing, without the category of land it can persevere and go on existing though albeit in a limping and crippled fashion. Thus, the phenomenon of Judaism did endure and survive diaspora-existence. True, it was (and indeed was perceived as such by Judaism itself) a truncated form of existence. In diaspora-existence Judaism could only mark time; it could only, so to speak, hold the fort but it could not actively pursue its redemptive vocation. For the resumption of the active pursuit of its redemptive vocation it had to await and hope for its restoration to the land.

Special Circumstances of the Modern World

We must add, however, that the situation has radically changed in modern times and that the assertions made above must, therefore, be qualified accordingly if they are to apply to Judaism in the modern world. Because of radical changes in the social structure of the host-nations and the rise of nationalism in its modern form which, in turn, lead to a radical change in the conditions of existence of Judaism in diaspora, i.e., leading to a transformation from ghetto-existence to what is commonly called Emancipation, the very possibility of the survival of Judaism in diaspora-existence is thrown into question. Evidently, we cannot analyze and expound in detail on this thesis here (we have done it, in a way, in our essay "The Dilemma of Identity for the Emancipated Jew," which appears in this volume as chapter six). We shall instead state dogmatically that in the conditions of existence afforded by the modern world, the phenomenon of Judaism, if it is to survive, must extricate itself from diaspora-existence. This means that it must regain its sovereignty, and since sovereignty is afforded only by the possession of land this means that Judaism must regain a land of its own. Thus, in the conditions of existence of the modern world or, to put the matter differently , vis-à-vis emancipated Judaism, the category of land is needed not only for the resumption of the active pursuit and the ultimate realization of the redemptive vocation but for the very existence of the phenomenon of Judaism. And of course the question of existence takes precedence over the question of pursuing the redemptive vocation, and therefore it is understandable that in the formulations we have surveyed, formulations dealing with and expressing the situation of Judaism in the modern world, the category of land is considered primarily with regard to the question of existence and not the redemptive vocation (though, of course, by regaining the land for the sake of existence the possibility to resume and ultimately realize the redemptive vocation is also given). Emancipated Judaism cannot survive in diaspora; for it the category of land is on an equal footing with the category of peoplehood—it is essential for the very existence of the phenomenon. But even so, even with regard to Judaism in the modern world, the category of land is not essential in the same sense as the category of peoplehood. For at least theoretically (though realistically it is very unlikely) Judaism can retreat from Emancipation and in this eventuality the impossibility of survival in diaspora-existence is not so definite. This, in turn, means that the need for the category of land for the sake of survival is once again removed. The category of peoplehood, on the other hand, is not affected by such contingent circumstances. The need for it for the very existence of the phenomenon is permanent, determined by the very structure of the phenomenon itself and independent of all conditions of existence; the need for it will persist in all conceivable situations.

(a) Requirement of the Category of Land in General
It should be clear, however, that when the inner logic operative here requires the category of land, it requires the category of land in general. It does not require any specific land to the exclusion of others. Any geographic location would satisfy the requirements of the inner logic here. This applies equally to the requirement of land for the sake of pursuing and realizing the redemptive vocation and to the requirement of land in modern times for the sake of the survival of emancipated Judaism. For the need for a land arises in both instances from the need for sovereignty. And sovereignty can be provided by the possession of any land; it is common to all lands. Affording sovereignty is not an attribute possessed by certain lands to the exclusion of others. Of course, again, this is purely on the theoretical level; in reality there are other considerations which bear heavily and significantly on this question and which do indeed particularize and focus on a specific geographic location, i.e., the specific land of Israel, to the exclusion of all other geographic locations.

(b) Peoplehood in the Full Sense of Ethnicity
Lastly, it should be also clear that the category of peoplehood indicated by the inner logic operative here is of a peoplehood in the sense of full ethnicity. Clearly, since the redemptive vocation is the establishment of the righteous community, the category of peoplehood that is required is the category of peoplehood that carries the social, economic and political dimensions. The category of peoplehood in the sense of restricted ethnicity would not be capable of providing the matrix for the realization of the redemptive vocation nor, indeed, for the striving for its realization. Of course, in diaspora-existence, since the social, economic, and political dimensions were not available anyway (indeed, the absence of these dimensions constitutes in essence diaspora-existence and characterizes it as a truncated existence), the formulation of the category of peoplehood in the sense of restricted ethnicity would readily suggest itself—it corresponds to, and indeed reflects, the reality of the category of peoplehood existing in these circumstances, i.e., in the conditions of diaspora-existence. Most of the formulations we have surveyed did indeed arise in the circumstances of diaspora-

existence so that it is understandable that the formulation of the category of peoplehood in the sense of restricted ethnicity was so wide-spread. Also, formulating the category of peoplehood in the sense of restricted ethnicity would remove, or at least mitigate, some issues on which a potential head-on collision between the claims of the host-nation and the claims of Jewish peoplehood in the sense of full ethnicity could potentially arise; as such, formulating the category of peoplehood in the sense of restricted ethnicity would be more congenial to emancipated Judaism in diaspora-existence, and it is to be expected that formulations arising in the circumstances of diaspora-existence would be disposed, even if unconsciously, towards it. Still, in terms of the phenomenon of Judaism itself, and irrespective of the contingent considerations arising from circumstances of diaspora-existence, the category of peoplehood that is required is the category of peoplehood in the sense of full ethnicity. Only as such can the category of peoplehood fulfill its task in the redemptive vocation and be the primary category that is essential and irremovable. The category of peoplehood in the sense of restricted ethnicity could maintain this status only in diaspora-existence when the active pursuance of the redemptive vocation of Judaism was suspended anyway (it thus maintains this status, in a way, by default due to diaspora-existence). It can maintain this status because the function of Judaism in diaspora-existence was, as we said, merely to mark time and hold the fort. This task the category of peoplehood in the sense of restricted ethnicity could fulfill—it could keep the ethnic identify (i.e., thus holding the fort) and it could endure through the flux of time (thus marking time). But in modern times, with respect to emancipated Judaism and with the need to be extricated from diaspora-existence and regain sovereignty, the need for full ethnicity is clearly reasserted, for sovereignty implicates full ethnicity. Only for the Judaism that retreats from Emancipation is restricted ethnicity still viable.

Concluding Evaluation

In view of this tracing of the inner logic and the structure of what constitutes the distinctive, mainstream expression of the religious phenomenon that is Judaism how are we to evaluate the formulations of modern Judaism surveyed above? Interestingly enough, the formulations belonging to the political-Zionist trend reflect most authentically this distinctive religious phenomenon of Judaism in its present emancipated situation in the modern world. In a way it is ironic, because these formulations professed all too often to be secular and not religious (and indeed were taken as such). But apparently their non-religious stance is in truth only a stance against the rabbinic expression of Judaism, i.e., a stance against the authentic, viable expression of Judaism when it found itself in the circumstances of diaspora-existence. Taking rabbinic Judaism as the criterion of religiousness, they may well appear secular; but vis-à-vis emancipated Judaism finding itself in the circumstances of the modern world they are, in a profound sense, authentic religious expressions of Judaism. Their great advantage is that they perceive the category of peoplehood in the sense of full ethnicity. On the other hand, the many formulations which perceived the category of peoplehood in the sense of restricted ethnicity, though in many ways reflecting authentically the distinctive religious phenomenon of Judaism, fall short of doing justice to the needs of emancipated Judaism in the modern world. They are still expressing the Judaism of diaspora-existence. In a way, they represent an inner, deep-seated contradiction—wanting to express emancipated Judaism while at the same time affirming diaspora-existence. Coupling emancipated Judaism with diaspora-existence is not really possible. Yet in expressing this impossible contradiction these formulations reflect authentically the state of mind and desire of emancipated Jewry. While falling short of reflecting authentically emancipated Judaism they nonetheless reflect authentically emancipated Jewry. Lastly, as regards the formulations in the mystical trend, they evidently express a Judaism that has a different religious structure and consequently a different inner logic than the religious structure and inner logic that we presented above as constituting what we claimed to be the distinctive religious phenomenon of Judaism. We are here, so to speak, in a different ball-park altogether. The two structures differ in their very foundations, i.e., what they conceive to be the ultimate predicament of man and, commensurate with this, the redemptive vocation for man. Naturally, the inner logic that would operate in the mystical trend would lead to a different understanding of the status of the category of peoplehood and the category of land in the phenomenon of Judaism. The crucial question here, of course, is which trend expresses the phenomenon of Judaism more authentically. We would want to claim that intriguing and attractive as the mystical trend is, it nonetheless does not reflect the phenomenon of Judaism in its distinctiveness; and although there is no denying (not after Scholem's work) that the mystical trend found widespread expression within Jewry, it was not the mainstream expression. But the case that must be made to support this contention must be left to another occasion.

Endnotes

[1] We did not include, in a separate heading, the non-mystical, halachic-rabbinic literature because essentially it reflects in its substance the pre-modern, traditional understanding of mainstream Judaism. The halachic-rabbinic literature of the modern period is a continued expression of rabbinic diaspora Judaism, not of the emancipated Judaism of the modern world. The interesting aspect of halachic-rabbinic Judaism in the modern era revolves around the question of how to relate to the Zionist program. But this is a question of strategy and policy, not of substance. To jump ahead of our story, it can be said that the halachic-rabbinic trend clearly affirmed the centrality of the category of peoplehood and of the category of the land, indeed specifically of the land of Israel. The question before this trend was whether Jewry should take action (and in this case, what action should be taken) to secure the return of Jewry to its homeland, or whether such action must be left in the hands of God so that Jewry must remain passive in its diaspora-existence awaiting patiently

for the time when God will act. Both sides to this question found expression within the halachic-rabbinic trend. Clearly, the latter view affirmed diaspora-existence and indeed it is the most viable expression among all other formulations affirming diaspora-existence in as much as it also, in essence, resisted the process of Emancipation (S. R. Hirsch may be an exception but his advocacy of emancipation coupled with loyalty to halachic-rabbinic Judaism is, in our judgment, not viable; the emancipation recommended was surface-Emancipation, thus not at all reflecting the process of Emancipation that was actually taking place). The former view which negated diaspora-existence was riddled with hedging and ambiguity regarding the Zionist program. This in a way is understandable, for it meant the readjustment of a religious stance, i.e., the halachic-rabbinic stance, that was geared to diaspora-existence, to existence outside profane history, to a program, i.e., the Zionist program, that negated diaspora-existence and involved the reentry of Jewry and Judaism into profane history—a readjustment that is, to say the least, very problematic.

Chapter 10
Exile and Redemption

Eliezer Berkovits

From the issues of enlandisement, Peoplehood and Land, we turn to the historical counterparts: exile and redemption. For the election of Israel makes sense only in the context of the ultimate redemption of Israel by the Messiah, its return from exile (however exile be interpreted) to the holy and promised land. No conceptions emerged from the Holocaust so profoundly affected as those—not the conception of God or of Israel—and none has enjoyed so much attention. The Hebrew words, galut, exile and ge'ulah, redemption, contain the entire theological doctrine that, for Judaists in the State of Israel and many overseas as well, explain the religious significance of the State of Israel. For them, it is not only a political entity, an expedient and instrumental agency for providing a homeland for the Jews who wanted and needed a state of their own. It is a fore-taste of redemption, the beginning of the advent of salvation. Berkovits's contribution is to provide the secular categories, exile and return, with religious consequence, so that exile takes on theological weight, and return, the meaning of redemption. Here once more we see how the classical theological categories have found renewal in the aftermath of the Holocaust, the intensity and the vitality of Berkovits's essay showing how the catastrophe infuses all thought with new, and nuanced, perspective.

***

1

If we divert our attention from the spiritual and religious problems of the day and try to focus on the external political situation of the Jewish people, what do we behold?

Once again, and even more dramatically, the moral and spiritual exhaustion of the human race leaps into view. The most glaring manifestation of the international collapse of values today is to be found in the United Nations. The U.N. has become a shameless organization of international hypocrisy, and thus the dangerous derider of truth, justice, and human decency. It has become the source from which the poison of international demoralization seeps into the councils of governments, paralyzing them, and rendering them impotent to deal effectively with the all-encompassing problems that threaten the very survival of man on this globe. Nothing could be more natural than that this spiritual debacle of the human race should be reflected in the

---

*From *Crisis and Faith*, by Eliezer Berkovits. Copyright 1976 by Eliezer Berkovits. Reprinted by permission of Sanhedrin Press, a division of Hebrew Publishing Company.

situation of the Jewish people. As in the past, so today, the plight of Israel, of the Jewish people, is the moral barometer of mankind. This is a heavy burden to bear, but we have every reason to be proud of it.

With the Hitler era, something entirely new entered Jewish and world history. Whereas during the specifically Christian era of Jewish persecution the genocidal criminality was normally limited to localized communities, from the beginning of Western civilization's Nazi phase the threat to Jewish survival became total. The crisis is all-comprehensive. The survival of the Jewish people in its entirety is at stake. This is what we sensed anew in the trying weeks that preceded the Six-Day War in 1967. We realized what the State of Israel meant for all of us. We could not have survived another holocaust. With the Yom Kippur War, we awoke to the same realization that total crisis was upon us. The truth is that, ever since the days of the European holocaust, the Jewish people the world over has been confronted with the ultimate question of Jewish existence. In the days of my rabbinate with the Jewish Community in Berlin under the Nazis, I would occasionally preach on the concept of *Am Olam*, the Eternal People, and would define it as the colossus of time in confrontation with the colossi of space. However, now that everything seems to be in the balance, can we still speak of ourselves as the *Am Olam*, with the same kind of self-assured faith and faithfulness? Already there are authors who write about the last Jew and the end of the Jewish people. Of course, one could have done the same—and perhaps with even greater justification—in the year 69–70 C.E., when we had as yet not withstood two millennia of exile. Yet we are still around, and have had—in spite of everything arrayed against us—an incomparable impact on the entire course of world history. But since this is another phase of the total crisis, we had better look to our faith, attempting to understand it anew in the light of these darkened horizons.

2

Since the earliest days, two concepts were essential to our self-understanding. They have accompanied us throughout our long history and we have lived with them through the ages. Precisely because of that, we have taken them so much for granted, so that by now we are hardly able to appreciate their mysterious—perhaps supernatural—quality. The two concepts are *Galut* and *Ge'ulah*, Exile and Redemption.

The idea of *Ge'ulah* is, of course, identical with the idea of Messianism, the faith that, no matter how long the Exile may last, one day the Jewish people will return to Zion and Jerusalem and find redemption in their ancient homeland. Such faith is not easy to explain. How was it possible for an entire people to hold on to this kind of an irrational faith during all the generations of their manifold exiles? The entire course of world history contradicted that faith. In the light of world-historic realities, in the midst of the bitter *Galut* experiences, the faith was an absurdity. But no less unique and inexplicable than the faith in Redemption "at the end of times" has been the exile history of the Jewish people. In the course of human history numerous nations were uprooted and exiled from their homeland. But as the result of such categories, they disintegrated and ultimately disappeared from the face of the earth. The only exception is Israel. True, faith in *Ge'ulah* gave us the strength to endure in *Galut*. However, as we have indicated, that faith itself requires explanation. It will not do to explain a puzzle with an enigma.

Perhaps even more surprising than the faith and the history is the nature of the mourning in our exiles, the emotional intensity with which the Jewish people, year in, year out, through the many centuries, wept for the loss of Zion and Jerusalem. On *Pesaḥ*, reciting the *Haggadah*, we speak that declaration of identity between the generations: "In every generation, a Jew is obliged to see himself as if he, in his own person, had been redeemed from Egypt." In the course of time, the sentence has received many penetrating interpretations. Yet I doubt that there have been, at any one time, too many Jews who succeeded in looking upon themselves as if, indeed, they themselves had been participating in the Exodus. But, as I recall the intensity of the mourning, the weeping, wailing and lamenting all through the ages up to our own age, it becomes obvious that in every generation Jews in their multitudes have conducted themselves as if they themselves had lost Zion and Jerusalem and were personally exiled from the holy land; as if they had witnessed the *Ḥurban*, the destruction, with their own eyes, as if it had happened to them directly. Possibly this wholly personalized *Avelut* (mourning) asks even more for an explanation than the faith in Redemption itself.

Consider the Jewish stance in history. On the one hand, there is *Avelut*, mourning of a kind that made manifest complete identification with the past. In every generation, we saw ourselves as if we ourselves had been exiled from Zion and Jerusalem. On the other hand, by the unwavering faith in *Ge'ulah*, we have always identified ourselves with the future. We were so sure that one day the Redeemer would come that at times we felt as if something of the promise had indeed been fulfilled. After the mourning period of the *Drei Wochen* (Three Weeks) and *Tisha B'Av* (the Ninth of Av), there follows *Shabbat Naḥamu*, the Sabbath of Consolation, which we have observed in every kind of exile as if indeed we had been comforted. The celebration of the *Seder* and the observance of the festival of *Pesaḥ*, *Zeman Herutenu*, (ibid.) the Season of our Freedom, often in the midst of the most abject oppression, has given the Jew a very real sense of personal redemption. Or again, in the joyous liberation from the burdens of the past year as the holy day of *Yom Kippur* comes to its climactic close, the Jew is granted, in anticipation, a measure of the bliss of the fulfillment of the times. The weekly *Shabbat*, too, has granted rest and peace *Me'en Olam Haba*, as if from the world to come. On the one hand, complete identification with the past, the origin of our Exile; on the other, complete identification with the future through anticipatory faith in Redemption. On the one side, mourning; on the other, consolation. Past and future, exile and redemption, embracing each other in every present moment. In all the exiles, the Jew has lived in the past and the future more than in the present; they were more important than the present. We have drawn the past from behind and the future from before us and sunk them into the contemporary moment in which we found ourselves in each generation. Thus, living with the past in memory and with the future in faith, we have saved the present from the domination of time. In every generation we have succeeded in establishing the present moment as a point in eternity. Without it we could not have remained on the stage of history.

3

Still, how was it possible for us to accomplish this? It may very well be that the secret of our eternity is hinted at in the nature of our national mourning, to which we have already referred. It is a matter of general experience, and the rabbis expressed it by saying that it has been decreed that as time passes the dead be forgotten. As times passes pain and sorrow subside, the wound heals. One is able to forget. Yet we have never been able to forget the death of the second Jewish commonwealth. On the contrary, ever since the *Ḥurban* we have been declaring: "If I forget thee, O Jerusalem." What kind of loss has this been that could never be forgotten?

One of the most tragic experiences in the life of one of the fathers of the Jewish people may perhaps provide the explanation. Our father Jacob mourned for his son Joseph all through the years. He believed his son was dead. Why could he not forget? The explanation the tradition gives is: it is a law of life that as the years pass the dead are gradually forgotten. Joseph, however, was not dead. Jacob's endless mourning contained within itself a glimmer of hope. Similarly, in the case of the national mourning of the Jewish people. The fact that through the centuries the Jewish people have not been able to act naturally and forget meant that, somehow, the mourning carried within itself the intimation that in spite of the *Ḥurban* there was no death. This kind of mourning that time could not soothe contained the seed of a hope, of the tiding of new life, of the coming redemption. Only an eternal people can hold on to its past with such intensity and save it from sinking away into unredeemed oblivion. Something of the very reality of *Ge'ulah* has been present in the *Galut*. The heart of the nation always knew throughout history, with some mysterious awareness that could never be doubted, of life eternal. There has never been an exile in which a measure of the redeeming force and vitality of the promised future has not been present. In all of his exiles, the Jew strove, built, and created. This redeeming vitality, present in all exiles, has been the source of our mysterious faith in ultimate redemption. In actual fact, an advanced share of *Ge'ulah* has forever accompanied the *Galut*.

4

Normally, we think of *Galut* as a phenomenon of Jewish history. It is, however, vital that we understand what *Galut* has meant in the foundation and formation of Judaism. *Galut* did not start with the destruction of Jerusalem and the dispersion of the Jewish people to the four corners of the world. It stands at the very beginning of the road. Even before there was a Jewish people there was always Jewish exile. It all started with the call to Abraham: "Get thee out of thy country, and from thy kindred, and from thy father's house, unto the land that I will show thee." This is how the path of the first Jew began—exile and promise. When the father of the nation-to-be was still childless, it was already decreed and revealed to him: "Know of a surety that thy seed shall be a stranger in a land that is not theirs, and shall serve them; and they shall afflict them four hundred years; and afterwards shall they come out with great substance." (Gen 15, 13) Once again, even before there was a Jewish people there was already Exile and the promise of Redemption. Not only did this exile not destroy the sovereignty of the Jewish people but, on the contrary, it was through Exile that Abraham became the father of Israel and it was in Exile that the children of Jacob became the people of Israel, the children of Israel of history. It happened in Egypt that they were for the first time referred to as a people, when Pharaoh said of them: "Behold, the *people* of the children of Israel are too many and too mighty for us." In our Egyptian exile we became a nation. What is the significance of all this?

There are two kind of exiles. There is a national exile which begins with *Ḥurban*, with the destruction of the sovereignty of the people and their dispersion into alien lands. However, prior to national exile, and more fundamental and universal, there is cosmic exile. National exile is a phenomenon in the history of nations; cosmic exile bespeaks the spiritual quality of the universal human condition at any one time in history.

What do we mean by "cosmic exile?" God has His plan for the world. The entire creation is infused with a divine purpose that longs for and seeks its realization in the cosmos in general and in human history in particular. Since, however, mankind has its own goals such as passion for power, desire for domination, for possessions and pleasures, such egotistic human drives deny the divine purpose in the creation of man. As a result, God's own purpose finds itself in Exile in the history of mankind. So long as the divine plan remains unrealized in history, the history of mankind tells the story of—what Jewish tradition calls—*Galut haShekhinah*, the Exile of the Divine Presence. God Himself is, as it were, a refugee in the world of men. It is this exile that is prior to, and at the root of, every national exile. It is on account of this that the history of the Jewish people begins with Exile. The call that went out to Abraham was a call for identification with the divine plan in history. This, however, compelled him to leave everything behind and to join the Exile of the Divine Presence in history. But by way of this identification with the divine purpose and the divine

Galut, he became Abraham, the father of a "multitude of nations." The Egyptian exile was of similar significance for his descendants. Egypt was one of the phases of the exile of the divine plan in history. To have been in *Galut* at the very beginning of their way meant that the starting point of the way was identification of the children of Jacob with the Exile of the Divine Presence. Yet it was through this identification that they became the people of Israel, *Am E ḥ ad*, one people in the world. The association of the children of Israel with the cosmic *Galut*, sharing in it right from their beginnings, made them the Jewish people.

However, precisely on this account, Exile is not only misery and disaster, but also challenge and responsibility with life-giving and life-sustaining meaning. The symbol of the Roman occupation in ancient Israel was the city of Caesarea. Comparing the symbol of Caesarea with that of Jerusalem, the Talmud says: If they tell you Caesarea and Jerusalem both are settled or that both are destroyed, do not believe it. But if they say Caesarea is settled and Jerusalem destroyed or Jerusalem is settled and Caesarea destroyed, believe it. For when one is safely established, the other cannot be so. (*b. Meg.* 6a). In this manner, the Talmud expressed the confrontation between two principles in history. In the world of triumphant Caesarea there is little room for Jerusalem, the Holy City, just as in the world of established Jerusalem, there is no place for the Caesarea of the Caesars. At the time just preceding the destruction of the second Jewish commonwealth, there was a very real choice before the people: either find a place in the world order of the Roman Empire which was wide open to them, or identify themselves with the destiny of the *Shekhinah*, of the Divine Presence, with the divine exile that was unavoidable within the *pax romana*. The Jewish people chose between these two possibilities. The result of their choice was the *Ḥurban*, the destruction of their state and their dispersion. But it is only because of that choice that the people of Israel are still the people of Israel and are still around in the world of men.

In other words, this *Ḥurban* was not just disaster. It was choice! We chose to side with the divine plan for man, which was denied in the world of Caesar. The destruction of Jerusalem and of the state was not a disaster that overwhelmed the Jewish people with the blind force of a natural catastrophe. What happened was the result of a free choice of unparalleled heroism in human history. True, it brought exile down upon our heads. Yet this consciously determined embracing of Jewish destiny granted us our eternal share in life. The source of our suffering has also been the source of our survival. So, too, has it been to this day, the source of our timelessness.

5

There is this difference between national and cosmic exile. National exile—the dispersal of an entire people from its homeland—is stagnation, loss of vitality, decline, and, ultimately, disappearance. This is the law in the world of Caesar. But in the cosmic exile of the divine purpose there is never stagnation, never irreversible stagnation. The realization of the divine purpose may be again and again tragically delayed, but it cannot be defeated. This exile is forever a process—often one of roundabout paths beyond immediate human understanding—towards its realization. As the Kabbalists would say, the fall is often the prerequisite for the rise. The Exile of the Divine Presence in history is a continuous progression toward Redemption. Because we have identified ourselves from the very beginning with the cosmic exile, which indeed constitutes the essence of our being, we have been able to find the certainty of our redemption—and often a measure of its fruition in anticipation—at the very heart of our various exiles. This is the secret of Israel eternal.

Our Exile, then, is twofold: national and universal, the exile of the people, and the exile of the *Shekhinah* in which we share. Because of that, Jewish messianism is also twofold. The Talmud teaches that the only difference between the present world and the days of the Messiah is the freedom from alien subjugation. But Isaiah prophesied: A nation will not raise the sword against another, nor will they learn the art of war any longer. Both are right; both redemptions are needed; national redemption for the national exile, universal redemption for the *Galut haShekhinah*, for the exile of God in human history. Jewish history seeks redemption in a twofold drive. It drives for national redemption among the nations, as well as universal redemption for all the nations. For this reason every form of national redemption can only be *At h alta deGe'ulah*, the beginning. Only universal redemption may be acknowledged as *Ge'ulah Shelemah*, redemption completed and time fulfilled. No separation between the two is possible. Jewish history has been moving on a double track. At times, we are warned "not to force the end;" at others, as at the time of the return from Babylon, we are punished for not having "gone up like a solid national phalanx."

6

The phase of the Exile in our times has to be recognized as total crisis because of the radically new event—the total threat—that entered Jewish history. It is usually referred to as the *Sho'ah*, the Holocaust. This is probably not the right term. In our exiles, we have experienced numerous holocausts—during the crusades, the Black Death, the Chmelnicki pogroms, the massacres in the Ukraine at the end of the First World War, etc., etc. This catastrophe, however, was different from all of them, not just in degree, but in kind, in its essential quality. The proper name for it is not *Sho'ah*, but *Hurban*, annihilation. For the first time in our history, the Exile itself was destroyed. After every other national catastrophe, there was still enough strength left in the Jewish people to continue, to rebuild and to recuperate. As we have indicated earlier, something of the awaited redemption was present in every one of our exiles. This time what happened was radically new. In our generation, the generation of

Nazism, of humanity's betrayal of all the values without which life itself becomes absurd indeed, the *Galut haShekhinah* (the Exile of the Divine Presence) reached its nadir, its most tragic intensification in history. Since Jewish existence interlocks with the *Galut* haShekhinah, we too were forced down to the depth of suffering and martyrdom and at the end of it we were left completely exhausted. Even that spark of *Ge'ulah* which was present before in every *Galut* and which alone enabled us to continue, to rebuild and to create anew, was extinguished this time. Our faith was shaken to its foundations.

At this fateful hour in Jewish history there was only one remedy left for the destruction of the *Galut*, and it had to be as radical and revolutionary as the destruction itself; national redemption in the sight of all men through the restoration of Israel's sovereignty in the land of Israel. Redemption was long overdue. It had to come. Without it, we would not have been able to continue. The rise of the State of Israel, after two millennia of such Exile and at the moment when it occurred, has become the reviving force, calling back to life the "dry bones" of the shattered *Galut*. Divine Providence had no choice but to grant us a measure of national redemption to meet the national *Ḥurban*. However, therein lies too the cause for this new phase of the total crisis that has broken over us since the Yom Kippur war. The national redemption, *because it had to come* for the sake of Jewish survival, was running ahead of *Galut haShekhinah*, of the redemption of the Divine Presence from its exile in the affairs of men and nations. The national redemption of the Jewish people came without a corresponding measure of universal redemption. This is the root of Israel's present problem. In our days, a civilization that has been drifting ever since its spiritual and moral collapse in the era of Nazism is once again being tested. What a degradation of the dignity of man that formerly proud nations can be treated today by oriental potentates like big daddy treats his little children to whom he grants pocket money according to whether they please him or displease him! Is a darker eclipse of human values imaginable than when the conscience and the standard of values of formerly great nations are determined by the amount of oil Arabia is willing to allow to reach them? What a demoralization of international order, what a derision of international justice! International cynicism is eating away the last shreds of the moral fibres of human society, already sickened by the universal catastrophe of Nazism. Mankind is on the road to universal chaos. As in the days of Nazism, with the selling out of the Jewish people to Hitlerism, the world was moving fast towards the second World War, so today with the cynical willingness of formerly great nations to sell the State of Israel and the Jewish people for a barrel of oil, the world is approaching the day of reckoning, the hour of the thermonuclear Armageddon.

7

We concede this is a metaphysical interpretation of Jewish existence. But Jewish survival testifies that we are a "metaphysical" people. As in the time of triumphant Nazism, so today the plight of the *Shekhinah* in human history is dramatically reflected in the destiny of Israel. If it were otherwise we would not be Jews. Because our destiny has been linked to *Galut haShekhinah*, to the Exile of the Divine Presence, once again in this hour of the total demoralization of the international order the crisis is total. Once again everything seems to be in the balance. But just because the crisis is total, the promise too is total. God's own destiny in human history is linked to our own destiny. He needs us no less than we need Him. This is probably the deepest meaning of the idea of being "a chosen people." God has joined His fortunes among men to our fortunes, as we have joined our destiny to Him on this earth. He let it be said by the mouth of His prophet, "Ye are My witnesses, saith God." And the rabbis commented: "If you are my witnesses, I am God; if not, I am not God." But since God will be, so must the witness too. This is the source of our suffering, the source of our dignity, the guarantee of our survival till the end of days. We have reached a juncture in world history when the existence of the Jewish people cannot be separated from the existence of the State of Israel. And the future of the people of Israel is inseparable from *Ge'ulat haShekhinah*, from the redemption of God Himself from His man-created exile. Because of that, Israel will still dwell in Zion and Jerusalem long after the wells of Arabia had been forced to surrender their last drop of oil.

The question, of course, is: what is the function of the Jewish people, in such a scheme of history? It would seem to us that no matter what our reaction to the scheme may be, we shall remain the witnesses. What God has started with us He will complete. Too much remains unfinished; too much awaits its justification; too much waits for its redemption. God will not die in His exile. As far as we are concerned the question is: shall we just endure our destiny or willingly embrace it? We shall not escape it. This is the lesson that we must learn from the Yom Kippur war. The State of Israel has been forced back into Jewish history. If the tragedy of the Yom Kippur war will bring home to us the futility of our desire to become a "normal" people and will induce us to recover the ethos of the Jewish stance in history in the context of *Galut* and *Ge'ulah*, it may yet be turned into a triumph of our struggle for survival within the messianic wave of world history. Only in that context can it be said that the state of Israel has come to stay. There is no escape for Israel from the historic destiny of Israel. The question again is: shall we only endure it, or shall we find the ultimate meaning of our human existence in it by embracing it with resolute determination and dedication. There has hardly ever been a more worthwhile moment in history to be a Jew in the classical context of *Galut* and *Ge'ulah* than at this time of moral and spiritual exhaustion of the human race.

Conclusion

We started our discussion with an analysis of the erosion of all standards of value and meaning in the world. Mankind seems to have reached a dead-end street. All the dreams have already been dreamt and found wanting; all the visions viewed and discarded; all the ideals deserted. Man seems to have already had his future and stands now in a wasteland of history with his only wretched preoccupation how to save his skin from the ultimate disaster.

Yet there are some bright spots even in this dark horizon. They harbor some promise; they represent the challenge and the opportunity. Young people were among the first to notice that something was amiss; they were among the first to sense the loss of purpose, of worthwhile goals, in this civilization. Many rebelled. Their rebellion was a symptom of the sickness, a manifestation of the need for spiritual integrity. The drug culture was such a symptom of the sickness. It was a desperate cry for some magic source of human salvation, as young people sensed that they were drowning in meaninglessness and absurdity. Salvation did not come; the sickness and the cry remained. Nearer to the present hour, we recognize the same restless search for new horizons among the young in the drift towards Eastern mysticism, in the longing for some secret formula to be received from the divine wisdom of some guru who happens to be in the vogue, some mystical incantation to which one may cling in order to save oneself from suffocation in the spiritual vacuum of this declining civilization. The same desperate search is motivating some of the new fangled faith-oriented fad groups like the Jesus freaks and others. All this is no solution, but still only the symptoms of the sickness. However, the direction of the search indicates a sensing of the dimension whence alone healing may come, pointing to the realm beyond the material, the domain of the spirit, the homeland of all meaning and worthwhile purpose to guide human existence. It is the dimension indwelt—as will ultimately be discovered—by the spirit of God.

Of late, one may notice how this longing for internal security of the spirit is gradually spreading to the adult population as well. This rather late and slow awakening is, of course, not unrelated to the economic insecurity and political imbalance that recently—and especially since the Yom Kippur war—threatens to engulf all of mankind. Energy crisis, the threat of international bankruptcy, social and political disorders, starving millions—and no vision, no ideals, no faith, but a spiritually and morally exhausted human race to cope with the world—encompassing problems of humanity's survival. It brings home the truth that science and technology alone will not do the job; that new foundations of the spirit, and in the spirit, are needed in this world that has lost its anchor and is drifting dangerously into the "Final Solution" of thermonuclear oblivion.

Chapter 11

The Personal Messiah

Steven S. Schwarzchild

Since issues concerning eternal Israel, such as election, sin and atonement, exile and redemption, come to cogent formulation in the doctrine of the Messiah, we complete our consideration of Israel as theological category with that encompassing matter. Schwarzchild begins with Reform Judaism's transformation of "redeemer" to "redemption," and he insists that that is an error, and that eternal Israel must hope and pray for a personal Messiah, a Messiah who is a specific human being. Reviewing arguments against a personal Messiah and in favor of a more generalized "messianic age," Schwarzchild finds in the presence in the world of false Messiahs (including, explicitly, the one of Christianity) testimony to the truth of the hope for the true, one, personal Messiah: "The false Messiah is as old as the hope for the true Messiah. He is the changing form of this changeless hope." Here is where Judaism and Christianity both meet and part company.

I. Phenomenolgy of the Jewish Spirit, 1945

When people think in 1968 about Jewish survival it can be assumed that the occasion for their consideration is the Six Day War of 1967 and its continuing consequences. We, too, will want to revert to that episode, but I wish to begin our exploration at another and more decisive point in contemporary Jewish history: the early summer of 1945—i.e., the hour when the Jewish people stood on both sides of the open doors of Bergen-Belsen, of Auschwitz, of Maidanek and Theresienstadt and the other camps of extermination, and when the full weight of what had happened to us there and throughout the Holocaust came bearing down on us.

The reality of the situation at that point was twofold: on the one hand, it was brutally clear that death and destruction, infinite pain and incurable physical and spiritual dislocations had reaped an abundant harvest in our midst. We were on the very verge of expiration; indeed, in some ways we had died, beyond revival. At the same time, we must remember, this condition prevailed, in varying ways and degrees, in all the countries and among all the peoples of the Old World, from the British Isles through the entire heartland of Eurasia to the islands of Japan and beyond. Slaughter and fire, the lie and the eraser had cut a wide swath not only through the peoples but also through the institutions and cultures of these continents. So we looked around

---

*From *Judaism and Ethics*, ed. Daniel Jeremy Silver Copyright 1970 by The Central Conference of American Rabbis Reprinted by permission.

us—we saw the scene—and, though with cracked voices and with bitter hearts, we first hummed softly and then sang in a swelling chorus the refrain of the Partisan song: *"Mir zennen do"*—"Never say we have walked our last road;" when all the roads will have been trod, and when all others will have fallen by the wayside, we—or at least a small remnant of Israel, the true שארית הפליטה—will yet present ourselves to proclaim: "We are still here—*mir zennen do*." The greatest, the world-shaking and heaven-rending, the inexpungeably traumatic tragedy of Israel was accompanied, contrapuntally, as it were, by the increasing consciousness of the ineluctable, unextirpatable, survival of the Jewish people throughout history—and if through that history then surely throughout eternity.¹

It is relatively easy to trace the spreading and deepening realization of this truth among Jews over the last twenty-three years. Indisputably the establishment of the State of Israel, in the face of apparently insuperable hostilities and difficulties, was undergirded by the psychology of שארית הפליטה: "We've come through so much—we'll come through this, too"—together with the historical lesson: אני לי מי לי אם אין. (I remember, for example, the passengers of the "Exodus" speaking like this, and acting on it, the second time around on this itinerary between West Germany and the shores of Israel.) Again, when one talked with or read the expressions of many of the participants in the Six Day War,² almost a quarter of a century later, this immediately post-Holocaust posture was clearly noticeable, usually formulated in just these terms—and this was, in fact, true throughout world Jewry. Even theologically the appropriation of this consciousness, though more slow, can be observed: Eliezer Berkovits ended his notable polemic against "interfaith dialogues" with a rousing peroration to the effect that we, the eternal people, were present and witnesses when the Christian era began—we are still present and witnesses now that it has come to an end.³ That was several years ago. Last fall this became, as we remember, virtually a stampede among rabbis, community leaders, and among the ranks of Jewry: "The Christian world has again stood by passively or even antagonistically. We're on our own. We're going to keep it that way."

II. The Classic Jewish View

If this is a correct phenomenology of the Jewish spirit after the Second World War, we do not need to stop long to prove that it stands in complete accord and direct line with the classic Biblical, Talmudic, medieval Jewish conception of the prospects of Jewish survival and its theology. I take it that the following is a legitimate summary of how our classic teachers envisaged the situation.

The model of the relationship between God and Israel in the Bible is, of course, the Covenant.⁴ There are two ways of understanding that covenant—let them be called the ethical and the metaphysical. The ethical interpretation makes the religious, moral, and historical honor of Israel the prerequisite for God's fulfillment of His part of the Covenant, *i.e.*, the preservation and advance of the Jewish people: if they do not do their share He is relieved of His obligation and will let it lapse.⁵ The advantage of this view is obviously the responsibility which it places upon the Jew and the ethical stimulus which it thus constitutes. Its corollary disadvantage is equally obvious: it is entirely too anthropocentric; it claims that history is determined by a large number of individual and collective subjective and irrational factors; it declares in effect that God's providence, or historical forces, can easily be detracked, rerouted, or even stopped cold by essentially trivial human incursions.⁶ The metaphysical view, then, represents the other part of the polarity. It speaks of the ברית עולם; it assures mankind that as long as the rainbow will be in the sky so long—which is to say eternally—will humanity persist, and it assures Israel that its survival is coeval with God's existence.⁷ Here the emphasis is not on man but on metaphysical factors—God, the world or mankind as totalities, the over-arching purpose of history, etc. Ezekiel and others will thus let ethical considerations ride, at least for the time being, and announce redemption שמו/ uml לא למעננו כי אם. In this interpretation of the Covenant the advantages and disadvantages of the ethical interpretation are precisely reversed: it obviously possesses a view of history which is objective and rational, but correspondingly it tends to lower the status of human ethical responsibility.⁸

These two views are not mutually exclusive, and they are certainly not chronological or Bible-critical *realia*. Their relationship to one another is rather dialectical. The case of Ezekiel just adduced makes this point all by itself and in Biblical terms: ethics are by no means ejected from this historiographical scheme, anymore than historiosophy is absent from, let us say, Amos, for whom, nonetheless, history seems to be a function of ethics rather than vice versa. Certainly for the Bible as such both interpretations of the nature of the Covenant come together in an integral, dialectical unity. God's plan for history is unalterably determined, and man's ethical decisions are indispensable as well as constitutive. If you will, הכל צפוי והרשות נתונה. One Biblical formulation of this unity of opposites is the very doctrine of the שאר ישוב of which we spoke at the outset as an historical reality. What the dialectical doctrine states at the very least is that, while Israel's actions are determinative of its survival, it is simultaneously true that this survival is divinely guaranteed in any case.

In classical Rabbinic Judaism this paradoxical view of the matter—empirically verified by Jewish history and doing justice both to the ethics as well as the metaphysics of the problem—becomes considerably more sophisticated and subtle. ישראל סבא, the eternity of Israel, founded on the eternity of God, נצח ישראל, is taken for granted by all.⁹ This in itself is wondrous enough when we remember that Rabbinic Judaism is, after all, largely the product of the destruction of the Second Commonwealth and of the bimillenial fate of Israel in a tragic and always radically tenuous *galut*. The full sophistication of the belief in the divinely guaranteed eternity of Israel becomes clear, however, only when one tries to understand the extremely complex teachings of the Rabbis in which, again, they synthesize dialectically the polar demands of the ethics and the metaphysics of Jewish survival and destiny. In פרק חלק, *Sanh.* 96b-98a, the *locus classicus* is to be found of Jewish messianism and thus of the eternity of Jewish life. Especially the debate between Rabbi Eliezer ben Hyrcanus, who advocates the ethical interpretation,[10] and Rabbi Joshua ben Hananya, who advocates what we have called the metaphysical interpretation, is to be noted.[11] By superficial students their debate might be regarded as merely a Billy Graham-like verse-slinging match; the usual but equally superficial view is that the two represent mutually exclusive doctrines, and their debate is then taken as another illustration of the unsystematic nature of Talmudic theology. The fact of the case is that, by the time the debate is over, in this passage and in a great number of others the final result is precisely the dialectical unity of ethics and metaphysics of which we have spoken. Its lovely poetic metaphor is found in *Midr. Tehillim* 45:3: "Just as this rose grows with its heart toward heaven, so do you repent before Me and turn your hearts heavenward, and, like the dew, I will thereupon cause your redeemer to appear."[12] It takes the form, for example, of saying that Israel must conduct itself morally so that its destiny can be fulfilled (ethics) but that God will, if need be, constrain it so to act (metaphysics). Another frequent way of putting it is to say that God has determined the end but that Israel can, by pious deeds, hasten its advent. (Note the sophisticated nature of this formulation: human evil cannot delay, or frustrate, God's providence, though human good can accelerate it; *i.e.* God acts, as it were, in a limit-situation fashion.)[13] Perhaps the most highly developed stage of this particular formulation of the combination of the contingency-*cum*-necessity, what Ezekiel Kaufman has called רצון והכרח, of Israel's meaningful existence is to be encountered in the greatest of all Jewish eschatologists, Isaac Abarbanel, who schematizes it by distinguishing between the first period of אפשרות ביאתו, when, depending on human actions, the Messiah may come, and the subsequent period of חיוב והכרחיות, when he will come regardless of human preparations, by divine fiat.

Of one thing there can, in any case, be no doubt: the Jewish consciousness of our generation that we and our children until the end-of-days will always proclaim *"mir zennen do"* is a simple perpetuation not only of the experience but also of the classic theology of Jewish history. Whatever the effect on it of the deeds of Jew and Gentile may or may not be, Jewish survival is guaranteed by God—subject, to be sure, to high costs and to qualifications in detail but not to fundamental anxiety. וקים עם ישראל חי.

III. Practical Applications

Let us, at this juncture, try to indicate one sociologico-psychological and one "pastoral" practical application of our theological truism before we return to our main *heilsgeschichtlich* concern in the perspective of the last year.

The sensationalistic notion of "the vanishing Jew" has been widely circulated. With reference to the *galut*-Jew in general and the American Jew in particular it serves diverse purposes. Some Israelis and other שוללי גלות use it in order to strengthen their exhortations to *aliyah*.[14] I always suspect that certain Christian circles use it because their notion of the religious conquest of Judaism is still very much operative in their minds, if not always on their lips. American mass media use it in order to increase their circulation, which, like most reading matter in this country, depends in large measure on a Jewish suburbanite middle-class clientele. Furthermore, it would appear that there is a clinically sick streak in many American Jews who gratify their masochism by reading about their own imminent collective demise. (The fact that they are so interested in reading about it refutes their prediction.) At the same time the diagnosis of Jewry's mortal illness and the prognosis of the death of Judaism come in handy for those who want to justify their own defection from ישראל כלל: they can now point to the public confirmation that their course of action is in line with the *Zeitgeist*, and, indeed, with the inevitable course of history; furthermore, they can legitimately argue that no man can be expected to tie up his and his family's faith in a foredoomed venture.[15]

We will not bother to polemicize against that notion of "the vanishing Jew" at any length. This prediction has been made in literally every single generation of Jewish history.[16] One of the more frequently told such tales is that of Steinschneider who, under historically and culturally similar conditions to our own, is supposed to have asked a rabbinical student why he had come late and, when told that the student had been detained at a Zionist meeting, replied with some anger that, in our time, our only task was to provide a decent funeral for the literary remains of Jewish history. The facts of history—many facts of a very long history—have empirically given the lie to all such predictions, to the point where no reasonable man can, on purely empirical grounds, any longer take them seriously.

No one should mistake this attitude for a vapid or any other kind of optimism: we referred at the outset to the symbiosis of death and resurrection in the barracks of Auschwitz—surely no one who proclaims: אני מאמין בביאת המשיח while he or his child is walking into the gas-oven can be accused of liberalistic euphoria. Furthermore, we are far from denying the sociological, cultural, and religious evisceration of the Jewish people anywhere, much less in America; on the contrary, we watch its vulgarities and mindlessness with horror. It is perfectly true: according to all the natural laws of history, demography, and sociology the people of Israel cannot much longer endure, and, certainly, it cannot be expected further to be ethically creative.

We have no hope in *homo Judaeus*. All that we are saying is that to deduce from this condition the demise of the Jewish people and of Judaism is itself a symptom of the sickness which the thesis claims to be describing: it is to study the Jewish phenomenon according to חוקות הגוים; it is to leave God and His covenantal promise out of account (as Laplace put it to Napoleon). One need not subscribe either to R. Yehuda Halevy's metaphysical biologicism or to Nachman Krochmal's Vicoism to accept the truth with which we, too, have been concerning ourselves, that there is a force at work in our history which overcomes and transcends all these perfectly correct laws of general human history. To put it epigrammatically: it is irrational not to believe in the miraculousness of Jewish history.

The most immediately pragmatic form which the notion of "the vanishing Jew" takes is the wide-spread worry about intermarriages. Statistics, analyses, papers, books, and conferences on this subject proliferate. Parents and rabbis constantly warn young people against its dangers—and the most flagrant of these dangers is supposed to be the survival of the Jewish people. I always visualize God sitting in heaven, surrounded by myriads of His serving angels, with the instruments of His omnipotent providence at His side, going into a panicky conference with His counselors when news comes through that little Gilbert Shapiro from Scarsdale has, for his own sociopathological reasons, decided to marry Christine Thomas from Dubuque on the campus of Omaha State Teachers College where they have met: the fate of the world and history, not to speak of the chosen people and its destiny, hangs in the balance! "He who sits in heaven laughs—the Lord mocks them" (Ps 2:4). There is, obviously, something ridiculous in this picture—even when it is multiplied a thousandfold. The main point, however, is that Gilbert and Christine are obviously not going to make their decision—if decision it be—in terms of Jewish destiny; indeed, if that meant much to them they would not be very likely to have reached their present condition in the first place. What is more, by inveighing against their allegedly great and injurious treason to the ethnic and religious ties of their families and people one is doing exactly what they—like their academic, bohemian, artistic, and intellectual counterparts—are looking for: they are conducting a small-scale raid against their parents, *milieu*, and the God of their backgrounds—they require a father's disapproval so that they can rebel against it and affirm their independence; by imploring their loyalty one confirms to them that, in the first place, the objects of their resentment are very weak and vulnerable and that, in the second place, their attacks are hitting their targets.

I should think that we ought to deal with the problems of intermarriage in the full and confident consciousness of the theologoumen that nothing that anyone, Jew or Gentile, does can ultimately affect the fate of Israel as a whole. When a Jew and a non-Jew come to us with marital intentions—in a period, incidentally, when marriages constitute only a limited portion of connubial relationships—we present to them the full strictness of Jewish law. (I mention only in passing the Reform rabbis who, also in my community, violate conspicuously not only Jewish law but also the explicit consensus of historic and contemporary Reform Judaism and who continue to injure the unity of the people of Israel and the effectiveness of their colleagues by officiating wholesale at mock-Jewish intermarriages.) The inviolability of Jewish law and religious substance affirms their sanctity and viability beyond impertinent individual or collective amputation to the point of death. A Judaism that declares its reliance on God rather than on—never mind kings—effervescent small-fry is considerably more persuasive than a weak beggar going down on his knees to beg for consideration. "The Lord is with me; I shall not fear; what can man do to me? The Lord is for me as my self; thus shall I be witness to my enemies. It is better to rely on God than to rely on man. It is better to rely on God than to rely on princes. All peoples have surrounded me, but I have escaped them. The right hand of the Lord is upright; the right hand of the Lord acts mightily. I shall not die but live and tell of the deeds of God. He has much tried me, but to death He has not given me over" (Ps 118). Especially in an age in which nothing succeeds as much as success I would hold that Jewish self-abnegation can be cured not with defeatism but only with—if you please —a divine, a messianic certainty of eventual triumph.

All of this does not, of course, mean that, relying on God's promise, we may lapse into human passivity. Jews have never done this: our metaphysics have always undergirded, not suspended, our ethics. Of course, we want to stop a Jew from defecting, in body or in spirit. But this is so because we hate to see any Jew—or any man—deprived of his share in the glory of Israel. We are worried about the incalculable deprivation which such a defection inflicts upon the defecting individual, not upon the people, faith and destiny from which he defects; we are anxious for the individual, not for God's providence.[16a] Of course, we want to do everything we can to strengthen, enrich, and disseminate *Yiddishkeit*, but this can be done not by begging unwilling—or, for that matter, even willing—individuals or groups, children, marriageable people, intellectuals, or what have you, to help us, the Jewish people, Judaism or God out of their respective troubles. What we must done is to externalize the resplendence of the spirit of God within them—to fan the sparks of the *schechinah* residing in the broken vessels of the Jewish community—to plumb the sophistication of the *sod* within the—usually misunderstood—*peshat* of Jewish reality.

IV. "Not by Power..."

We now return to our main theme—the significance of Jewish survival as we experienced it in 1945. The crucial question which—consciously or unconsciously—has arisen for all who have lived since is this: how did this survival, broken yet triumphant, tortured yet exultant, decimated yet fortified, come about? What can we learn about how we are to survive from how we did survive?

At the Eichmann trial the Israeli attorney-general Hausner asked most European-Jewish survivors of the Holocaust who gave testimony: Why did you not resist? Ben-Gurion, among others, said that one of the major purposes of the trial was to purge Jewish consciousness of a haunting guilt-feeling for not having fought back against the Nazis but—as the biblical phrase, frighteningly transvalued, which is usually cited at this point, goes—having "gone like sheep to the slaughter." Clearly, the premise of the question is, in the first place, that it is better to "fight back" than to die, without physical retaliation or defense, as martyrs, and, in the second place, that the survival of the שארית הפליטה was due to those who, as heros on the walls of the Warsaw Ghetto, soldiers in the Jewish Brigade, members of the roaming Partisan groups, or after the war as soldiers in the Haganah or other military or quasi-military outfits, fought against the Nazis and for the establishment of the State of Israel. There can be little doubt that it is on the basis of essentially such premises that organized Jewry concentrates its memorializations of the victims of the Holocaust on anniversaries of the Warsaw Ghetto Revolt. Hence issues forth also a new worldwide Jewish admiration for heroes of brawn—Israeli, healthy, clear-eyed, wiry boys and girls with machine-guns under their arms, Colonels Marcus, tanks and planes on Sunday-school bulletin boards, etc.

This view of how Israel survived its most horrible threat has undergone a rapid escalation. It began, shortly after the war, with the glorification of the Jewish military and paramilitary fighter while the "passive" martyrs were lamented but, for the rest, relatively neglected. From this followed shortly two different but supplementary theses: the Hausner thesis we have mentioned, that there was something, perhaps something crucial, that was demeaning, immoral, possibly even traitorous about not having physically fought back, and the Hannah Arendt thesis that significant elements of the Jewish leadership and communities in Europe had actually collaborated with their people's exterminators. Mind you, even most of those who vehemently argued against the Arendt thesis accepted the premise that to die unresistingly is somehow shameful, and they, therefore, concentrated their attention on revolts in ghettos and concentration camps and on Jewish leaders who were active in the war against the Nazis in order to try to refute Arendt's thesis.[17] The next step in the escalation was, of course, the resolution, in Israel and abroad, not to let ourselves be decoyed into such a situation again but rather, from the outset, to be ready to take to arms and other counter-aggressive measures against any actual or potential (and thus preemptive) enemy. This was certainly the underlying and usually proclaimed psychological posture immediately before and during the Six Day War; it was part of the *déja-vu*, the *déja-senti* atmosphere of those weeks when the beleaguered spirit of the Second World War was rife in the Jewish community—and it is the source of the predominant "hawkishness" in Jewish circles since then. The last and grotesquely Satanic degree of escalation which this interpretation of the Jewish history of our time has hitherto undergone is the doctrine enunciated in the current wave of Polish, neo-Stalinist Communist anti-semitism—that, by and large, it was the Poles—*mirabile dictu!*—who fought against the Nazis while the ranks of Jewry were shot through with traitors, collaborators, and cowards.

The subject is too painful, and I, therefore, want to try to summarize what is historically and morally wrong with this attitude as briefly as possible. In Israel and in this country a Jewish triumphalism has spread which is not lovely to behold. In the phrases תנועה למען ארץ ישראל השלמה are slung around which sound most ominous to anyone who has lived through the 'thirties of our century: "liberated territories," "the Greater Israel," "the call of the historic soil," "the metaphysical unity of the people and the land," "the irresistible destiny of the millennia," etc. Policy discussions are held about how to keep the numbers and the fertility of the Arabs (and sometimes even also of the Sephardim) in manageable proportion to those of the rest of Israel—satellite states are proposed as a more liberal way of dealing with the Near Eastern problem than wholesale removal of populations—the Israeli army is further enhanced as the chief tool of integration, education, and decision-making, where the Kibbutz had, surely, been originally cast in that role—generals become cabinet-members and ambassadors, together with previously proscribed terrorist leaders and right-wing chauvinists—let these examples stand for others as well.[18]

In a more technically theological sense the Israeli victory in the Six Day War has produced an immensely aggravated danger of pseudo-faith and pseudo-messianism. It is by now a cliché how Israeli as well as *galut* Jews without religious faith suddenly came to believe in miracles (performed by a non-existent God) and thought they were witnessing the אתחלתא דגאולה.[19] To which my teacher Prof. Akiba Ernst Simon replied epigrammatically: "I, too, would believe that it was a miracle—if I didn't believe in God so much."[20]

In March 1968 the "Newsletter on Religious and Cultural Affairs" put out by the Consulate General of Israel in New York[21] carried a rather stunning and worrisome summary of the pseudo-messianic mood in certain circles. The Israeli chief-rabbinate called for *hallel* on the anniversary of the conquest of Jerusalem—the laws of the restoration of the Temple were to be studied (in fact, of course, a great military parade was held)—the possibility of proclaiming Iyyar 28 a permanent holiday was discussed—"Chief Rabbi Untermann reiterated his considered view that 'the cardinal duty of פרסום הנס—publicizing the miracle, made the recital of Hallel on the anniversary of Israel's victory literally a biblical ordinance דין דאורייתא גמור, and one was also authorized to say the Beracha accompanying it.'" (The Torah Education Department of the World Zionist Organization promises an early publication of Rabbi Untermann's מצות פרסומא נסא וגודל השמעתא. Here one may ask: why do non-Orthodox Jews hasten to protest against bureaucratic discriminations against them in Israel but not about substantive matters, ברומו של עולם העומדים, such as this? Rabbi M. Fogelman of Kiryat Motzkin is quoted: "Is the miracle of our day less than that of Hanukkah?" Rabbi Techorsh, member of the Chief Rabbinate Council, advocated the recital of

שהחיינו and על הנסים. Rabbi Y. Abuhatzirach, also a member of the Council and spiritual head of Israel's North African community, maintained (and, perhaps such views can be indulged depending on the history of those who hold them) that last year's "recovery of ארץ ישראל constituted the final step before the advent of the Messiah," warranting special readings from Torah and Prophets.[21a]

This is extremely dangerous talk. Theologically I would adduce at least three arguments against it, the first two cited from—if you please—the Satmerer Rebbe's recent hlwagh קונתרס, והתמורה על; (1) "Miracles" are miracles only when they are in accord with the Torah and the *halachah*; otherwise, like the miracles of the Egyptian magicians, they are deceptions of Satan;[22] (2) Victories in wars, even those of the few over the many, are always natural events, not miracles. Thus Hanukkah celebrates the miracle of the oil, not the victory of the Hasmoneans.[23] Indeed, military victories are special opportunities for the seductions of Satan.[24] I should like to add a third reason for not regarding a victory in war a divine act, and I regret that this kind of thinking is hard to come by nowadays in Orthodox, Reform, or any other Jewish circles: R. Yochanan, the central teacher in the eschatological discussion of פרק חלק, interpreting Jeremiah 30:6, asks why, in the messianic fulfillment, "all faces will turn pale."[25] He answers that the angels and Israel will turn pale because the salvation of Israel carries along with it a comparative demotion of other peoples: "At that time the Holy One, praised be He, will say: 'Those (Israel) are the works of My hands, and the others (Gentiles) are the works of My hands. How can I cause the ones to perish in favor of the others!' "[26] And Rav Pappa (and Rashi *ad locum*) expatiate further on this consideration. It might be argued that, despite their misgivings, all the parties concerned nevertheless pray for the messianic fulfillment and therefore the corollary derogation of the Gentiles—but it must be remembered that R. Yochanan makes the statement which we have quoted in order to explain why he, like a number of others, exclaims: ייתי ולא איתמיניה—*i.e.*, R. Yochanan prefers not to experience the messianic advent rather than be an accessory to the plight of the non-Jews. Much further genuine Jewish morality—or any other—cannot go! Can we say less in the presence of Moslems and Arabs?

Turning to American Jewry, the triumphalism which we have illustrated manifests itself here perhaps more flagrantly than in Israel, perhaps precisely because it is at one remove. Hundreds of rabbis sign full-page newspaper ads insisting that all of the conquered land must be retained by Israel because—if you please—otherwise the Soviet Union will have succeeded in pushing the United States out of its strategic strongholds in the Near East. Liberal Jewish professors, who had been in the vanguard of the movement against the Vietman War, demand full American political and military commitment on the side of Israel, and, though their dissenting voices are heard on every other subject, a strange silence prevails toward the Israeli government on the delicate but crucial question of Arab-Jewish relations; the center of Jewish attention in this country has now become "Negro anti-Semitism" and campus anarchism where previously it had been equality and peace, etc.[27] I confess, with great sadness, that I see a dominant note of rampant self-assertiveness and self-righteousness in world Jewry, which may be compared with the ideology of those against whom Jeremiah prophesied, who thought that their strength lay in their own arms and in alliances with foreign, pagan powers.

One is sorely tempted, at this point, to want to assert one's Jewish "patriotism" against the inevitable accusations which will be leveled. But let us, instead, go back to the original thesis about the nature of Jewish survival as we witnessed it in 1945, and let us see what happens to the real interests of the Jewish people when that fragmented survival is looked at in another light.

Certainly the Jews in the Warsaw Ghetto had every human right to defend themselves and to fight back. The same is true of all the other military or paramilitary expressions of resistance and counter-attack. Rightly do we honor their memories. But let us remember: in the first place, we lament to say that they, too, died—if survival is to be the yardstick of tactical or ethical worth, then we mourn to have to conclude that neither military resistance nor martyrdom availed. In the second place, it has been and is a terrible defamation of the third of the Jewish people who went to their deaths to claim or to imply that because they did not fight back they either did not resist or—חס וחלילה—collaborated. To be *mentshen* in the midst of inhumanity, to sanctify the name of God while surrounded by a flood of heathenism, to study, teach, and pray in a world in which only murder, rape, and brutality reigned, to squeeze a precious drop of life through the sieve of all-consuming death, and finally to go to one's death in ranks of thousands because the world had turned into hell and no longer had a place for decent human beings—who will rise and have the forwardness to claim that this was not, in its way, the greatest, the most admirable, the most heroic form of resistance,[28]—that the more than five million who did not, as it happens, resort to guns, knives, stones, and fire did not plant the banner of Israel, God, and humanity fluttering high on the battlefield of history?[29]

Two thousand years of Jewish exilic history had taught the Jewish people that the tree planted by the waters could bend its branches to the storm and afterwards rise up again and grow its fruit for the coming season. One has to be an assimilated, Westernized secularist to see something dishonorable—as Bialik did in עיר ההרגה and as so many Jews do today—in crouching in cellars until, it is hoped, the beasts have passed by, in order to save one's own and one's family's lives. To be sure, the gentlemanly thing to do is to stand up straight, meet the badman in the open street and get the first draw on him, but then, as Maurice Samuel has put it, we choose to be Jews, not gentlemen. And, when all was said and done, in 1945 a small but viable remnant from the Holocaust had in fact survived. They stumbled out of the camps, they raised their heads from the floor, they walked blinkingly into the light, they came out of hiding and disguise, and whispered: *"Mir zennen do."* And this was not a very small minority of our surviving people—it was the overwhelming majority of whose who had, by God's unfathomable and cruel grace, somehow or other come through. They *were*, indeed, the Jewish people. They own our unqualified piety and love—as do all those who, to the end and into horrible deaths, exemplified what it is to be Jews, human beings, citizens of "the lands of the living."

It is almost universally said that the Holocaust is an irrefutable blemish on—if not denial of—God. This is true. It is equally true that the survival of the Jewish people—at all times and especially through the Holocaust—is an inexplicable handiwork of His. (It is, incidentally, little less cruel than the slaughter, as Elie Wiesel and others make clear.) We are entitled to put it blasphemously: God was so vicious as to kill us, and He was so vicious as to preserve us; to Him go all blame and all glory. The Jew came out of this furnace—dead or alive—pure as the driven snow. Under the Law הרוגי מלכות are, regardless of their personal merits or previous conditions, martyrs על קדוש השם.[30] Again we conclude: we survive by God's harsh decree, and those who survive testify, willingly or no, knowingly or no, gladly or sadly, to His majesty and sovereignty.[31]

Now we can once more jump forward to the Jewish history of the decades since 1945. We presented ourselves—"a brand plucked from the fire"—to the world in 1945, we pressed against the shores of the Holy Land and the doors of governments, and in 1948 the United Nations established the State of Israel. We ought to recall that at that time and for a while thereafter there were no more eloquent protagonists of the United Nations than we Jews. It is one of the sorrier consequences of the superciliousness and arrogance of the last few years that now in most Jewish circles "the United Nations" is a term of deprecation. One need not have any exaggerated notions of its present capacities or wisdom to perceive the fundamental dangers and immoralities of this attitude. With respect to all three wars that Israel has had to wage since 1948 it is perfectly obvious that the idea that "with the strength of my hand have I acted and with my wisdom, for I am smart—and I remove the boundaries of nations" (Isa 10:13) is foolish even in purely political terms: but for the support that literally all the great powers of our age, the U.S.S.R., the U.S. and their satellites in 1948, Britain and France in 1956, and America in 1967, provided, disaster could easily have overtaken us. How long do we think we can live in the Near East surrounded, indeed interpenetrated, by hundreds of millions of Moslems and Arabs in the middle of millions of square miles of hostile territory and, in each blood-letting round, come out victors? (Unlike the Arab countries, we cannot afford a single defeat!) The Jew who is really committed to the survival of Israel not just for another generation but לעולמי עולמים will contemplate the needs of the hour in such a *specie aeternitatis*, however unpopular he may be among his fellows at the moment. And even if it were conceivable that in the longest run the Jewish people could maintain itself in the midst of such a sea of enmity, what human, spiritual and moral price would we have to pay for it? I always remember that when my son was less than ten years old he came home from a summer in an Israeli children's camp and said that his chief impression was of barbed wire all over the country. The transvaluation of all Jewish values which has already seriously set in in Israeli and world Jewry would soon completely overwhelm us.[32] The problem of our Jewish generation and of our children is whether we can live with the ethics and politics of the נרדפים, having, in some ways, ceased to be נרדפים.[33] I implore you and me and all of us not to prove Nietzsche to have been right—that morality is the rationalization of the weak.

At this point, finally, I can articulate my own form of Jewish super-chauvinism. What we have been saying is simply that the survival of the Jewish people is guaranteed by God—that we need not really concern ourselves with it—that to preoccupy oneself with it is a form of sickness, as health-faddists are invariably sick people[33a]—that to attribute our survival to human instrumentalities including and primarily our own, inevitably leads to the acts of *hybris*, גאוה, which victimize other human beings and result in unending conflict and eventual defeat—and that, on the contrary, the God Who has brought us this far will also redeem His other promises to Israel. Like the השלמה תנועה למען ארץ I, too, am unable to surrender—לבא לעתיד—one inch of the sacred soil of ארץ ישראל. We may implicitly believe that in the Redemption not only will the historic land revert to its divinely designated occupants but that, as Rabbinic literature amply proclaims,[34] it will be vastly expanded—yes, Hebron and Jericho, the cedars of Lebanon and the great river: "And He said to me: 'These waters go out into the eastern Galilee, descend into the Arabah, and end in the sea'" (Ezek 47:8). The late Chayim Weizman was asked about this messianic claim by a member of the Peel Commission when, back in 1936, he was ready to accept the first partition plan for Palestine, and he answered, not facetiously: God made the promise—God, not we, will redeem it. Our task is to be *mentshen* and thus—and thus only—to hasten the Messiah's coming, not by force or by magic or by superarrogation.

The kind of pseudo-messianism which we have previously had occasion to consider[35] is not limited to the "old-fashioned" circles of the Israeli chief-rabbinate.[36] The pop song that became the hymn of the Six Day War is suffused with messianic connotations: "The *Shofar* sounds on the Temple Mount, in the Old City,/ And within the caves in the rock rays of the Light shine, . . ." etc. Nothing less than the glossy official magazine of French Jewry, *L'Arche*, for Oct–Nov 1967 (No. 128) appeared under the red headline: *"Jerusalem 5728—Le Méssie, va-t-il Arriver?"* Inside there is an article by Alex Derczansky still moderately entitled: *"Le Royaume de Dieu Reste à Construire . . . Mais on Sait Maintenant que Godot Doit Arriver,"* whereas Arnold Mandel, one of the intellectual mentors of contemporary French Jewry and presumably a sensitive and sophisticated man, the title of whose article graces the front cover, is quite sure that, at the least, the Messiah son of Joseph, "the political and national Messiah," has arrived *hic et nunc* "on our territory in the Jewish year 5728."

We cannot here analyze the whole complex and profound subject of Jewish messianology. The least that must be said, however,[37] is that this kind of thinking is grist for the mills of all the "realists," anti-utopians, and neo-conservative thinkers of our time—Reinhold Niebuhr, Jakob Talmon, Norman Cohn, Hannah Arendt, etc. Their argument invariably boils down to this—that utopianism and Jewish messianism are forms of *hybris*, עבודה זרה, which claim to be able to accomplish humanly what in truth only God can accomplish and, what is worse, which will always play havoc with human beings who do not completely fall in line with the messianic claims, on the grounds that they are not only political dissenters but blasphemers who want to undermine the reign of God Himself. This is, of course, a willful and purposeful distortion of the messianic belief. This belief in fact dictates that men must exert themselves as much as and more than they are capable of doing toward the messianic goal, in the hope—*nota bene*: not in the arrogantly sure expectation—that God will—in His own good time and for His own good reasons, not in any proportionality to these human efforts: "Not on our righteous acts do we make our petitions dependent"—bring about Redemption. It thus self-evidently subsumes the human part in bringing about the consummation to the onus of human fallibility, inadequacy, and sinfulness and to the divine prerogative of grace. Nonetheless, the "anti-utopians" have enough evidence, of course, with which to support their case, by the simple device of procuring it from the rich arsenal of pseudo-messianisms, which they proceed to identify with authentic messianism: their evidence of fanaticism, *hybris*, ruthlessness and inhumanity invariably stems from those who violate the fundamental Jewish messianic dictates: "Do not press the End!"[38] and "May those be devastated who calculate the End."[39]

An apparent contradiction might be pointed to in our argumentation: on the one hand, we reject the view of the anti-utopian neo-conservatives who advocate, at best, slow, small steps of melioration within the established structures of society—yet, on the other hand, we now raise the old Jewish motto "Do not press the End!"

Here we turn, for the last time, to the dialectical polarity of the ethics and the metaphysics of the Covenant. The ethics of the Covenant do, indeed, require us to act in such a way as to hasten the coming of the Messiah, *i.e.* to endeavor to establish the radical reign of peace, justice, and goodness on earth. But ethics are concerned with other men, not ourselves. Therefore, with respect to the peace movement, the Black movement, the social movement in our time (movements, that is to say, which are primarily concerned with men other than ourselves) our motto must be theirs: "All of it—here and now!" and on this motto we must act. This must apply, too, to the genuine problems of Palestine Arabs: no reasonable Zionist has denied the at least partial justice of their case, and the plight of many of their people has lasted much, much too long. The metaphysics of the Covenant, on the other hand, are concerned, as we have seen, with the persistence of the people of Israel throughout history, *i.e* primarily with ourselves. This God has assumed as His responsibility. Elie Wiesel quotes a midrash[40] that explains why the Jews opposed to Haman's attempt to exterminate them physically the spiritual resistance of repentance, fasting and prayer: "When our physical existence was threatened we simply reminded God of His duties and the promises deriving from the Covenant." In short, the Torah is our business, Israel's survival is God's.[41]

It all comes down to the simple formula of the Levitical and Deuteronomic blessings-and-curses: if we fulfill the commandments of His will He will bless and keep us—it is not the other way around, that, if we maintain ourselves, He or we will be able to act as He desires us to: "If you walk in My statutes and keep My commandments and do them . . .,then will I walk Myself in your midst: I will become your God for you, and you will become a people for Me. I am the Lord your God, Who brought you out of the land of Egypt, so that you would no more be their slaves; I will break the bands of your yoke, and I will lead you integrally" (Lev 26:1-13).

Endnotes

[1]Cf. Emil Fackenheim on what he calls "the *mitzvah* of surviving," *Judaism* 16/3 (Summer 1967): 272.—One might make a comparison with the famous wisecrack attributed to the Abbé Sieyés: when asked what he had done during the French Revolution, he is supposed to have said: *"J'ai vécu."* Jewishly one might say that not to have lived but to have "lived above" and thus to have "sur-vived" is at issue.

[2]Cf. שיח לוחמים ed. A. Shapira (Tel Aviv 5728); cp. M. Rosenak, "Moments of the Heart," *Judaism* 17/2 (Spring 1968): 211-24.

[3]"Judaism in the Post-Christian Era," *Judaism* 15/1 (Winter 1966): 84: "No one can foretell what this new era holds in store for mankind. But we are here at the threshold of the new age. We who were there when the Christian era began; in whose martyrdom Christianity suffered its worst moral debacle; we in whose blood the Christian era found its end—we are here as this new era opens. And we shall be here when this new era reaches its close—we, the *edim*, God's own witnesses, the *am olam*, the eternal witness of history."

[4]*Cf.* e.g., Deut 26:17, *et. al.*

[5]Lev 26:23f.: "If you walk with Me cavalierly, then also I will walk with you cavalierly." Cf. Exod 19:5f., Deut 11:17, 28:24, Josh 23:16, 1 Kgs 9:7, Jer 7, especially vv. 4f., 11, 15, 33f, Amos 9:7 and Rashi *ad locum*, Micah 3:11f., etc.

[6]Goethe said that "no one is a hero to his butler." To which Hegel replied, "That is so not because he is not a hero but because the butler is a butler." I.e., the personal idiosyncrasies, even the ethical failures of a man, cannot ultimately be believed to be history-shaping forces. Otherwise, instead of studying the laws of economics we would have to investigate how a corporation executive liked his eggs on any given morning. Cf. *Phaenomenologie des Geistes*, ed. Lasson, 81, 93, *et. al.*

[7]E.g., Ps 105:7-10: "He is the Lord our God. His statutes are valid in all the earth. He remembers His covenant forever, the word of His commandment unto the thousandth generation, which He made with Abraham and His oath unto Isaac. He has established it as a statute for Jacob, an everlasting covenant for Israel." Cf. 1 Chron 16:16; also Deut 4:29ff, Isa 49:14-26, Jer 31-34f.: "Thus says the Lord, Who sets the sun as light by day and the laws of the moon and stars as light

by night, Who stirs up the sea so that its waves billow, Whose name is Lord of hosts: If these statutes vanish from before Me, says the Lord, then only will the seed of Israel cease being a people before Me forever." Cf. Gen 17:7f., Exod 13:16, Deut 7:9, 33:27, Isa 54:9f., 59:21, Jer 30:11, 33:25f., Hos 2:21f., etc.

[8]Thus one arrives at the immoralism—either of a Hegel or the mechanism of a Marxism.

[9]Cf., e.g., ספר האגדה, ביאליק ורבניצקי, ישראל קימם לעולם, Cf., Mena ḥ. 53b:11, 24-26. "R. Joshua b. Levi said: 'Israel will not experience complete extinction either in this world or in the text.'" Cf. also A. Marmorstein, *Studies in Jewish Theology* (Oxford, 1950), א־חד בדרשות התנאים והאמוראים, האמונה בנצח ישראל

[10]In this passage as well as throughout Rabbinic literature, חשובה is usually mistranslated as "repentance," whereas in fact, of course, it means "moral conduct" in such instances.

[11]For a good beginning of the kind of ethico-conceptual analysis to which this kind of literature ought to be subjected, see Emmanuel Lévinas, "Temps Messianiques et Temps Historiques dans le Chapitre XI du Traité 'Sanhedrin,'" *La Conscience Juive*, ed. E. A. Lévy-Valensi and J. Halperin (Paris, 1963). For the theological dialectics of the Talmud, *cf.* also e.g., J. Petuchowski, "The Concept of 'Teshuvah' in the Bible and Talmud," *Judaism* 17/2 (Spring 1968): esp. 184f.

[12]Cf. also *Deut. Rab. 5:6.*

[13]Cf. Saadia Gaon, *Emunot ve'Deot* III/7: "Our nation is a nation only by virtue of its *torot*, and since the Creator has declared that the nation will persist as long as the heavens and the earth do it follows necessarily that its *torot* will persist as long as the heavens and the earth. See Jer 31:34f." *Cf. Kuzari*, 2/34: "Do not believe that I, though agreeing with you, admit that we are dead. We still hold connection with that divine influence through the laws which He has placed as a link between us and Him. There is circumcision, of which it is said: 'My covenant shall be in your flesh for an everlasting covenant.' (Gen 17:13) There is further the Sabbath: 'It is a sign between Me and you throughout your generations' (Exod 31:13). Besides this there is the 'covenant of the Fathers,' and the covenant of the Law first granted on Horeb and then in the plains of Moab in connection with the promises and warnings laid down in the section 'When you will beget children and grandchildren' (Deut 4:25). Compare further the antithesis 'If any of yours be driven out to the utmost parts of heaven' (ibid., 30:10)—'You shall return unto the Lord your God' (*ibid.*, v. 2); finally the song, 'Give ear . . .' (ibid., 32:1), etc. We are not like dead but rather like a sick and weakened person who has been given up by the physicians and yet awaits a miracle or an extraordinary recovery, as it is said: 'Can these bones live?'" (Ezek 37:3)—*Ibid.*, 3/10f.: "I have discovered that God has a secret purpose in keeping you in existence. . . . If an evil thought makes a man despair, saying: 'Can these bones live?' (ibid.)—our greatness having been negated and our history having been forgotten, as it is said,: 'Our bones are dried up and our hope lost; we have been condemned' (ibid., v. 11)—let him think of the nature of the exodus from Egypt and all that is said in the section 'For how many beneficences unto us do we owe gratitude unto God!' (Passover *Haggadah*). Then he will have no difficulty in imagining how we will be restored to our estate even if all but one of us will disappear. For it is written: 'Fear not, oh worm Jacob (Isa 41:14), i.e., what remains of a man when he returns to be a worm in his grave!"—Cf. also Maimonides, *Epistle to Yemen*, ed. A .S. Halkin (New York, 1952), 25: "God has long ago given us the guarantee through His prophets that we will not perish and that we will not cease to be a significant people. As the existence of God cannot be terminated so our disappearance from the world is impossible. It is said (Mal 3:6): 'For I, the Lord, do not change, and you, the children of Jacob, will not perish' (Cf. *So ṭ a* 9a). Furthermore, God has informed and promised us that He cannot possibly reject us completely and, though we may disobey Him and turn back His commandments, it is said (Jer 31:37): 'For God has said: "As much as the heavens above can be

measured and the foundations of the earth beneath can be plumbed, so will I reject all of the seed of Israel because of all that they have done"—says the Lord.' This very point was even earlier made known to us by Moses our teacher, peace be upon him (Lev 26:44): 'Yet for all that, when they are in the land of their enemies I will not reject them, nor will I abhor them, to destroy them utterly and to break My covenant with them—for I am the Lord their God.' " Ibid., 35: "It has been explained to us by Isaiah, the messenger of the nation, that the sign between us and God and the proof that teaches us that we will not perish is the persistence of God's Torah and His word among us. He said (Isa 59:21): 'As for Me, this is My covenant with them, says the Lord—My spirit which is upon you.' . . . And it is written (Isa 44:23): 'For You have we been killed at all times and treated as sheep suitable for slaughter.'" Cf. also *Yalkut Shimeoni*, 27b, beginning, to Exod 19:2, where God's "eternal salvation of Israel" is counterposed to Israel's previsioned "offensiveness and blasphemy," on the basis of its function of "purloining worlds for Him."

[14]Cf. the classic writings of Jacob Klatzkin—Cf. *The Zionist Idea*, A. Hertzberg (NewYork, 1960) 314-28, esp. 320ff.

[15]Arthur Koestler's *Thieves in the Night* was an anticipation of this attitude in our time, and his "Letter to a Parent of a British Soldier in Palestine" (cf. *Under Fire*, ed. D. Robinson [NewYork, 1968]) is a proterrorist corollary.

[16]*E.g.* Arthur Ruppin's classic *Die Juden der Gegenwart* (Berlin, 1920).

[16a]Cf. H. Slonimsky, *Essays* (NewYork, 1967) 62: "The individual Jew may drop away, but Israel as a whole is held inexorably fast. Thus Johanan, the prince of the Agada, has the following to say in explanation of God's ontological definition of himself as אהיה אשר אהיה 'I can be whatever I may be to individuals, but as for the mass I rule over them even against their desires and will, even though they break their teeth' (referring to Ezek 20:33): על כורחם שלא בטובתם כשהם משוברות שניהם אהיה לאשר אהיה ביחידים, אבל במרובים (*Exod. Rab.*, Romn 11b, col. 2)."

[17]I wish I had kept count of the young Jews with whom I have spoken who, validly or no, are, as a result, finding themselves in the most serious of ethical perplexities now when they have to try to buttress their universal conscientious objections to waging war with Jewish reasoning.

[18]There is by now much literature that can be adduced on this score. Cf., e.g., C. Potok's review of a cluster of recent books on the Six Day War in the *New York Times*, June 9, 1968, which ends: "a new kind of Jew has been in the making during these past decades, the concept of the exile, with its picture of the cringing, long-suffering Jew (whose picture?!), is now coming to an end." Cf. D. Lang, "After the Sixth Day," *The New Yorker*, May 18, 1968, 104. The most frightening religio-political chauvinism comes from Prof. Harold Fisch of Bar-Ilan University: see "Land of Israel Movement," *Congress Bi-Weekly*, 35/3, Feb 5, 1968, and *Niv HaMidrashiya*, (Winter–Spring 1968): 44-49, where he even rather likes Arah intransigence since it leads to Israeli expansion.

[19]Mandel, "Le Méssie, va-t-il Arriver?" *L'Arche* (Oct–Nov 1967): no. 128, quotes an Israeli: "I don't believe in God, but of one thing I'm sure: this time He was with us."

[20]Cf. Maimonides' striking position on miracles, which we cannot here rehearse but which can fairly be summarized as maintaining the possibility of miracles while denying in virtually every single case that one has occurred.

[21]Why does this publication always carry the front-page notation: "This publication is for your information and use, in any way you deem fit—therefore, please do not give any credit to the publisher"?

[21a]See further relevant halachic discussions summarized in I. Jakobovits, "Survey of Recent Halakhic Periodical Literature—The Occupied Territories," *Tradition*, 9/4 (Spring 1968): 101-104. Rabbi J. B. Soloveitchik's position represents a humane and wise bright spot in the spectrum. Cf.

also *Or Ha-Mizrach*, 17/3 (July 1968), Y. Gershoni, "Is it Halachically Permitted to Surrender Palestinian Territories?" and I. Y. Untermann, "The Commandment to Publicize the Miracle" (Hebrew). ²²Ibid., 69, et al.

²³This argument occurs, of course, throughout Jewish history but especially in 19th-century liberalism. I have been sorely tempted to write a review of the Satmerer Rebbe's book to be entitled, for the reason here mentioned as well as others, "The Reform Judaism of Satmer."

²⁴Ibid., 34f., et al.   ²⁵*Sanh.* 98b.

²⁶Cf. the famous midrash about God rebuking the angels while Egypt drowns in the Red Sea.

²⁷Cf. e.g., R. J. Isaac, "Good Guys (Arabs), Bad Guys (Israel): The View from the Left," *Congress Bi-Weekly*, loc. cit.; A. S. Maller, "The New Politics," *The Jewish Spectator* (June 1968); J. L. Teller, "The New Populism and the Jews," *Conservative Judaism* 22/3 (Spring 1968); M. Wyshograd, "The Jewish Interest in Vietnam," *Tradition* 9/4 (Winter 1966). Quite an interesting bibliography of this new American-Jewish turn away from "the Left" could be compiled—although, on the whole, it is not so much the writers who would make the point, since they almost always were conservatives all along and are merely making use of the new situation for their purposes (like the latter two mentioned here), as rather the obviously increased receptivity to and respectability of their views among the Jewish community.

²⁸See Ernst Simon, the very title of whose book tells part of this story: *Creation in the Midst of Destruction—Jewish Adult Education in Nazi Germany as Spiritual Resistance* (German) (Tübingen 1959).

²⁹Dr. Nathan Eck, of Yad VaShem in Jerusalem, reports the doctrine of Rabbi Nissenbaum of Warsaw that in the past, in order to save one's soul, one had to sacrifice one's life, i.e., in the face of the Inquisition one had to perform קדוש השם whereas now the Nazis want to exterminate Jewish life, and, therefore, in order to save the Jewish mind one has to perform, above all, קדוש החיים i.e., preserve Jewish life. (These questions were discussed at a Conference on Problems of the Resistance held at Yad VaShem the week before Passover 1968.)

³⁰*Kuzari*, I/113ff.: "Rabbi: 'I see that you are reproaching us with our degradation and poverty. But the best of other religions boast of both.' The Kuzari: 'This might be so if your humiliation were voluntary. But it is involuntary, and if you had the power you would kill.' Rabbi: 'Yet the majority may expect reward, because they bear their degradation partly from necessity, partly of their own free will. For whoever wishes to do so can become the friend and equal of his oppressor by uttering one word (*"credo"*) and without any difficulty.... If we bear our exile and degradation for God's sake, as is proper, we shall be the pride of the generation which will come with the Messiah and accelerate the day of the deliverance for which we hope.' " C.f. also H. Cohen, *Religion der Vernunft*, Frankfurt am Main 1929, chap. XII, last para., Eng. trans., *Judaism* 17/3 (Summer 1968), "From the Classics."—This is, all together, one of the most distressing *heilsgeschichtlich* points brought to the fore by the experience of the Holocaust. (Some of the following points have crystallized in my mind as a result of a long and searching conversation on this subject with Dr. Erich Fromm.) It is often argued that "the six million" are not מקדשי השם because many of them were not, of course, practicing religious Jews or even believers in God. The answer of *pietas*, theology, *halachah*, and historiosophy must be and is that anyone slain as a Jew—on whom the name of God was thus called, whether he knew or liked it or no—is a martyr. If a "martyr" is, etymologically, a witness, then witnesses witness regardless of their own subjective attitude to the content of their testimony. I.e., we are dealing with an objective, rational postulate (cf. footnote 6): it is not that one deduces a martyr's status from the fact that he was a Jew but rather the reverse, the Jew's status from the fact that he was a martyr. (Cf., *Protest: Pacifism and Politics*, ed. J. Finn (New York, 1967) 126ff.) See *Encyclopedia Talmudit*, "Haruge Malchut," X:

622-27: "Those slain by a government attain to atonement even though they had been wicked men—see Ps 79:1f.: 'Thy servants' refers to such as were deserving of death but who, by virtue of the fact that they were killed, are called 'Thy servants. . . . The atonement of those slain by a government is immediate, . . . as, for example, those who were killed in the destruction of the Temple, who had done all the evils which God hates, as is expounded by the Prophets, and yet Scripture says about them: 'They gave the bodies of Thy servants as food for the fowl of heaven.' . . . Those slain by a government attain to atonement even though they have not done repentance, i.e., even though they were 'killed in the midst of their wickedness' (See *Sanh.* 47). . . . Those slain by a government are to be properly mourned, and they are not to be deprived of any form of mourning. . . . Referring to those slain by a government that refuses permission to bury them, since it is thus impossible to count the seven and the thirty days of mourning from the time that the grave is closed, one begins to count the period of mourning at the time that hope is abandoned for asking the return of the bodies." Cf. also the moving words written in 1912 by Rav Kook regarding the HaShomer socialists who lost their lives in defense of the *Yishuv, Zichron,* ed. R. Y. L. HaCohen Fishman (Jerusalem, 1945) 5-9: he cites *Yoreh Deah,* 340-*Pess.* 50a: "No one can be compared to Jews killed by alien sovereignties," and says: "We are fortune's children when it comes to tears. . . . It is our happiness-*cum*-catastrophe that we may mourn these beloved victims according to our heart's desires, not only out of the emotions of our heart but also by virtue of the *halachah.* . . . But woe unto us that we are forced to make use of this good fortune."—Another aspect of the current Polish episode into which we cannot, unfortunately, enter is the astounding reconfirmation, which Nazi Germany first supplied in our century on a grand scale, of the eschatological thesis of Isaac Abarbanel (see B. Netanyahu, *Don Isaac Abarvanel* . . . (Philadelphia, 1956) 202f., 315f.) and of others that the God of Israel and of universal history stamps His indelible will for the Jewishness of His chosen even on those who most actively deny it, Marranos, communists, etc. Adam Schaff, perhaps the best-known Polish academic philosopher, who, in his debate with Sartre, went so far in his self-deJudaization that he made vulgar anti-Semitic wisecracks, has now—as one example out of many—been removed from official and public life on the ground that he is a Jewish nationalist and—of all things—a Stalinist! I would go so far as to be prepared to argue that the Six Day War lies significantly at the root of the current Czech and French quasi-revolutions and the Polish quasi-counter-revolution. (Cf. *Jews in Eastern Europe* 3/9 (May 1968): "World Communist Disunity over Jews and the Middle East.")

[31]Let anyone still wishing to quarrel with this thesis look at the case of Richard Rubenstein. Without going into his psychopathology, the least that can be said about his doctrine is that he thinks he has decided to divorce himself from this cruel God—thus he declares Him to be Nothing and teaches a revived religion of paganism, a return to the mother-goddess earth and her Canaanitish ways.

[32]Compare what was said in this country during the weeks after the assassination of Senator Kennedy about the psychological relationship between the Vietnam War and the predilection for violence at home.

[33]Cf. *B. K.* 93a, *Lev. R.* 27:5, *Pesiqta de Rab Kahana* (ed. Mandelbaum), 153; cf. generally and importantly, R. Kimmelman, "Non-Violence in the Talmud," *Judaism* 17/3 (Summer 1968) esp. sect. 3. Cf. the very title *The Religions of the Oppressed (A Study of Modern Messianic Cults),* V. Lanternari (NewYork, 1963). Cf. S. H. Bergman's lovely statement, quoted in D. Lang, *loc. cit.*, about being a minority as a majority, 92.

[33a]Freud said to Marie Bonaparte: anyone who asks about the meaning of life is already sick.

[34]Cf. *Šabb.* 30b, *Ketub.* 111b, etc.; also my forthcoming "A Note on the Nature of Ideal Society—A Rabbinic Study," *Curt Silberman Festschrift* (New York, 1969).

[35]See 254, supra.
[36]E.g., Chayim Shevili, חשבונות הגאולה (Jerusalem 1967).
[37]See also supra, 254f.   [38]*Sanh.* 97a.
[39]Ibid., 97b.
[40]*Judaism* 16/3 (Summer 1967): 281.
[41]In G. B. Shaw's *Joan of Arc*, Joan says: "Minding your own business is like minding your own body; it's the shortest way to make yourself sick. . . . I tell thee it is God's business we are here to do; not our own."

Chapter 12

Judaism and the Zionist Problem, Zionism and the Jewish Problem

Jacob Neusner

The success of Zionism in solving the central Jewish problems of the modern age also creates new dilemmas for the Judaic religious tradition. Since Zionism functions for Jewry in much the same way as religions do for other peoples, the role and function of *Judaism*—the complex of myths, rituals, social and cultural forms by which classical Jews experienced and interpreted reality—now prove exceptionally ambiguous. Because Zionism appropriates the eschatological language and symbolism of classical Judaism, Judaists face an unwanted alternative: either to repudiate Zionism or to acquiesce in the historicization, the politicization, of what had formerly stood above politics and beyond history. The choice to be sure was recognized and faced by small Reform and Orthodox circles, as everyone knows. The classical reformers repudiated Zionism in the name of the mission of Israel, which, they held, required Jewry to take a decisive role in the universal achievement by all men of the messianic age. Their last, and unworthy, heirs accurately repeat the rhetoric, but do not possess the oral authority, of the nineteenth-century reformers. Likewise, Orthodox leadership in Eastern Europe and the U.S.A. quite early discerned what they understood to be the heretical tendency of Zionism: the advocacy that Jews save themselves, rather than depend on the Messiah, and return to Zion before the foreordained end of time. Their repulsive continuators present no interesting differences from the anti-Zionist reformers.

For the great mass of American Jews, who take literally the Zionist interpretation of Jewish history and innocently identify Zionism with Judaism, but regard themselves also both as Americans by nationality and Jews by religion, naive belief substitutes for and precludes close analysis. They have yet to come to grips with the inner contradictions recognized by the extremists of Reform and Orthodox Judaism. Indeed, they exasperate Israeli Zionists as much as Diaspora anti-Zionists. If Zionist, then why American? If the end has come, why not accept the discipline of the eschaton? If the end has not come, how to justify the revision of the Judaic consciousness and its reformation along Zionist lines? Nor has U.S. Jewry taken seriously the demands of logic and intellect for the formation of a credible ideology to explain the status quo and justify it.

But the problem is not American alone, nor does it face only those who articulately espouse the Zionist idea. And, rightly understood, the problem is not a new

---

*From *Stranger at Home:"The Holocaust," Zionism, and American Judaism*, by Jacob Neusner. Copyright © 1981 by University of Chicago Press. Reprinted by permission.

one. The tension between ethnicism and religion, between "enlandisement" and universality, between Jewish nationalism and the mission of Israel, characterizes the history of the Jewish people and of Judaism throughout. Take, for example, the conflict of symbolism represented by Torah and Messiah. One achieves salvation through study of Torah and carrying out its precepts. *Or* one will be saved at the end of days by the Messiah of the House of David. But if Messiah, what need of Torah? And if Torah, why the Messiah? To be sure, the two are harmonized: If all Israel will keep a single Sabbath as the Torah teaches, then the Messiah will come. So the one is made to depend on the other. For the Talmudic rabbis, the Messiah depends upon Torah, and is therefore subordinate. Torah is an essentially particularist means of attaining salvation. Its observance is the obligation of Jews. Of all the commandments therein, only seven apply to non-Jews. The Messiah is primarily a universal figure. His action affects all mankind. Both nature and the nations, as much as Israel and its Land, are the objects of his solicitude. Israel first, to be sure, but everyone at last comes to the end of days.

The tension between *holy land* and *holy Torah* as salvific symbols is pointed out by 'Abd al-Tafāhum in a remarkable essay "Doctrine."[1] What is remarkable is that al-Tafāhum (who is, I presume, a Moslem, though he is not identified by the editor) writes informedly and sympathetically about all three Middle Eastern religions. He writes, "The whole self-understanding of the Hebrews turns on 'enlandisement' and habitation and then, centuries later, on 'disenlandisement' and dispersion. Its two poles are Exodus and Exile. . . . The triangular relationship is that of God, people, and territory."[2]

With the Exile, the physical symbol is reenforced, and, in time, moved into the framework of the last things. Internalizing the effects of historical weakness, Jews understood the exile as punishment for their sins in the Land—"unrighteous tenancy" —and, as al-Tafāhum says, "The single theme of 'enlandisement' as the sign and pledge of the divine will and the human response" becomes paramount. To this is added a second understanding of Exile: "the nationhood to education nations, the awareness of election and particularity that embraces a universal parable for all the segments of mankind and all the diversified economic and spiritual tenancies of terrestrial habitation by peoples and races in those interactions that make culture and history."

The meaning of Jewish history therefore becomes the philosophy of "experienced Zion"—an experience available both in the Land and outside of it. The symbolism of Judaic religious experience was ever more shaped by having *and* not having the Land. Having the Land means standing in a proper relationship with the natural order. Al-Tafāhum refers to A. D. Gordon: "everything creaturely is material for sanctification. . . . The land of promise is properly not merely a divine bestowal but human fulfillment." Love of Zion produces the marriage of Messiahship and kingship, land

and nation. Above all, it bears the intense particularities of Jewish existence, the overwhelming love for Israel—Land, people, faith—characteristic of Jews through time.

"Disenlandisement," by contrast, produces the universal concern of Israel for all people: the willingness to enter into intimate relationship with each and every civilization. Election stands over against universality, but not wholly so: "Only you have I known among the families of man, therefore I shall visit on you all your iniquities." The unresolved tension in the history of Judaism is between privilege and particularity, on the one side, and the privilege of service to men on the other. Unlike Christianity, Judaism never chose to transcend its history, its intimacy with the Jews.

Al-Tafāhum poses the question: "If Jewry disapproves the universalizing of its human mission which has happened in the Church, how does it continue to reconcile its sense of privilege with the self-transcending obligation, confessed and prized, within that very identity?" Is Israel, the Jewish people, a mere ethnic continuity? Can it equate spiritual vocation with biological persistence? "Can the 'seed of Abraham' in any case be, in these times, a physically guaranteed notion? Is destiny identical with heredity and fidelity with birth?" "Can [Jewry] either delegate its universal duty or realize it merely by the percentage of literal seed?"

In former times, these questions found a response in the allegation that Israel had a mission to carry out among the nations. Israel was a presence within the world, "absorbing its values, using its languages and participating in its life, while casting off, sometimes almost in embarrassment, the distinctiveness of its own history and cultic life." But that response has its limitations, for in discounting the "historic elements of dogma and sanctity," Jews lost also all sense of particularity and readily gave us what was unique to themselves to join the commonalities of mankind. The mission ended in assimilation among those to be missionized.

Zionism, al-Tafāhum observes, "posits in new and more incisive form the old question of universality." It contains within itself "an ever sharper ambiguity about the final questions of the universal meaning and obligation of the chosen people. . . . By its own deepest convictions Judaism is committed to the benediction of all people and without this loyalty its very particularity is disqualified."

The question therefore stands: "Has the new 'enlandisement' betrayed the old? Was Diaspora the true symbol or the tragic negation of what vocation meant? Are chosen-ness and the law, identity as God's and duty to man, still proper and feasible clues to Jewish existence? Or is the land now no more than the territorial location of a secular nationality apostate from itself?" Al-Tafāhum rightly asserts that these issues are not of merely political interest, for "they reach most deeply into . . . the doctrinal heart." It would be difficult to improve upon this statement of the dilemma raised for modern Judaism by Zionism. If Zionism solves "the Jewish problem," it also creates interesting problems for Judaism.

Jews, too, have recognized this paradoxical quality of Jewish existence, amid a universal, international situation. Writing in *The New Yorker*,[3] I. B. Singer has a character state,

> The modern Jew can't live without anti-Semitism. If it's not there, he's driven to create it. He has to bleed for humanity—battle the reactionaries, worry about the Chinese, the Manchurians, the Russians, the untouchables in India, the Negroes in America. He preaches revolution and at the same time he wants all the privileges of capitalism for himself. He tries to destroy nationalism in others but prides himself on belonging to the Chosen People. How can a tribe like this exist among strangers.

One can hardly regard Singer's insight as mere fiction, when the Lakeville studies have shown it is fact.

There, suburban Jews, studied by Marshall Sklare and Joseph Greenblum,[4] raise Jewish children in a culture of equalitarianism and send them to colleges where ethnic liberalism predominates. At the same time they expect the children to develop strong Jewish identification. To be a good Jew in Lakeville is to be ethical, kind, helpful. But moral excellence does not derive from the particular ethic of Judaism, though people suppose it does. It is a function of the generalized upper-class liberalism of the community.

The authors wonder, "Will not a sectarianism which is unsupported ideologically wither away when social conditions change? Will future generations be prepared to live with the dichotomy which the Lakeville Jew abides: a universal humanitarianism as the prime value in combination with the practice of giving priority to Jewish causes? May [future generations] not conclude that their humanitarian aspirations dictate that they place the accent on the general rather than the Jewish?"

The paradox expressed by Singer accurately describes Lakeville Jews, who espouse universal values and teach them to their children, while at the same time wanting to preserve their own particular group, to marry their children off only to Jews. If the people is unique, then what is universal about it? If the people wishes to preserve its ethnic existence, then why should it claim to stand with, and for, all mankind?

Zionism solves "the Jewish problem." Its success lies only partially in politics. The more profound problems for which it serves as a satisfactory solution are inward, spiritual, and, ultimately, religious. Just as the Judaic tradition had formerly told Jews what it meant to be Jewish—had supplied them with a considerable definition of their identity—so does Zionism in the modern age. Jews who had lost hold of the mythic structure of the past were given a grasp on a new myth, one composed of the restructured remnants of the old one.

The Jew had formerly been a member of a religious nation, believing in Torah revealed at Sinai, in one God who had chosen Israel, hoping for the Messiah and return to the Land in the end of days. Jews who gave up that story of where they came from and who they are tell a new story based on the old, but in superficially secular form. To be Jewish means to live in the Land and share in the life of the Jewish nation, which became the State of Israel.

To a hostile observer, things looked like this: The elements of "Jewishness" and the components of "Israelism" are to be one and the same—sacrifice, regeneration, resurrection. The sacrifice is no longer in the Temple: no prophets need decry the multitudes of fatted beasts. What now must be sacrificed is the blood of Israelis and the treasure of the Diaspora. The regeneration is no longer to be the turning of sinners to repentance—*teshuvah*—but rather the reformation of the economic and cultural realities of the Jewish people. No longer "parasites," but farmers, no longer dependent upon the cultural achievements of the nations but creators of a Hebrew, and "enlandised," culture, the Jews would be reborn into a new being and a new age. The resurrection is no longer of the dead at the end of time, but of the people at the end of the Holocaust.

The unfriendly witness sees matters this way: The new Zionist identity, like the old Judaic one, supplied a law for the rituals and attitudes of the faith. The old *halakhah* was made irrelevant, the object of party politics. The new as not partisan at all. All believed in, all fulfilled the law, except for sinners and heretics beyond the pale. The new law requires of Jewish men and women one great commandment: support Israel. Those who do it best, live there. Those who do not, pay a costly atonement in guilt and ransom for the absent body. The ransom is paid through the perpetual mobilization of the community in an unending campaign for funds. The guilt is exorcised through political rituals: letters to Congressmen and—for bourgeois Jews, what would normally be unheard of—mass rallies and street demonstrations. The guilt of Auschwitz and the sin of living in the Diaspora become intertwined: "On account of our sin do we live today, and in the wrong place at that!" Above all, the guilty and the sinner forever atone by turning to the *qiblah* of the Land: There is no Land but Israel, and the Jewish people are its product. The development of an American Jewish, or Judaic, culture is seen as irrelevant to the faith. The philanthropists will not support it, for no funds are left after allocations for Israel and for domestic humanitarian institutions. The rabbis will not speak of it, for the people will not listen. The people will hear of nothing but victories, and victories are won in this world, upon a fleshly battlefield, with weapons of war.

The old self-hatred, the vile anti-Semitism of an Alexander Portnoy—is left behind. No longer weak, one hardly needs to compensate for weakness by pretensions to moral superiority, and then to pay the price of that compensation by hatred of one's own weakness. Jews no longer look down on *goyim*, for they feel like them. The universal humanism, the cosmopolitanism of the old Jew are abandoned in the new particularism. The old grandmother who looked for Jewish names in reports of plane crashes has given way to the new grandson who turns off the news after the Middle Eastern reports are done with.

The Jews no longer make contradictory demands on society. They no longer want to be accepted into the tradition of society. In the new ethnicism of the hour, they seek only their share. The liberal dilemma has been resolved. Jews now quite honestly interpret the universe in terms of their particular concerns. Self-hatred, liberalism, the crisis of identity—the three characteristics of the mid-twentieth-century American Jew—all fade into the background. The end of the old myths no longer matters much, for new ones have arisen in their place. The American Jews who did not want to be so Jewish that they could not also be part of the undifferentiated majority have had their wish fulfilled. Some have indeed ceased to be Jewish at all, and no one cares. Many others have found a place in the new, well-differentiated majority—so goes the hostile view.

In my view, it is reactionary to cavil at these developments. Only an antiquarian cares about the end of old myths and the solution of the dilemmas that followed. Zionists need make no apologies to those who point out the profound changes Zionism effects in Jewish existence. They need only ask, Is self-hatred better than what we have done? Is a crisis of identity to be preferred over its resolution? Are people better off living among the remnants of disappointed otherworldly hopes, or shaping new aspirations? Surely it is healthier to recover a normal life than to lament the end of an abnormal one. Granted that the Jewish situation has radically changed, I contend it is no worse, and a good deal better, than what has been left behind. All the invidious contrasts in the world change nothing.

Zionism has had a uniformly beneficial effect upon Jewry. It achieves the reconstruction of Jewish identity by its reaffirmation of the nationhood of Israel in the face of the disintegration of the religious foundations of Jewish peoplehood. Zionism indeed supplies a satisfactory explanation for the continued life of the Jewish group. It reintegrates the realities of Jewish group life with an emotional, intellectual, and mythic explanation for those realities. If Zionism really is a new religion for the Jews, then I think, on that account, it is not obligated to apologize for its success. On the contrary, Zionism works a miracle by making it possible for the Jewish group to renew its life. It redeems the broken lives of the remnants of the Holocaust. But it also breathes new life into the survivors of a different sort of holocaust, the erosion of Jewish self-respect, dignity, and loyalty throughout the Western Diaspora. Jews who want more than anything else to become Americans are enabled to reaffirm their Jewishness. Throughout the world, Jews who had lost a religious, Judaic way of viewing reality regain a Jewish understanding of themselves.

Zionism indeed serves as a religion because it does what a religion must do: it supplies the meaning of felt history; it explains reality, makes sense of chaos, and supplies a worthwhile dream for people who find in Jewishness nothing more than neurotic nightmares. Neither metaphysics nor theology proves necessary, for Zionism explains what the people already know and take for granted as fact. Zionism legitimates what Alexander Portnoy observed but could not accept: that Jews are men of flesh and blood, that (in Portnoy's phrase), *there is an id in Yid.* What is remarkable is that the early Zionists sought to do just that: to normalize the existence of the Jewish people.

In what way, then, does Zionism constitute a problem for Judaism? In my view, it is not its secularity and worldliness, but the mythic insufficiency of Zionism that renders its success a dilemma for contemporary American Jews, and for Israeli ones as well. To be sure, for some Israelis and American Jews, to be a Jew is to be a citizen of the State of Israel—but that definition hardly serves when Israeli Moslems and Christians are taken into account. If one ignores the exceptions, the rule is still wanting. If to be a Jew is to be—or to dream of being—an Israeli, then the Israeli who chooses to settle in a foreign country ceases to be a Jew on giving up Israeli citizenship for some other. If all Jews are on the road to Zion, then those who either do not get there or, once there, choose another way are to be abandoned. That makes Jewishness depend upon quite worldly issues: This one cannot make his living in Tel Aviv, that one does not like the climate of Afula, the other is frustrated by the bureaucracy of Jerusalem. Are they then supposed to give up their share in the "God of Israel"?

More seriously still, the complete "enlandisement" of Judaism for the first time since 586 B.C.E. forces the Judaic tradition to depend upon the historical fortunes of a single population in a small country. The chances for the survival of the Jewish people have surely been enhanced by the dispersion of the Jews among differing political systems. Until World War II Jews had stood on both sides of every international contest from most remote antiquity. Now, we enter an age in which the fate of Jewry and destiny of Judaism are supposed to depend on the fortunes of one state and one community alone.

That, to be sure, is not a fact, for even now the great Jewish communities in the U.S.S.R., Western Europe, Latin America, and North America, as well as smaller ones elsewhere, continue to conform to the historical pattern. But, ideologically, things have vastly changed. With all the Jewish eggs in one basket, the consequence of military actions is supposed to determine the future of the whole of Jewry and Judaism. So the excellence of some eight hundred pilots and the availability of a few dozen fighter bombers are what it all comes down to. Instead of the thirty-six righteous men of classical myth are seventy-two Phantoms—Mirages—a curious revision of the old symbolism.

Just what is *important* about being Jewish and in Judaism? In my view, the answer must pertain both to the State of Israel and to the *Golah* communities in equal measure. It cannot be right only for American Jewry, for we are not seeking a *Galut* ideology and no one would accept it. Such an ideology—right for here but irrelevant to Israelis—would obviously serve the selfish interests and the peculiar situation of American Jews alone. But the answer cannot pertain only to the situation of the Israeli Jews, for precisely the same reasons.

What is important about being Jewish is the capacity of the Jewish people and its mythic creations to preserve the tension between the intense particularities of their life and the humanity they have in common with the rest of mankind. That tension, practically unique to Jewry, derives from its exceptional historical experience. Until now, it has been the basis for the Jews' remarkable role in human history.

Others have not felt such a tension. To be human and to be English—or Navaho—were hardly differentiated. And why should they have been, when pretty much everyone one cared for and knew was English, or Navaho? To be a Jew in any civilization was, and is, to share the values held by everyone *but* to stand in some ways apart from (not above) the others. It was, and is, to love one's native land with open arms, to preserve the awareness of other ways of living life and shaping culture.

To be sure, before the destruction of the First Temple, Jewish people may well have been much like others. But from that time forward the Land was loved with an uncommon intensity, for it had been lost, then regained, therefore could never again be taken for granted. Alongside land, the people found, as few have *had* to, that Jews live by truths that could endure outside a single land and culture. Jewry discovered in itself an international culture, to be created and recreated in every land and in every language. It found in its central moral and ethical convictions something of value for all of civilizations. Its apprehension of God and its peculiar method of receiving and spelling out revelation in the commonplaces of everyday life were divorced from a single place, even the holiest place in the world, where they had begun.

But al-Tafāhum is wrong in supposing that the Jews' "disenlandisement" was the precondition for recognition of what was of universal importance about themselves. On the contrary, it was in the Land itself that the awareness of ethnic differentiation proved the least valid. Outside of it the group turned inward, and rightly so, for it became most acutely sensitive to its differences from others. In this respect the gentile students of Judaism do not understand what it is to be a Jew. The Diaspora Jew addresses the nations and in their own language, but in doing so speaks as a *Jew*. It is the "enlandised" Jew who sees himself or herself as no different from everyone within range of vision, therefore as human among humans, rather than Jew among gentiles. The willingness and necessity to enter into intimate relationship with each and every civilization therefore produced two sorts of encounters, the one, between the Jew in his land and others who might come there, or who might be known elsewhere, who held in common the knowledge of what it means to belong to some one place; the other, between the world and the always self-aware Jew living in other lands, a Jew sensitive to the language and experience of those lands precisely because he or she was forever at the margins of the common life.

Jewry did not disapprove the universalizing of its mission in the Church. It simply did not recognize that the Church ever truly carried out that mission. Jewry perceived no discontinuity requiring reconciliation between its sense of peoplehood (privilege) and its "self-transcending obligation." The Jews long ago ceased to be a mere ethnic continuity, and no one, in either the State of Israel or the Diaspora, regards the Jews as merely an ethnic group. One can, after all, become a Jew by other than ethnic and territorial assimilation, through *conversion*. That fact predominates in all discussions of what it is to be a Jew. The issue comes from the other side: *Can one become a Jew not through conversion, but through mere assimilation?* The dogged resistance of Jewry to the reduction of Jewishness to mere ethnicity testifies to the falseness of al-Tafāhum's reading of the Jewish situation.

But his other question is indeed troubling: Is destiny to be equated with heredity and fidelity with birth? The answer to that question can be found only in the working out of the potentialities of both Israeli and Diaspora Jewish life.

To be sure, the old Diaspora—the one before 1948—absorbed the values of the nations and could locate no one center where the distinctiveness, hence the universality, of Jewish history and civilization might be explored. Zionism does indeed posit in new and more incisive form the old question of universality, *but it also answers that question*. In the Jewish state Jews lose their sense of peculiarity. They reenter the human situation common to everyone but Jews. In the State of Israel everyone is Jewish, therefore no one is the Jew. And this, in my view, opens the way to an interesting development: the reconsideration of Jewish humanity in relationship with the other sorts of humanity in the world. It is now possible for the normal to communicate with the normal.

What the Israelis have to communicate is clear to one and all. They have not divorced themselves from important elements of the Jewish past, but have retained and enhanced them. The possession of the land, after all, represents such an important element. What does it mean to believe that one's moral life is somehow related to the destiny of the land in which one lives? In times past the question would have seemed nonsensical. But today no people is able to take its land, its environment, for granted. Everyone is required to pay attention to what one does with one's blessings. Today each land is endangered by immoral men who live upon and make use of it. The moral pollution of which the prophets spoke may infect not only a society but the way a society makes use of its resources. So the intimate relationship between Israel and the Land is no longer so alien to the existence of other nations. And the ecological-moral answers found in the Land and State of Israel are bound to have universal meaning.

I choose this example because it is the least obvious. The record of the State of Israel is, in my view, not ambiguous about "the final questions of the universal meaning and obligation of the chosen people." One need not be an Israeli apologist to recognize the numerous ways in which the State of Israel has sought to make war without fanaticism, to wage peace with selflessness. Only indifference to the actual day record of the State of Israel, with its technical assistance, its thirst for peace, its fundamentally decent society at home, and above all its hatred of what it must do to survive, justifies questions concerning Israel's "universal duty." On the contrary, it seems to me that Israeli society has, within the limits of its wisdom and power, committed itself to the benediction of all peoples, and with its loyalty to that very blessing its very particularity is verified and justified.

I therefore do not agree that the new "enlandisement" has betrayed the old. It has fulfilled it.

The other half of the question pertains to the Diaspora. The Diaspora was neither the true symbol nor the tragic negation of Israel's vocation. "Chosen-ness and law, obligation to God and duty to man," are still proper and feasible clues to Jewish existence *both* at home and abroad. The Land never was, and is not now, merely the territorial locus of a secular nationality. The existence of the Diaspora guarantees otherwise. The Diaspora supplies the certainty that people of many languages and civilizations will look to Zion for more than a parochial message, just as the Israelis make certain the Diaspora Jews will hear that message. But, as I said, things are the reverse of what al-Tafāhum supposes. The Diaspora brings its acute consciousness of being different from others, therefore turns to the State to discover the ways in which it is like the others. The Diaspora contributes its variety and range of human experience to the consciousness of the State of Israel. But the State offers the Diaspora the datum of normality.

One cannot divide the Jewish people into two parts, the "enlandised" and the "disenlandised." Those in the Land look outward. Those outside look toward the Land. Those in the Land identify with normal peoples. Those abroad see in the Land what it means to be extraordinary. But it is what happens to the whole, altogether, that is decisive for the Judaic tradition. And together, the Diaspora Jew and the Israeli represent a single tradition, a single memory. That memory is of having had a land and lost it—*and* never having repudiated either the memory of the Land *or* the experience of living elsewhere. No one in the State of Israel can imagine that to be in the Land is for the Jew what being in England is to the Englishman. The Englishman has never lost England and come back. So one cannot distinguish between the Israeli and the Diaspora Jew. Neither one remembers or looks upon a world in which his particular values and ideals are verified by society. Neither ceases to be cosmopolitan. Both preserve a universal concern for *all* Israel. Both know diversities of culture and recognize therefore the relativity of values, even as they affirm their own.

This forms what is unique in the Jewish experience: the denial of men's need to judge all values by their particular, self-authenticating system of thought. In this regard the Diaspora reciprocates. Both see as transitory and merely useful what others understand to be absolute and perfected. Behind the superficial eschatological self-confidence of Zionism lies an awareness everywhere present that that is just what Zionism adds up to: a *merely* secular eschatology. No one imagines that Zionism has completed its task or that the world has been perfected. The world is seen by both parts of the Jewish people to be insufficient and incomplete.

The Israeli's very sense of necessity preserves the Jews' neatest insight: without choice, necessity imposes duty, responsibility, unimagined possibilities. The Jews are not so foolish as to have forgotten the ancient eternal cities—theirs and others'—which are no more. They know therefore that it is not the place, but the quality of life within it, that truly matters. No city is holy, not even Jerusalem, but men and women must live in some one place and assume the responsibilities of the mundane city. But if no city is holy, at least Jerusalem may be made into a paradigm of sanctity. Though all they have for mortar may be slime, Jewish men and women will indeed build what they must, endure as they have to. The opposite is not to wander, but to die.

But have Diaspora Jews strayed so far from those same truths? In sharing the lives of many civilizations, do they do other than to assume responsibility for place? Do they see the particular city as holy, because they want to sanctify life in it? Or do they, too, know that the quality of life *anywhere* is what must truly matter? People must live in some one place and in so far as Jewish people have something to teach of all they have learned in thirty centuries, they should live and learn and teach in whatever place they love. And one may err if one underestimates the capacity of the outsider, of the Diaspora Jew, to love.

I therefore see no need either to repudiate Zionism or to give up the other elements that have made *being Jewish* a magnificent mode of humanity. Zionism, on the contrary, supplies Jewry with still another set of experiences, another set of insights into what it means to be human. Only those who repudiate the unity of Israel, the Jewish people, in favor of either of its segments can see things otherwise. But viscerally American Jews know better, and I think they are right in refusing to resolve the tensions of their several commitments. Zionism creates problems for Judaism only when Zionists think that all that being Jewish means is "enlandisement" and, thereby, redemption. But Zionists *cannot* think so when they contemplate the range of human needs and experiences they as human beings must face. Zionism is a part of Judaism. It cannot be made the whole, because Jews are more than people who need either a place to live or a place on which to focus fantasies. The profound existential necessities of Jews—both those they share with everyone and those they have to themselves—are not met by Zionism or "enlandisement" alone. Zionism provides much of the vigor and excitement of contemporary Jewish affairs, but in so far as Jews live and suffer, are born and die, reflect and doubt, raise children and worry over them, love and work—in so far as Jews are human, they require Judaism.

Zionism and "The Jewish Problem"

When Herzl proposed Zionism as the solution to the Jewish problem, the "Zionism" of which he spoke and the "Jewish problem" which he proposed to solve constituted chiefly political realities. But, as Arthur Hertzberg trenchantly argues in *The Zionist*

Idea, Zionism actually represented not a merely secular and political ideology, but the transvaluation of Jewish values. If so, the same must be said of the "Jewish problem" to which it addresses itself. Zionism as an external force faced the world, but what shall we say of its inner spirit? The inwardness of Zionism—its "piety" and spirituality—is not to be comprehended by the world, only by the Jew, for, like the Judaism it transformed and transcended, to the world it was worldly and political, stiff-necked and stubborn (in Christian theological terms), but to the Jew it was something other, not to be comprehended by the gentile.

In his celebrated correspondence with Eugen Rosenstock-Huessy, Franz Rosenzweig wrote:

> I find that everything I want to write is something I can't express to you. For now I would have to show you Judaism from within, that is, to be able to show it to you in a hymn, just as you are able to show me, the outsider, Christianity. And for the very reason that you can do it, I cannot. Christianity has its soul in its externals; Judaism, on the outside, has only its hard protecting shell, and one can speak of its soul only from within.[5]

Following Hertzberg, one can hardly see Zionism except as a New Judaism, a completely new view of all that had gone before and an utterly different conception of what should come hereafter. But this Zionism—neither spiritual nor political, but in a measure a unique amalgam of the spirit and the *polis*—is hidden by its hard protecting shell. What then can we say of its soul from within?

The Zionism of which I speak is the effort to realize through political means the hope supposed to have been lost in the time of Ezekiel, proclaimed imperishable in the time of Imber, the continuous hope of restoration and renaissance first of the Land of Israel, then of the people of Israel through the Land, finally, since 1948, of the people and the Land together, wherever the people should be found. This Zionism did not come about at Basel, for its roots go back to the point in the ages at which Jewry first recognized, then rejected, its separation from the Land. Zionism is the old-new Judaism, a Judaism transformed through old-new values. It is a set of paradoxes through which the secular and the religious, separated in the nineteenth century, were again fused—re-fused—in the twentieth. Zionism to be sure is a complex phenomenon; within it are tendencies which are apt to cancel each other. But all forms of Zionism are subsumed under the definition offered here, which represents, I think, the lowest common denominator for all Zionist phenomena.

The Jewish problems which Zionism successfully solved were the consequence of the disintegration of what had been whole, the identity, consciousness, and the culture of the Jew. It was, as I said, Zionism which reconstructed the whole and reshaped the tradition in a wholly new heuristic framework.

In former times it was conventional to speak of the "Jewish problem." Most people understood that problem in political and economic terms. What shall we do about the vast Jewish populations of Eastern and Central Europe, which live a marginal economic life and have no place in the political structures of the several nations? Herzl proposed the Zionist solution to the "Jewish problem." Dubnow wished to solve the "Jewish problem" by the creation of Jewish autonomous units in Europe. The Socialists and Communists proposed to solve the "Jewish problem" by the integration of Jewry into the movement of the international proletariat and to complete the solution of the problems of the smaller group within those of the working classes.

Today we hear less talk about the "Jewish problem" because Hitler brought it to a final solution: by exterminating the masses of European Jews, he left unsolved no social, economic, or political problems. The Western Jewries are more or less well integrated into the democratic societies. The State of Israel has no "Jewish problem" in the classic sense. The oppressed communities remaining in the Arab countries are relatively small, and the solution of their problems is to be found in migration to the West and to the State of Israel. The "Jewish problem" to be sure continues to confront Soviet Russia, and there the classic Marxist formulation of the problem still persuades people. But, for the rest, the "Jewish problem" does not describe reality or evoke a recognized, real-life perplexity. (That does not mean Jews do not have problems, or that gentiles do not have problems in relating to and understanding both Jews and Judaism.)

I shall concentrate on three aspects of the contemporary Jewish situation, all closely related, and all the result of secularism. The first is the crisis of identity, the second, the liberal dilemma, the third, the problem of self-hatred. The Jewish identity crisis may be simply stated: There is no consensus shared by most Jews about what a Jew is, how Judaism should be defined, what "being Jewish" and "Judaism" are supposed to mean for individuals and the community. The liberal dilemma is this: How can I espouse universal principles and yet remain part of a particular community? The problem of self-hatred needs little definition, but provokes much illustration, for many of the phenomena of contemporary Jewish life reflect the low self-esteem attached to being Jewish.

For Jews the secular revolution is not new. From the Haskalah, the Jewish Enlightenment in the eighteenth century, onward, Jews have come forward to propose a nonreligious interpretation of "being Jewish," an interpretation divorced from the classic mythic structure of Judaism. The God-Is-Dead movement evoked little response among Jewish theologians and ideologists because they found nothing new in it. If the issue was naturalistic, instead of supernatural, theology, Jewish theologians had heard Mordecai Kaplan for half-a-century or more. If the issue was atheism, it had been formulated by Jewish secularists, socialists, and assimilationists in various ways from the mid-nineteenth century forward. If the secular revolution means that large numbers of people cease to look to religion, or to religious institutions, for the meaning of their lives and cease to practice religious traditions and to affirm religious beliefs, then this is neither news nor a revolution. Jews have participated in that sort of "revolution" for two centuries. They have done so without ceasing to regard themselves, and to be regarded by others, as Jews. That does not mean the Jews have found antidotes to the secular fever, but it does mean that they by now have a considerable heritage of experience, a substantial corpus of cases and precedents, for what Christians find to be new and revolutionary: the loosing of the world from all religious and supernatural interpretations.

The secular revolution has imposed upon Jews a profound crisis of identity. In former times everyone knew who was a Jew and what being a Jew meant. A Jew was a member of a religious nation, living among other nations by its own laws, believing in Torah revealed at Sinai and in one God who had chosen Israel, and hoping for the coming of the Messiah. The gentile world shared the philosophical presuppositions of Jewish beliefs. Everyone believed in God. Everyone believed in prophecy, in revelation, in the Jews' holy book. Everyone believed in the coming of the Messiah. Above all, everyone interpreted reality by supernaturalist principles. To be sure groups differed in the nature of God, the particular prophets to be regarded as true, the book God had revealed. But these differences took place within a vast range of agreement.

When religious understandings of the world lost their hold on masses of Western people, "being Jewish" became as problematic as any other aspect of archaic reality. If to be Jewish meant to be part of a Jewish religious community, then when Jews ceased to believe in religious propositions, they ought to have ceased being Jewish. Yet that is not what happened. For several generations Jewish atheists and agnostics have continued to take an active role in the Jewish community—indeed, functionally to constitute the majority in it—and have seen nothing unusual either in their participation in Jewish life or in their lack of religious commitment. Indeed today the American Jewish community is nearly unique in interpreting "being Jewish" primarily in religious, or at least rhetorically religious, terms. Other Jewish communities see themselves as a community, a nation, a people, whether or not religion plays a role in defining what is particular about that community. The secular revolution immensely complicated the definition of Jewish identity, not only by breaking down the uniform classical definition, but also by supplying a variety of new, complex definitions in its place.

Today, therefore, if we ask ourselves, "What are the components of 'Jewishness'?" we are hard put to find an answer. What are the attitudes, associations, rituals both secular and religious, psychology and culture, which both Jews and others conceive to be Jewish? The truth is, today there is no such thing as a single Jewish identity, as there assuredly was in times past an identity one could define in meaningful terms. Jewishness now is a function of various social and cultural settings, and is meaningful in those settings only.

The Jews obviously are not a nation in the accepted sense; but they also are hardly a people in the sense that an outsider can investigate or understand the components of that peoplehood. There is no "Jewish way" of organizing experience and interpreting reality, although there was and is a Judaic way. There is no single Jewish ideology, indeed no single, unitary Jewish history, although there once was a cogent Judaic theology and a Judaic view of a unitary and meaningful progression of events to be called "Jewish history." Only if we impose upon discrete events of scarcely related groups in widely separated places and ages the concept of a single unitary history can we speak of "Jewish history." Jewish peoplehood in a concrete, secular, this-worldly historical sense is largely a matter of faith, that is, the construction of historians acting as do theologians in other settings. There once was a single Jewish ideological system, a coherent body of shared images, ideas, and ideals, which provided for participants a coherent overall orientation in space and time, in means and ends. There once was such a system, but in the secular revolution it has collapsed.

It is indeed, the secular revolution that has imposed on Jewry a lingering crisis of identity. Jews today may find in common a set of emotions and responses. These do not constitute an "identity," but rather, a set of common characteristics based upon differing verbal explanations and experiences. That does not mean no one knows what a Jew is. In particular settings Jews *can* be defined and understood in terms applicable to those settings. But as an abstraction the "Jewish people" is a theological or ideological construct not to be imposed upon the disparate, discrete data known as Jews or even as Jewish communities in various times and places. Lacking a common language and culture, even a common religion, the Jews do not have what they once had. Today Jewish identity so greatly varies that we need to reconsider the viability of the very concept of "Jewishness" as a universal attribute, for today Jewishness cannot be defined in neutral, cultural terms.

If there are no inherent and essential Jewish qualities in the world, then nothing about "being Jewish" is natural, to be taken for granted. Being Jewish becomes something one must achieve, define, strive for. It is today liberated from the forms and content of the recent past, from the "culture-Judaism" of the American and Canadian Jewish communities. If the artifacts of that "culture-Judaism"—matters of cuisine, or philanthropy, or cliquishness—are not part of some immutable and universal Jewish identity, then they may well be criticized from within, not merely abandoned and left behind in disgust. One can freely repudiate them in favor of other ways.

Omissions in contemporary Jewish "identity" are as striking as the inclusions. Among the things taken for granted are a sense of group loyalty, a desire to transmit "pride in Judaism" to the next generation, in sum a desire to survive. But the identity of large numbers of Jews, whether they regard themselves as secular or not, does not include a concept of God, of the meaning of life, of the direction and purpose of history. The uncriticized, but widely accepted Jewish identity syndrome is formed of the remnants of the piety of the recent past, a piety one may best call residual, cultural, and habitual, rather than self-conscious, critical, and theological (or ideological). That identity is not even ethnic, but rather a conglomeration of traits picked up in particular historical and social experiences. it is certainly flat and one-dimensional, leaving Jews to wander in strange paths in search of the answers to the most fundamental human perplexities.

Why are Jews in the forefront of universal causes, to the exclusion of their own interest and identity? Charles Liebman, writing in *The Religious Situation 1969*, examines the reasons given for this phenomenon. He rejects the notion that Jewish liberalism, cosmopolitanism, and internationalism rest on "traditional" Jewish values, for, he points out, it is the secular, not the religious, Jew who espouses cosmopolitanism. Jewish religious values in fact are folk-oriented rather than universalistic.

Liebman likewise rejects the view that the Jews' social status, far below what they might anticipate from their economic attainments, accounts for their attraction to the fringes of politics. This theory accounts, Liebman says, for Jewish radicalism rather than Jewish liberalism, that is, for only a small element of the community. Further, Jewish radicals normally abandon Jewish community life; liberals dominate it.

A third explanation derives from the facts of history. Liberal parties supported the emancipation of the Jews; conservative ones opposed it. But for the U.S. this was not the case. Indeed, until the New Deal, Jews tended to be Republican, not Democratic or Socialist. Liebman posits that the appeal of liberalism is among Jews estranged from the religious tradition. This appeal, he says, "lies in the search for a universalistic ethic to which a Jew can adhere *but* which is seemingly irrelevant to specific Jewish concerns and, unlike radical socialism, does not demand total commitment at the expense of all other values."

Since the Emancipation, Jews have constantly driven to free themselves from the condition which Judaism thrusts on them. This Liebman calls estrangement: "The impetus for intellectual and religious reform among Jews, the adoption of new ideologies and life styles, but above all else the changing self-perception by the Jew of himself and his condition was not simply a desire to find amelioration from the physical oppression of the ghetto. It was rather a desire for emancipation from the very essence of the Jewish condition.... The Jew's problem was his alienation from the roots and the traditions of the society."

Here is the point at which the phenomenon of secularization becomes important. Jews earlier knew they were different, estranged. But with the collapse of religious evaluations of difference, the Jews ceased to affirm that difference. Secularization changed the nature of the Jew's perception of his condition, transferred the estrangement from theology to the realm of contemporary culture and civilization.

Jews supported universal humanism and cosmopolitanism with a vengeance. They brought these ideals home to the community so that Jewish difference was played down. Look, for example, at the Union Prayerbook, and count the number of times the congregation prays for "all mankind." The New Liberal Prayerbook in England so emphasizes the universal to the exclusion of the particular that one might write to the English liberal rabbi responsible for the liturgy: "Warm and affectionate regards to your wife and children, and to all mankind." Liebman concludes, "The Jew wished to be accepted as an equal in society *not* because he was a Jew, but because his Jewishness was *irrelevant*. Yet at the same time, the Jew refused to make his own Jewishness irrelevant. . . . He made . . . contradictory demands on society. He wants to be accepted into the tradition of society without adapting to the society's dominant tradition." This constitutes the liberal dilemma: how to affirm universalism and remain particular.

However complex the liberal identity of secular Jews, it is still more complicated by the phenomena of anti-Semitism and consequent self-hatred. The "Jewish problem" is most commonly phrased by young Jews as, Why should I be Jewish? I believe in universal ideals—who needs particular ones as well?

Minorities feel themselves "particular," see their traditions as "ritual," and distinguish between the private, unique, and personal and the public, universal and commonplace. Majorities do not. Standing at the center, not on the fringe, they accept the given. Those who are marginal, as the Jews are, regard the given as something to be criticized, elevated, in any event distinguished from their own essential being.

Jews who ask, Why be Jewish? testify that "being Jewish" somehow repels, separates persons from the things they want. American society, though it is opening still is not so open that those who are different from the majority can serenely and happily accept that difference. True, they frequently affirm it—but the affirmation contains such excessive protest that it is not much different from denial. The quintessential datum of American Jewish existence is anti-Semitism, along with uncertainty of status, denial of normality, and self-doubt. The results are many, but two stand out. Some overemphasize their Jewishness, respond to it not naturally but excessively, to the exclusion of other parts of their being. Others question and implicitly deny it. The one compensates too much; the other finds no reward at all.

As Kurt Lewin pointed out in *Resolving Social Conflicts: Selected Papers on Group Dynamics*, "Every underprivileged minority group is kept together not only by cohesive forces among its members but also by the boundary which the majority erects against the crossing of an individual from the minority to the majority group."[6] An underprivileged group member will try to gain in social status by joining the majority—to pass, to assimilate. The basic fact of life is this wish to cross the boundary, and hence, as Lewin says, "he [the minority group member] lives almost perpetually in a state of conflict and tension. He dislikes . . . his own group because it is nothing but a burden to him. . . . A Jew of this type will dislike everything specifically Jewish, for he will see in it that which keeps him away from the majority for which he is longing." Such a Jew is the one who will constantly ask, Why be Jewish?—who will see, or at least fantasize about, a common religion of humanity, universalism or universal values that transcend, and incidentally obliterate, denominational and sectarian boundaries. It is no accident that the universal language, Esperanto, the universal movement, Communism, the universal psychology, Freudianism, all were in large measure attractive to marginal Jews.

True, Jews may find a place in social groups indifferent to their particularity as Jews. But a closer look shows that these groups are formed chiefly by deracinated, dejudaized Jews, along with a few exceptionally liberal non-Jews standing in a similar relationship to their own origins. Jews do assimilate. They do try to blot out the marks of their particularity, in ways more sophisticated, to be sure, than the ancient Hellenistic Jews who submitted to painful operations to wipe away the marks of circumcision. But in doing so, they become not something else entirely, but another type of Jew. The real issue is never, to be or not to be a Jew, any more than it is, to be or not to be my father's son.

Lewin makes this wholly clear: "It is not similarity or dissimilarity of individuals that constitutes a group, but interdependence of fate." Jews brought up to suppose being Jewish is chiefly, or only, a matter of religion think that through atheism they cease to be Jews, only to discover that disbelieving in God helps not at all. They still are Jews. They still are obsessed by that fact and compelled to confront it, whether under the name of Warren or of Weinstein, whether within the society of Jews or elsewhere.

Indeed, outside of that society Jewish consciousness becomes most intense. Among Jews one is a human being, with peculiarities and virtues of one's own. Among gentiles he is a Jew, with traits common to the group he rejects. That is probably why Jews still live in mostly Jewish neighborhoods and associate, outside of economic life, mostly with other Jews, whether or not these associations exhibit traits supposed to be Jewish. And when crisis comes, as it frequently does, then no one doubts that he or she shares a common cause, a common fate, with other Jews. Then it is hardest to isolate oneself from Jews, because only among Jewry are these intense concerns shared.

The Jewish community has yet to face up to the self-hatred endemic on its life. Jews are subtle enough to explain they are too busy with non-Jewish activities to associate with Jews. Students coming to college do not say to themselves or others, "I do not want to be a Jew, and now that I have the chance not to be, I shall take it." They say, "I do not like the Hillel rabbi; I am not religious so won't go to services; I am too busy with studies, dates, or political and social programs to participate in Jewish life." From here it is a short step to the affirmation of transcendent, universal values, and the denial of particular "religious" identity. That those who take that step do so mostly with other Jews is, as I said, proof of the real intent.

The organized Jewish community differs not at all from the assimilationist sector of this student generation. Indeed, it shows the way. Leadership in Jewry is sought by talented and able people, particularly those whose talents and abilities do not produce commensurate results in the non-Jewish world. Status denied elsewhere is readily available, for the right reasons, in Jewry, but in Jewry status is measured by the values of the gentile establishment.

Lewin says, "In any group, those sections are apt to gain leadership which are more generally successful. In a minority group, individual members who are economically successful . . . usually gain a higher degree of acceptance by the majority group. This places them culturally on the periphery of the underprivileged group and makes them more likely to be 'marginal' persons. . . . Nevertheless, they are frequently called for leadership by the underprivileged group because of their status and power. They themselves are usually eager to accept the leading role in the minority, partly as a substitute for gaining status in the majority. As a result, we find the rather paradoxical phenomenon of what one might call 'the leader from the periphery.' Instead of having a group led by people who are proud of the group, who wish to stay in it and to promote it, we see minority leaders who are lukewarm toward the group." This, I think, is very much true of U. S. Jewry.

American Jews want to be Jewish, but not too much so, not so much that they cannot be just "people," part of the imaginary undifferentiated majority. And herein lies their pathology: they suppose one can distinguish between one's Jewishness, humanity, personality, individuality, and religion. Human beings, however, do not begin as part of an undifferentiated mass. Once they leave the maternity ward, they go to a home of real people with a history, a home that comes from somewhere and that was made by some specific people. They inherit the psychic, not to mention social and cultural, legacy of many generations.

What has Zionism to do with these Jewish problems? It is, after all, supposedly a secular movement, called "secular messianism," and the problems I have described are the consequences of secularity. How then has an allegedly secular movement posited solutions to the challenges of secularity faced by the formerly religious community?

Zionism provides a reconstruction of Jewish identity, for it reaffirms the nationhood of Israel in the face of the disintegration of the religious bases of Jewish peoplehood. If in times past the Jews saw themselves as a people because they were the children of the promise, the children of Abraham, Isaac, and Jacob, called together at Sinai, instructed by God through prophets, led by rabbis guided by the "whole Torah"—written and oral—of Sinai, then with the end of a singularly religious self-consciousness, the people lost its understanding of itself. The fact is that the people remained a community of fate, but, until the flourishing of Zionism, the facts of its continued existence were deprived of a heuristic foundation. Jews continued as a group, but could not persuasively say why or what this meant. Zionism provided the explanation: The Jews indeed remain a people, but the foundation of their peoplehood lies in the unity of their concern for Zion, in devotion to rebuilding the Land and establishing Jewish sovereignty in it. The realities of continuing emotional and social commitment to Jewish "grouphood" or separateness thus made sense. Mere secular difference, once seen to be destiny—"who has not made us like the nations"—once again stood forth as destiny.

Herein lies the ambiguity of Zionism. It was supposedly a secular movement, yet in reinterpreting the classic mythic structures of Judaism, it compromised its secularity and exposed its fundamental unity with the classic mythic being of Judaism. If, as I suggested, groups with like attributes do not necessarily represent "peoples" or "nations," and if the common attributes, in the Jewish case, are neither intrinsically Jewish (whatever that might mean) nor widely present to begin with, then the primary conviction of Zionism constitutes an extraordinary reaffirmation of the primary element in the classical mythic structure: salvation. What has happened in Zionism is that the old has been in one instant destroyed and resurrected. The holy people are no more, the nation-people take their place. How much has changed in the religious tradition, when the allegedly secular successor continuator has preserved not only the essential perspective of the tradition, but done so pretty much in the tradition's own symbols and language?

Nor should it be supposed that the Zionist solution to the Jews' crisis of identity is a merely theological or ideological one. We cannot ignore the practical result of Zionist success in conquering the Jewish community. For the middle and older generations, as everyone knows, the Zionist enterprise provided the primary vehicle for Jewish identity. The Reform solution to the identity problem—we are Americans by nationality, Jews by religion—was hardly congruent to the profound Jewish passion of the immigrant generations and their children. The former generations were *not* merely Jewish by religion. Religion was the least important aspect of their Jewishness. They deeply felt themselves Jewish in their bone and marrow and did not feel sufficiently marginal as Jews to *need* to affirm their Americanness/Judaism at all. Rather they participated in a reality; they were in a situation so real and intimate as to make unnecessary such an uncomfortable, defensive affirmation. They did not doubt they were Americans. They did not need to explain what being Jewish had to do with it. Zionism was congruent to these realities, and because of that fact, being Jewish and being Zionist were inextricably joined together.

But how different is the newer generation? True, extreme aberrant Jewish elements in the New Left are prepared to turn against the State of Israel. But what, more than anything else, has weakened the New Left and caused its split into numerous bickering factions, if not the defection of considerable numbers of Jewish radicals, unable to stomach both the crude anti-Semitism and the mindless pro-Nasserism of the Communist-line New Left groups? If so, we can only conclude that the younger generation is as viscerally Zionist as the older generations. The rock on which the New Left split was none other than 1967 Zion. I cannot think of more striking evidence of the persistence of the Zionist conception of Jewish identity among the younger generation.

The Zionist critique of the Jews' liberal dilemma is no less apt. Zionism has not stood against liberal causes and issues. On the contrary, Zionist Socialists have stood at the forefront of the liberal cause, have struggled for the working-class ideals, have identified the working class cause with their own. The record of Israeli and American Zionist thought on liberal issues is unambiguous and consistent. The liberalism of which Liebman writes is of a different order. It is a liberalism not born in Jewish nationhood but despite and against it. The liberal cosmopolitan Jew, devoted to internationalist and universal causes to the exclusion of "parochial" Jewish concerns, is no Zionist, but the opposite. He or she is a Jew acting out the consequences of deracination in the political arena. His or her universal liberalism takes the place of a profound commitment to the Jews and their welfare. Indeed, it is a liberalism that would like to deny that Jews have special, particular interests and needs to begin with. "Struggling humanity" in all its forms but one claims his sympathy: when Jews suffer, they *have* to do so as part of undifferentiated humanity.

In so far as this Jewish liberalism was nonsectarian and hostile to the things that concern Jews as Jews—as in those Jewish welfare federations which articulately state their purpose as humanitarian to the exclusion of Judaism—Zionism has rejected that liberalism. It has done so because of its critical view of the Emancipation. Unlike the Jewish liberals, Zionism saw the Emancipation as a problem, not a solution. It was dubious of its promises and aware of its hypocrisies. It saw Emancipation as a threat to Jewry and in slight measure a benefit for Jews. The Jews' problem was that Emancipation represented dejudaization. The price of admission to the roots and traditions of "society" was the surrender of the roots and traditions of the Jew, so said Zionist thought.

At the same time Zionism stood between the religious party, which utterly rejected Emancipation and its works, and the secular-reform-liberal party, which wholly affirmed them. It faced the reality of Emancipation without claiming in its behalf a messianic valence. Emancipation is here, therefore to be criticized, but coped with; not utterly rejected, like the Orthodox, nor wholeheartedly affirmed, like the secular, reform, and liberal groups. Zionism therefore demanded that the Jew be accepted as an equal in society because he or she was a Jew, *not* because Jewishness was irrelevant. Its suspicion of the liberal stance was based, correctly, in my opinion, on the Jews' ambivalence toward Jewishness. Zionism clearly recognized that the Jewishness of the Jew could never be irrelevant, not to the gentile, not to the Jew. It therefore saw more clearly than the liberals the failures of the European Emancipation and the dangers of American liberalism to Jewish self-respect and Jewish interests. Zionists were quick to perceive the readiness of non-Jewish allies of Jewish liberals to take the Jewish liberals at their word: We Jews have no special interests, nothing to fight for in our own behalf. Zionists saw Jews had considerable interests, just like other groups, and exposed the self-deceit (or hypocrisy) of those who said otherwise. The liberal Jew wanted to be accepted into the traditions of society without complete assimilation, on the one side, but also without much Jewishness, on the other. The Zionist assessment of the situation differed, as I said, for it saw that Jews could achieve a place in the common life *only* as Jews; and, rightly for Europe, it held this was impossible.

In its gloomy assessment of the European Emancipation, Zionism found itself in a position to cope with the third component in the Jewish problem, the immense, deep-rooted, and wide-ranging self-hatred of Jews. The Zionist affirmation of Jewish peoplehood, of Jewish being, stood in stark contrast to the inability of marginal and liberal Jews to cope with anti-Semitism. Cases too numerous to list demonstrate the therapeutic impact of Zionism on the faltering psychological health of European Jews, particularly of more sensitive and intellectual individuals.

The American situation is different in degree, for here anti-Semitism in recent times has made its impact in more subtle ways, but its presence is best attested by the Jews themselves. Yet if a single factor in the self-respect American Jewry does possess can be isolated, it is its pride in the State of Israel and its achievements. Zionism lies at the foundation of American Jewry's capacity to affirm its Jewishness. Without Zionism religious conviction, forced to bear the whole burden by itself, would prove a slender reed. To be a Jew "by religion," and to make much of that fact in an increasingly secular environment, would not represent an attractive option to many. The contributions to Jewry's psychological health by the State of Israel and the Zionist presence in the Diaspora cannot be overestimated. It is striking, for example, that Kurt Lewin, Milton Steinberg, and other students of the phenomena of Jewish self-hatred invariably reached the single conclusion that only through Zionism would self-hatred be mitigated, even overcome.

The role of Zionism as a therapy for self-hatred cannot be described only in terms of the public opinion of U. S. Jewry. That would tell us much about the impact of mass communications, but little about the specific value of the Zionist idea for healing the Jewish pathology. In my view, the Israelis' claim "to live a full Jewish life" is a valid one. In Zionist conception and Israeli reality, the Jew is indeed a thoroughly integrated, whole human being. Here, in conception and reality, the Jew who believes in justice, truth, and peace, in universal brotherhood and dignity, does so not despite his or her peculiarity as a Jew, but through it, making no distinction between Jewishness, humanity, individuality, way of living, and ultimate values. These constitute a single, undivided and fully integrated existential reality.

Part of the reason is the condition of life: The State of Israel is the largest Jewish neighborhood in the world. But part of the reason is ideological, and not merely circumstantial: Zionists always have rejected the possibility of Jews' "humanity" without Jewishness, just as they denied the reality of distinctions between Jewishness, nationality and faith. They were not only *not* Germans of the Mosaic persuasion, but also *not* human beings of the Jewish genus. The several sorts of bifurcations attempted by non-Zionists to account for their Jewishness along with other sorts of putatively non-Jewish commitments and loyalties were rejected by Zionists. It was not that Zionists did not comprehend the dilemmas faced by other sorts of Jews, but rather that they supposed through Zionism they had found the solution. They correctly held that through Zionist ideology and activity they had overcome the disintegrating Jewish identity crisis of others.

At the outset I suggested that, like Judaism, Zionism can be understood from within, from its soul. My claim is that Zionism is to be understood as a solution to Jewish problems best perceived by the Jews who face those problems. The "Jewish problem" imposed by the effects of secularism took the form of a severe and complex crisis of identity, a partial commitment to universalism and cosmopolitan liberalism while claiming the right to be a little different, and a severe psychopathological epidemic of self-hatred. But the way Zionism actually solved those problems is more difficult to explain. If, as I suppose, because of Zionism contemporary Jewries have a clearer perception of who they are, what their interests consist of, and of their value as human beings, then Zionism and the State of Israel are in substantial measure the source of the saving knowledge. But *how* has Zionism worked its salvation on the Jews? Here I think we come to realities only Jews can understand. They understand them *not* because of rational reflection but because of experience and unreflective, natural response.

Zionism, and Zionism alone, proved capable of interpreting to contemporary Jews the meaning of felt history, *and* of doing so in terms congruent to what the Jews derived from their tradition. It was Zionism which properly assessed the limitations of the Emancipation and proposed sound and practical programs to cope with those limitations. It was Zionism which gave Jews strength to affirm themselves when faced with the anti-Semitism of European and American life in the first half of the twentieth century. It was Zionism and that alone which showed a way forward from the nihilism and despair of the D.P. camps. It was Zionism and that alone which provided a basis for unity in U.S. Jewry in the fifties and sixties of this century, a ground for common action among otherwise utterly divided groups.

These achievements of Zionism were based not on their practicality, though Zionism time and again was proved "right" by history. The Jews were moved and responded to Zionism before, not after the fact. And they were moved because of the capacity of Zionism to resurrect the single most powerful force in the history of Judaism: Messianism. Zionism did so in ways too numerous to list, but the central fact is that it represented, as Hertzberg perceptively showed, not "secular Messianism" but a profound restatement in new ways of classical Messianism. Zionism recovered the old, still evocative messianic symbolism and imagery and filled them with new meaning. And *this* meaning was taken for granted by vast numbers of Jews because it accurately described not what they believed or hoped for—not faith—but rather what they took to be mundane reality. Zionism took within its heuristic framework each and every important event in twentieth-century Jewish history and gave to all a single, comprehensive, and sensible interpretation. Events were no longer random or unrelated, but all were part of a single pattern, pointing toward an attainable messianic result. It was not the random degradation of individuals in Germany and Poland, not the meaningless murder of unfortunates, not the creation of another state in the Middle East. All of these events were related to one another. It was Holocaust and rebirth, and the state was the State of *Israel*.

In so stating the meaning of contemporary events, Zionism made it possible for Jews not only to understand what they witnessed, but to draw meaning from it. And even more, Zionism breathed new life into ancient Scriptures, by providing a contemporary interpretation—subtle and not fundamentalist to be sure—for the prophets. "Our hope is lost," Ezekiel denied in the name of God. "Our hope is not lost," was the response of Zionism. These things were no accident, still less the result of an exceptionally clever publicist's imagination. They demonstrate the center and core of Zionist spirituality and piety: the old-new myth of peoplehood, land, redemption above all. The astonishing achievements of Zionism are the result of the capacity of Zionism to reintegrate the tradition with contemporary reality, to do so in an entirely factual, matter-of-fact framework, thus to eschew faith and to elicit credence. Zionism speaks in terms of Judaic myth, indeed so profoundly that myth and reality coincide.

Endnotes

[1] In A. J. Arberry, ed., *Religion in the Middle East* (Cambridge, 1969) 2/2: *The Three Religions in Concord and Conflict*.
[2] Ibid., 367.   [3] 21 March 1970.
[4] *Jewish Identity on the Suburban Frontier* (NewYork, 1967).
[5] In *Judaism Despite Christianity, The "Letters on Christianity and Judaism" Between Eugen Rosenstock-Huessy and Franz Rosenzweig*, ed. Eugen Rosenzstock-Huessy (University of Alabama Press, 1969).
[6] (NewYork: Harper, 1948).